Today's HOMEOWNER ®

Around the Home & Yard

MORE THAN 800 TIPS & PROJECTS

Creative Publishing international, Inc.
5900 Green Oak Drive
Minnetonka, Minnesota 55343
1-800-328-3895
www.howtobookstore.com

CREATIVE
PUBLISHING
international

President: David D. Murphy
VP/Editor-in-Chief: Patricia K. Jacobsen
VP/Retail Sales & Marketing: Richard M. Miller

Executive Editor: Bryan Trandem
Associate Creative Director: Tim Himsel
Editorial Director: Jerri Farris
Managing Editor: Michelle Skudlarek

TODAY'S HOMEOWNER is a registered
trademark of Times Mirror Magazines, Inc.,
and is used under license.

Today's HOMEOWNER ®

VP/Editor-in-Chief: Paul Spring
Executive Editor: Fran J. Donegan
Managing Editor: Steven H. Saltzman

VP/Publisher: John W. Young
General Manager: Jill Raufman
President, Today's Homeow⌐   ⌐⌐ F. Klein

All rights reserved.
Printed by Quebecor Worl⌐
10 9 8 7 6 5 4 3 2 1

Library of Congress Catal⌐

Around the home & yard : ...
    p. cm.
At head of title: Today's homeowner.
ISBN 0-86573-586-7 (hard cover)
ISBN 0-86573-486-0 (soft cover)
1. Dwellings—Remodeling—Amateurs' manuals. 2. Landscape
construction—Amateurs' manuals. I. Title: Around the home and
yard. II. Creative Publishing Internationa. III. Today's homeowner.

TH4816.A76 2000
712'.6—dc21   00-025701

D1279405

Contents

Sprucing Up Walls

*Add new style and
personality to drab,
ordinary walls
with paint, wallpaper,
molding and mirrors.*

Sprucing Up Walls

Although the walls of our homes are backdrops for all our indoor activities, too often we simply paint them white and maybe put up a picture or two. So it's easy to overlook the potential that a relatively simple wall improvement may have to significantly enhance a room's style, function and livability.

In this chapter, we'll look at a variety of simple ways to add interest to walls by using decorative painting and wallpapering techniques, wall trim and mirrors. The projects in this chapter require only simple do-it-yourself skills.

Wall Treatments

There are many excellent books that describe basic paint and wall-covering techniques; this section focuses specifically on decorative techniques that can add a creative finishing touch to your walls. They include texture painting, decorative painting, wallpaper borders and upholstered walls.

If you're new to painting or wall-papering, start small until you gain confidence and master the basic techniques involved.

Wall Trim

Another relatively easy way to add personality to a dull wall is to install trim, such as a wall frame molding, crown molding or wainscoting. All these wall trim projects require only basic carpentry skills.

Wall frame molding is very simple to install and offers an excellent design solution for a large expanse of unadorned wall.

Although crown molding can add great character to a room, traditional installation techniques require you to cut tricky compound and angled joints. The project shown here presents a much simpler approach.

Wainscoting

Wainscoting is a covering over the lower part of a wall that has both decorative and practical uses. In addition to adding the warmth of natural wood to a room, it helps protect the wall from wear and tear. Wainscoting is traditionally used in kitchens, baths, dining rooms, libraries and hallways.

Here we show you two easy and inexpensive styles: pressed-metal wainscoting (the embossed squares used for tin ceilings) and prefabricated oak veneer library panels. Either of these wainscotings can be installed in a medium-size room in a weekend.

Mirrors

Mirrors are perhaps the best way to create the illusion of space in a small or cramped room—and compared to other wall options, they're inexpensive and easy to install. Here you'll learn how to select and place mirrors to create the effect you're looking for, and how to mount and clean a mirror properly.

This section also offers several suggestions for using mirrors in a bathroom or kitchen. In many homes, the bathroom and kitchen are the smallest rooms—which means they have the most to gain from the space-expanding effect of a well-placed mirror.

TEXTURE PAINTING

Tools
- power drill with paint mixer
- tools to create texture:
  whisk broom, trowel, sponge,
  long-nap paint roller,
  paintbrush, etc.

Materials
- premixed latex texture paint or
  dry powder texture paint

Although texture is an important element of our homes, we often overlook the subtle background surfaces that surround us. Texture painting is a way to bring that element to the fore by adding a third dimension to walls.

The possibilities for texture painting variations are almost limitless. The depth of the texture you'll get will depend on the stiffness of the paint, the amount you apply to the surface and the tool you use to create the texture pattern.

As with any painting project, begin by washing and drying the walls thoroughly, to ensure that the paint will adhere properly to the surface. For best results, experiment with different textures on sheets of cardboard until you get the effect you're looking for.

Use a small whisk broom to create a swirl pattern.

Pile up thick paint with a trowel to create an adobe pattern.

Texture Painting Suggestions

Texture painting involves working thickened paint into an interesting pattern that adds a three-dimensional effect to a wall. You can use specially designed texture paint or powder and almost any kind of tool or instrument to create a textured effect.

Use a premixed latex texture paint to produce light stipple patterns, and a thicker powder texture to create heavier adobe or stucco finishes. To mix the powder texture with water, use a power drill fitted with a paint mixer attachment.

Here are some ideas for texture painting techniques to help you get started.

Stipple Texture

Use a long-nap roller. For different patterns, vary the pressure on the roller and the amount of texture paint on the surface of the wall.

Swirl Pattern

Apply the texture paint with a roller, then use a small whisk broom to create a repeated swirl design.

Adobe Pattern

Trowel texture material onto the surface and pile it up in ridges.

Brocade Design

Trowel over the partially dried paint to flatten the peaks. Clean the trowel after each stroke with a wet brush or sponge.

Stucco Pattern

Dab, drag or swirl a sponge over texture paint until you find a texture you like.

Two-Tone Stucco

Sponge on a layer of texture paint. Let the paint dry, then sponge another color over it.

Crow's-foot Design

Apply texture paint with a roller. Brush it level, then randomly strike the surface with the flat of a brush.

Stomp Design

Randomly press the flat side of a trowel into the texture paint, then pull it away.

Use a long-nap paint roller to create a stipple effect.

For a crow's-foot look, strike the wall with the side of a brush.

DECORATIVE PAINTING

Decorative painting techniques offer an easy and inexpensive way to add visual texture to walls. All you need is a sponge, some paint and a clean, dry wall.

For a watercolor effect, use soft, light colors. For a bolder look, select colors with strong contrasts. Often, the second-darkest color is used as the base coat, and the accent colors are applied from darkest to lightest.

You can use the techniques shown here either together or separately. Before you start, experiment on cardboard to see the effect you'll get.

Sponging

A. Apply a base coat of the desired background color to a clean, prepared surface. Allow to dry.

B. Rinse a natural sea sponge in water to soften it; squeeze it dry.

C. Pour a little of the first accent color onto a paint tray. Dab the sponge in the paint, taking care not to overload it. Blot it on newsprint until it makes a light impression.

D. Using a quick, light touch, press the sponge gently onto the wall (don't drag it). Turn it often to produce an irregular effect. (If you'll be adding another color, apply the first color sparingly.)

E. Apply the first color to the entire area, until the individual sponge marks are no longer obvious. Stand back often to examine the wall, and fill in as necessary.

Tools
- natural sea sponge
- paint tray
- newsprint or scrap paper
- veining feather or fine fan brush
- paintbrush

Materials
- 1 quart low-luster latex enamel interior paint per color
- metallic paint (for veining)

Sponging. Press the sponge gently onto the wall with a quick, light touch. Allow the first accent color to dry before adding the next one.

F. Allow the first color to dry. Rinse the sponge and the paint tray.

G. Repeat these steps for each color of paint. When you apply the last color, fill in between the earlier sponge marks, to blend the colors.

Marbling

A. Following the instructions for Sponging, apply the first accent paint in diagonal drifts that meander randomly up the wall.

B. Soften the edges of the drifts by gently blotting wet paint with a tissue and lightly whisking a dry paintbrush over the surface.

C. Apply the second color of paint or glaze in a lighter tone, blending the textures and colors.

D. Embellish the surface by veining it (see below).

Veining

A. Select a metallic paint or an accent color. If you'd like a translucent effect, thin the paint with water.

B. Dip the tip of a turkey quill feather or fine fan brush into the paint. (Veining feathers are available in the paint department of home improvement stores.) Remove excess paint on a piece of newsprint.

C. Draw the tip of the feather or brush lightly along the surface at a 45-degree angle. Use a trembling motion so the veins wave, break off and reappear. Fork the veins, and cross one over another.

D. When crossing over a vein, lift the feather or brush and shift direction.

E. To vary the width of a vein, twist your wrist as you move the feather along.

Marbling. After sponging on the first color in diagonal drifts, apply a lighter color of paint or glaze over it.

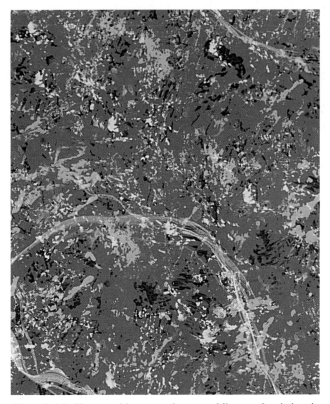

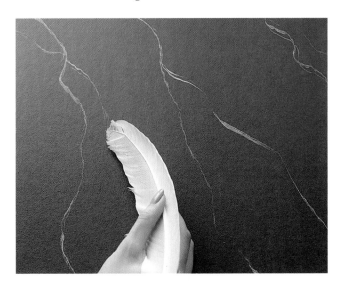

Veining. Using a trembling motion, draw the tip of a feather or a fan brush lightly over the prepared surface.

For a bold effect, combine sponging, marbling and veining in high-contrast colors with metallic paint highlights.

WALLPAPER BORDERS

Border strips made of wallcovering materials are a unique way to add style to a room or to highlight an architectural feature, such as a fireplace mantel. You can use these borders in any room and on both painted and wallpapered surfaces.

Interesting borders are easy to find or make. Matching borders are available for many wallcovering designs (check the sample books in a wallpaper store). You can also create your own customized borders by cutting full-size wallpaper into narrow strips. To make this job easier, use a striped pattern with a nondirectional design. For another interesting effect, trim around the outline of a pattern inside a wide stripe.

There are many possible ways to place a wallpaper border in a room. Use it as a crown molding around the perimeter of a ceiling. Position the border so that it frames a window, door or fireplace. On a painted wall, create a chair rail border or place a line of wallpaper along the top of the wainscoting.

Tools
- ruler
- level
- sharp utility knife
- wide broadknife
- straightedge
- smoothing brush
- seam roller
- sponge

Materials
- wallcovering border
- wallcovering paste
- seam adhesive

Step 1
A. Plan the layout of the border, starting in the least conspicuous corner of the room.

B. If the border isn't being placed along a ceiling or baseboard, draw a light pencil line around the wall at the desired height, using a level as a guide. Measure the line down from the ceiling or up from the floor, whichever is shorter.

Step 2
A. Cut and prepare the first border strip.

B. Beginning at the selected corner, apply the border along the reference line, overlapping it onto the adjacent wall by ½ in.

C. Press the border flat along the wall with a smoothing brush. Have a helper unfold the unused portion of the border as you apply and brush it into place.

Begin by overlapping the border ½ in. around the first corner. Press it down with a smoothing brush.

Form a ¼-in. tuck just beyond the inside corner, then continue applying the border and cut it at the corner.

Step 3

A. Form a ¼-in. tuck just beyond each inside corner, then continue to apply the border.

B. Cut the border at the corner using a utility knife and broadknife.

C. Peel back the tucked strip and smooth it around the corner. Press the border flat.

D. Apply seam adhesive to the lapped seam, if necessary.

Step 4

A. For seams that fall in the middle of a wall, overlap the border strips so the patterns match.

B. Cut through both layers with a utility knife, then peel back the border and remove the cut ends.

C. Press the border flat. After half an hour, roll the seam.

D. Rinse excess adhesive from the border, using a damp sponge.

Step 5

A. To cut-in the border flush with wallcovering, overlap the border onto the wallcovering.

B. Use a straightedge and a utility knife to cut through the underlying wallcovering along the border edge.

C. Pull up the border; remove excess wallcovering. Press the border down flat.

HOW TO MITER BORDER CORNERS

Step 1

A. Apply the horizontal border strip first. Extend it past the corner farther than the width of the border.

B. Apply the vertical border strip the same way, overlapping the horizontal strip.

C. Check the strips to make sure the pattern will meet at the diagonal cut. If necessary, adjust the position of the strips.

Step 2

A. Cut through both layers of border at a 45-degree angle, using a utility knife and a straightedge.

B. Peel back the end of the border; remove both cut sections.

C. Press the border flat. Wait half an hour, then roll the seam.

D. Wipe any remaining adhesive from the seam with a damp sponge.

Cut through both layers of border at a 45-degree angle. Peel the border back, remove the cut pieces and press flat.

UPHOLSTERED WALLS

Tools
- staple gun
- 3/8-in. to 1/2-in. staples
- pushpins
- single-edged razor blades
- hot glue gun
- glue sticks
- thick craft glue

Materials
- decorator fabric
- polyester upholstery batting

Step 1

A. Buy and cut the fabric, welting and batting (see fabric worksheet). Don't trim the selvages unless they show through the fabric.

B. Measure around doors and windows and along the ceiling and baseboard. Measure from the floor to the ceiling at each corner.

C. Cut 3-in.-wide fabric strips, equal to the total of these measurements, for the double welting.

Step 2

A. Remove switch plates and outlet covers from the walls. Don't remove moldings or baseboards—the double welting will cover the fabric edges.

B. Staple batting to the wall every 6 in., leaving a 1-in. gap between the batting and the edge of the ceiling, corners, baseboard and moldings.

C. Butt the edges between widths of batting and cut the batting to fit around switch and outlet openings.

Step 3

A. Stitch the fabric panels together for each wall separately, matching the pattern. Avoid placing seams next to windows and doors.

B. Beginning at an inconspicuous corner, hang the fabric from the top,

Upholstering walls with decorator fabric offers practical benefits as well as a striking, elegant appearance. The fabric covers any imperfections in the wall surface, and its padding insulates the room and absorbs sound.

However, there are a few things to watch out for. Avoid fabrics with plaids or stripes; they'll call attention to walls that aren't square. It's easy to staple fabric to paneling, but drywall requires a little more planning. Staples won't penetrate the metal corner bead used on outside corners, so you'll have to wrap the fabric around them. If you have plaster walls, make sure the staples will hold before you begin.

Step 3

Anchor fabric to the corners, pulling it taut and stapling it close to corners.

Step 5

Cut openings for doors and windows with diagonal cuts into the corners.

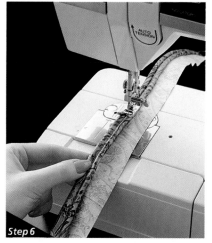

Step 6

To finish the double welting, stitch between the cords.

turning under ½ in. and stapling every 3 to 4 in. Don't cut around the windows and doors.

C. Anchor the fabric in the corners, pulling it taut and stapling close to the corner (the staples will be covered with double welting).

D. Trim the excess fabric and start the next panel at the next corner.

Step 4

A. Staple along the baseboard, pulling and smoothing the fabric taut to remove any wrinkles.

B. Use a single-edged razor blade to trim the excess fabric along the baseboard.

Step 5

A. Mark the outside corners of the windows and doors with pushpins. Cut out openings with diagonal cuts into the corners.

B. Turn under the raw edges and staple around the molding.

Step 6

A. Make the double welting by placing cording on the wrong side of a 3-in.-wide fabric strip. Fold the fabric over the cording with a ½-in. seam allowance extending. Use a

zipper foot to stitch next to the cording.

B. Place the second cord next to the first. Bring the fabric over the second length of cording.

C. Stitch between the two cords on the previous stitching line. Trim off excess fabric next to the stitching; the raw edge is on the back of finished double welting.

Step 7

A. Apply hot glue to the back of the double welting, about 5 in. at a time. Secure the double welting to the upper and lower edges of the wall and around window and door frames, covering the staples.

B. Press the double welting into the corners and around any openings, using a screwdriver to push it into the corners. After the glue dries, peel off any excess.

Step 8

A. Apply fabric to the switch plates and outlet covers, securing it with diluted craft glue.

B. Clip and trim the fabric around the openings. Turn the raw edges to the back of the plate and glue them in place.

Fabric Worksheet

Cut Length		in.
Measurement from floor to ceiling, plus 3 in.*	=	_____
Cut Width		
Width of fabric minus selvages	=	_____
Number of Fabric Widths Needed for Each Wall		
Width of wall	=	_____
Divided by cut width of fabric	/	_____
Number of fabric widths for wall**	=	_____
Amount of Fabric Needed for Double Welting		
Total welting length (see Step 1)	=	_____
Divided by cut width of fabric	/	_____
Number of strips**	=	_____
Multiplied by 3 in.	x	3
Fabric needed for double welting	=	_____
Total Fabric Needed		
Cut length (figured above)	=	_____
Number of fabric widths (figured above) for all walls	x	_____
Fabric needed for all walls	=	_____
Fabric needed for double welting	+	_____
Total length needed	=	_____
Divided by 36 in.	/	36
Number of yds. needed	=	_____

*Allow extra for pattern repeat; don't subtract for windows and doors unless they cover most of the wall.

**Round up to the nearest whole number.

WALL FRAME MOLDING

Wall frame moldings are an elegant way to add a distinctive touch to a wall. They can accent special features, divide large walls into smaller sections or add interest to an otherwise plain surface.

The molding can be single or double, the same color as the walls or a contrasting shade. You can highlight the frames by wallpapering the area within the frame or painting it a different color than the surrounding wall.

To plan the size and location of the frames, cut paper strips the width of the moldings and experiment by taping them to the wall. Try to repeat the shape, size or visual line of other design elements in the room, such as the windows or a fireplace mantel.

Install the molding with small finishing nails placed near the outside corners of the molding and through the wall studs (use nails long enough to go through the wall and into the studs). If the vertical pieces aren't placed over a wall stud, apply wood glue to the back of the molding pieces to keep them from pulling away from the wall.

Add interest to an otherwise plain wall by covering the framed area with wallpaper.

Tools	Materials
• level	• paper
• backsaw & miter box or power miter saw	• tape
	• decorative molding
	• wood glue
• drill with ¹⁄₁₆-in. bit	• paint or stain
• carpenter's square	• putty to match paint or stain
• nailset	• finishing nails

Cut paper strips in the form of the molding and tape them to the wall. Mark the upper corners with a pencil.

Nail the upper molding strip to the wall, aligning it with the pencil marks.

Step 1

A. Cut paper strips the width and length of the molding.

B. Tape the strips to the wall exactly as you want to position the wall moldings, making sure the upper strip is level.

C. Lightly mark the outer corners of the upper strip with a pencil.

Step 2

A. Measure the molding and mark the miters on the top and bottom molding pieces.

B. Cut the ends of the molding at opposite 45-degree angles, using a backsaw and a miter box or a power miter saw. The two pieces must be exactly the same length.

C. Repeat steps 2A and 2B for the side strips.

D. Paint or stain the moldings as desired. Predrill nail holes near the ends of all the molding pieces.

Step 3

A. Position the top molding piece on the wall, aligning it with the pencil marks.

B. If the molding won't be nailed into wall studs, place dots of glue sparingly on the back.

C. Nail the molding to the wall, leaving the nails slightly raised.

Step 4

A. Position the side frame molding pieces on the wall, making sure they're square. Nail the upper corners only.

B. Position the lower piece on the wall, making sure it's square and level. Nail it to the wall.

C. Drive the remaining nails into the side frame pieces.

Step 5

A. Using the nailset and a hammer, tap the nails slightly below the surface of the frame.

B. Touch up the nail holes and the mitered corners using wood putty and paint, or tinted wood putty.

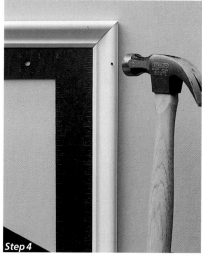

Check to make sure that the corners are square, then nail the molding in place.

CROWN MOLDING

Crown molding is a powerful architectural accent that can dramatically change the look of a room without overpowering other elements. While it has graced cottages and castles alike for centuries, it's less common in modern homes, because installing it takes time and requires a highly skilled carpenter.

Traditionally, crown molding has been nailed to the wall and the ceiling at an angle—which involves cutting a tricky compound-angle miter joint where the molding turns an outside corner. Inside corners are traditionally just as difficult, requiring another compound-angle joint or a coped cut. These are all fussy joints to fit, and mistakes are expensive.

However, there's now a fast, foolproof way to add the classic beauty of crown molding to your home—and it doesn't require making a single angle cut.

The beautiful dentil crown molding shown here looks as if it's made of solid mahogany, but it's actually molded from lightweight, high-density urethane foam. It features premolded corner blocks, which eliminate the need to cut angled joints. You simply nail up the corner blocks and square-cut the molding to fit between them. In addition to the corner blocks, there are also divider blocks that simplify joining two lengths of molding along a long wall.

Hundreds of urethane molding styles are available in both 8- and 12-ft. lengths. Most are available in both a stainable wood-grain finish and a paint-grade white finish that resembles traditional plaster moldings.

See **Grand Entrance**, pages 90-93, for another way to use urethane millwork to add the elegance of classic wood trim to your home.

Tools
- hammer
- power miter saw, radial arm saw, or fine-tooth handsaw
- nailset
- 1-in. paintbrush

Materials
- molded urethane molding, corner blocks & divider blocks (if needed)
- paint or stain
- 2-in. (6d) finishing nails
- caulk to match the molding
- crayon-type putty stick to match the molding

Step 1

Before installing all the moldings and accessories, you need to paint or stain them to match the existing wood trim.

Painting: No primer is needed; the moldings are preprimed and will accept any good-quality latex or oil-based paint.

Staining: Use a thick-bodied gel stain or a controlled-penetration stain. Don't use a semitransparent stain; it's too thin to tint the non-porous urethane.

Apply the paint or stain with a 1-in.-wide paintbrush, taking care to fully cover the dentil detailing.

Step 2

A. Nail up all the inside corner blocks. If the wall corners are out of square (as most are), slip a few narrow shims behind the blocks to fill the gaps.

B. Nail up any outside corner blocks in the same way.

C. If you need to put up two lengths of molding to complete a long wall, center a divider block between them.

Outside corner blocks eliminate the need to cut compound angles in the molding. Secure them with nails.

Step 3

A. Carefully measure the distance between one pair of corner blocks.

B. Add ⅛ in. to that dimension and cut a length of crown molding to match.

The most accurate way to crosscut the molding is with a power miter saw or a radial arm saw, but you can also get excellent results with a fine-tooth handsaw. To get a square cut, clamp a short 1×4 to the molding and use it as a saw guide.

Step 4

A. Hold the molding in place and butt one end tightly against a corner block. Bow it slightly and insert the other end in the other corner block. Press the molding to the wall until it pops into place. Secure it with 6d finishing nails driven into every other wall stud.

B. Drive a nail up into a ceiling joist every few feet. (If you can't find the ceiling joists, they may be running parallel to the molding. In that case, angle a nail up into the drywall or the plaster ceiling.)

Step 5

Continue cutting and installing the molding to fit between the corner (and divider) blocks. If you cut a piece slightly too short, fill the gap with a matching caulk. Also fill any gaps along the wall or ceiling.

Step 6

When all the molding is up, set the nailheads and fill the holes with a crayon-type putty stick. Remove any excess putty with a damp cloth.

Nail up the inside corner blocks, after shimming them as needed.

Raise the molding into position and pop it into place between the corner blocks. Continue until all the molding is installed, then caulk any gaps.

PRESSED-METAL WAINSCOTING

Embossed pressed-metal sheets are actually reproductions of the old tin plates used on ceilings. They're affordable and available in many styles and sizes.

All you need to install them are a few hand tools and a good pair of tin snips. However, since the edges are very sharp, always wear leather work gloves when you handle them.

To provide support for nailing the metal sheets, screw furring strips to the wall.

Step 2

Step 1

Paint the back of each metal sheet with an oil-based primer to protect against rusting.

Step 2

Secure 1×3 furring strips to the wall with screws.

Space the horizontal strips to provide a nailing base for the top, middle and bottom of the pressed-metal sheets, the chair rail and the baseboard molding.

Space the vertical strips 24 in. on center, to align with the ends and middle of the metal sheets.

Step 3

Install the baseboard molding.

Step 4

Starting in the most visible corner of the room, attach the metal sheets to the furring strips, using the decorative cone-head nails that come with them. When you get to a corner, use the tin snips to cut the panels to fit.

Step 5

Install the chair rail. Refer to the diagram at right for a simple chair rail made from two pieces of pine and base cap molding.

¾" x 1¾" shop-made rail cap

⅜" x 1¾" pine

1⅛" base cap molding

1x3

24"-high x 48"-long metal panel

1x3

1⅛" base cap molding

1x3 ripped to fit

1x4

1x3

Shoe molding

Tools
- paintbrush
- tin snips
- hammer
- leather work gloves
- screwdriver

Materials
- pressed-metal sheets, with decorative cone-head nails
- oil-based primer
- 1x3 furring strips
- chair rail
- baseboard molding
- screws

LIBRARY PANELS

Prefabricated frame-and-panel wainscoting can evoke the traditional look of cherry, mahogany, walnut or oak library panels—but is far easier to install.

The design shown mimics the look of red oak. The sheets are 30 in. high × 48 in. wide, and divided into three recessed panels. The frame is made of red oak-veneer fiberboard bonded to an oak plywood backboard. The exposed edges of the fiberboard frame are trimmed with a decorative solid-oak molding.

Fasten the wainscoting panels with drywall screws. Install a plywood strip to support the baseboard molding.

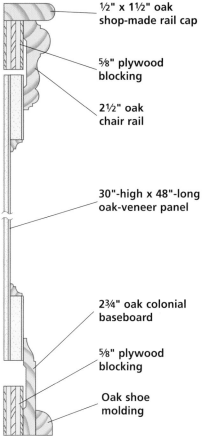

½" x 1½" oak shop-made rail cap

⅝" plywood blocking

2½" oak chair rail

30"-high x 48"-long oak-veneer panel

2¾" oak colonial baseboard

⅝" plywood blocking

Oak shoe molding

Step 1

Plan the layout of the panels from the most visible corner of the room outward. Ideally, electrical outlets will be centered in a frame. (You may want to have an electrician move outlets before you install the wainscoting.)

Step 2

Fasten the panels into place with drywall screws driven into wall studs. Drive the screws along the top and bottom edges of the panels so they'll be concealed by the chair rail and baseboard moldings. Butt the edges of the panels together to form a tight joint.

Step 3

Install strips of ⅝-in. plywood to provide a nailing base for the chair rail and baseboard moldings.

Step 4

Nail the chair rail and baseboard moldings to the plywood strips.

Step 5

If the panels are unfinished, apply two coats of varnish. You can stain them first, if you wish.

Materials
- prefabricated wood-veneer frame-and-panel sheets
- drywall screws
- ⅝-in. plywood strips
- chair rail
- baseboard molding
- stain (optional)
- varnish
- finishing nails

Tools
- screwdriver
- hammer

DESIGNING WITH MIRRORS

Mirrors can enhance almost any room—but the most effective type, size and location of the mirrors you choose will depend on the room's size and what you want to accomplish. Do you want to expand the space, multiply the light, add drama to the room—or all three?

To create the illusion of expanded space, use a few large floor-to-ceiling mirror panels and hide their seams (as shown above). Use an odd number of panels and avoid dividing the wall in the center. For example, on a 12-ft. wall, use three 4-ft. panels or one 6-ft. panel flanked by two 3-ft. panels.

To make a room look brighter, use large panels and be sure to reflect the light sources in the mirror. Consider using a lattice over the mirror—the mirror will reflect light, and the lattice will diffuse it. Don't

use smoked mirrors, which will make the room look darker.

If adding drama is your top priority, consider using several narrow strips applied to the walls or ceiling.

To avoid visual confusion, don't mirror more than two walls in one room. And finally, don't forget that the mirrors must be able to fit through all the doors that lead to the installation site.

Tools
- screwdriver
- drill

Materials
- ¼-in. mirror panels (from a glazier)
- mechanical mirror supports: screws, frames, clips, L-channel or J-channel
- mirror mastic

Using Mastic & Fasteners

Wall- and ceiling-mounted mirrors are held in place by mastic. Since mastic remains pliable even when fully cured, it's able to absorb vibrations in the mounting surface. However, be sure to use only mastic that's specifically labeled for mirrors; some adhesives, including silicone, contain solvents that will corrode the mirror backing.

Mirror mastic is available in both rubber- or asphalt-based formulas, as well as quick-setting varieties.

Asphalt-based mastic is the most common variety. If you're using it, the wall surface behind the mirror must be primed—untreated drywall or plywood will ruin the mastic. Asphalt-based mastic requires three to four days to cure. Use shims and double-stick tape to keep the mirror in place in the meantime.

This multipanel mirror reflects an outside view, creating a sense of endless space.

Rubber-based mastic forms a strong bond that's almost impossible to break. This can be a problem if you ever want to remove the mirror. Rubber-based mastic usually cures within six hours.

Quick-setting mastic sets up in about four hours. Some varieties are designed only for unprimed, porous substrates, while others are designed for nonporous surfaces, such as tile. Check the label to be sure you get the type you need.

Although mirror mastic is strong, it's best to provide additional support along the bottom of large mirrors, especially if they will be subjected to a lot of movement (such as on the back of a door). Another option is to make a lip for a mirror by setting it into drywall or tile.

Install support hardware for the bottom edge before mounting the mirror. (The side or top supports can be added after the mirror is in place.) If you choose not to install any mechanical supports, use temporary supports (cardboard or wood shims) to hold the mirror in place until the mastic sets.

Mounting a Mirror

Actually, the hardest part of mounting a mirror isn't attaching it, but getting it straight. Here are the steps involved in mounting a mirror properly.

Step 1
Install the mechanical supports for the lower edge of the mirror, making sure that they're level.

Step 2
Cover the back of the mirror with mastic, spacing dabs about the size of a chocolate kiss about 8 in. apart.

If the wall behind the mirror isn't plumb, use a stiffer mastic, such as building mastic, which requires dabs about the size of Ping-Pong balls. The gap-filling capability of stiffer mastics makes them the best choice for walls that are irregular or slightly bowed.

Step 3
Slip the mirror into the bottom supports and then push it up against the wall.

Adjust it for position. If the bottom supports were carefully leveled, any adjustments should be minor.

Step 4
Install mechanical supports for the sides and top of the mirror, if necessary.

BUYING MIRRORS

Home centers sell precut, full-length mirrors that are ready to install on the back of a closet, bedroom or bathroom door. But if you want to mirror a wall or replace the broken mirror above your bath vanity, you'll need to find a local shop that specializes in cutting and installing mirror and glass.

In general, consider hiring a glazier if you're dealing with a mirror bigger than about 2×3 ft. Trying to transport, cut and mount anything much larger is risky and not really cost-effective.

Mirror stock comes in three thicknesses: ⅛ and ³/₁₆ in., which are both used in frames, and ¼ in., which can be attached to walls in large sections with mastic and mechanical fasteners.

The mirror stock from all sources is basically the same; it's the finishing and the installation that determine the final appearance and expense of a mirror.

MIRRORED BATH IDEAS

Mirrors are one of the best ways to create a feeling of spaciousness in a dark or cramped area—and perhaps nowhere is this illusion more effective than in bathrooms, which can be both dark and small. In addition, using plenty of mirrors in the bath means you won't have to vie with your spouse for the one over the vanity in the morning.

Avoid installing bathroom mirrors from the floor to the ceiling. Begin the mirror at waist height or above so it won't reflect the plumbing or the toilet.

Here are two creative ways to use reflective surfaces to brighten up a bathroom.

Glass Ceiling

This 5 × 8-ft. bathroom feels spacious because of the mirror panels that cover the ceiling.

In addition, placing mirrors at either side of the short wall over the vanity visually doubles the length of this wall. Ending the mirrors at the front edge of the vanity prevents you from seeing infinite reflected images of yourself every time you stand at the sink.

While mechanical fasteners are usually necessary to hold mirrors on ceilings, here a marble wall tile forms a ⅜-in. lip to support the mirror. The mirror panels are also glued to the ceiling with mastic.

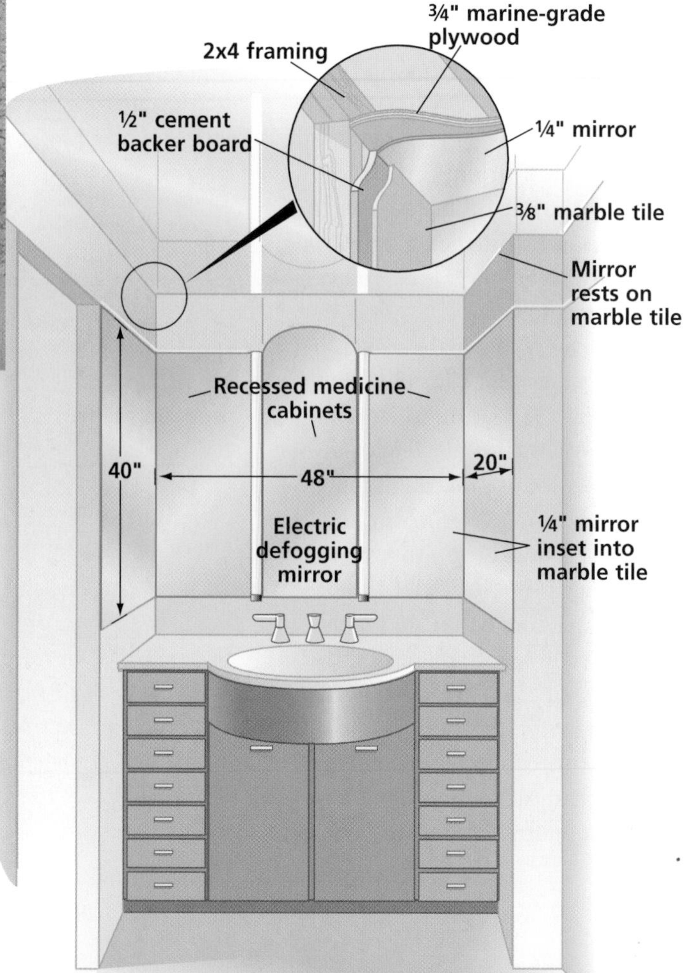

Tools
- screwdriver
- drill

Materials
- ¼-in. mirror panel (from a glazier)
- mechanical mirror supports: screws, frames, clips, L-channel or J-channel
- mirror mastic

Diagram labels:
- 2x4 framing
- ¾" marine-grade plywood
- ½" cement backer board
- ¼" mirror
- ⅜" marble tile
- Mirror rests on marble tile
- Recessed medicine cabinets
- Electric defogging mirror
- 40"
- 48"
- 20"
- ¼" mirror inset into marble tile

Mirrored Sky

This cramped, windowless bath used to feel claustrophobic. But now a 1-ft. band of mirrors, combined with a trompe l'oeil overhead scene, make the low ceiling look as if it's floating in space—giving a bather an expansive skylike view.

The ⅜-in. tile and the ¼-in. mirrors are both laid over the same backer board, and the mirror seams are aligned to the tile grout lines. Since the mastic adds some thickness to the back of the mirror, the finished surfaces are flush, and the look is sleek and elegant.

THE RIGHT WAY TO CLEAN MIRRORS

Moisture is a mirror's number one enemy. When you spray wet glass cleaner onto a mirror, it can puddle in the seams and edges, invade the mirror's protective coating and eventually deteriorate its reflective surface. That's the cause of those ugly black spots on old mirrors.

Instead of spritzing glass cleaner onto the mirror, follow these suggestions:

• Use a lint-free paper towel or a clean, soft cotton cloth. Old diapers and T-shirts work great.

• Spray a nonabrasive, low-ammonia cleaner onto the cloth, not the mirror, so it won't seep into the seams.

• Another option is to moisten the cloth in 1 gal. of water mixed with 1 cup rubbing alcohol or ¾ cup distilled white vinegar.

• Finish the process by drying the mirror thoroughly with a soft, grit-free cloth, paying special attention to the seams and edges.

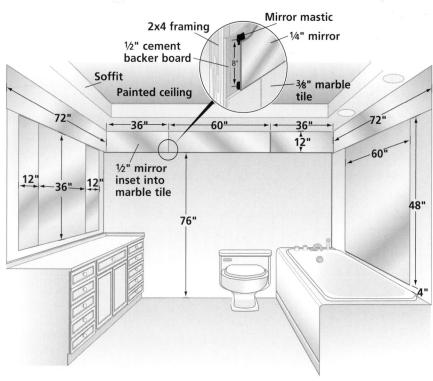

Jewel Box Bath

Measuring just 5 × 5½ ft., this windowless bathroom is hardly bigger than a modest walk-in closet. However, three mirrored and lighted niches have turned it into a bright, delightful retreat. The niches are lined with ¼-in. mirror panels and lighted with miniature halogen fixtures that are magnified by reflection. Here's how to create this look in your bathroom:

Step 1

A. Cut open three recessed niches in the wall between studs (usually they'll be 14½ in. wide × 4 in. deep).

B. Purchase small "hockey-puck" halogen light fixtures. Position them and determine where the wiring will run. Prepare the wiring for the fixtures in the wall.

C. Nail blocking between the studs to form the top and bottom of each niche. Drill a hole for the fixture wires through the blocking at the top of the niche.

D. Cut pieces of ¼-in. plywood to line the top, bottom, sides and back of the niches. Drill a hole for the fixture wires in the top piece. Glue the back piece in place, then nail or screw in the other pieces.

Step 2

Measure the wall niches carefully and figure the exact dimensions of the glass shelves and the top, bottom, side and back mirror panels. Design each side mirror panel in three sections, allowing for ¼-in. voids between the sections. Also mark a wiring hole in the top mirror panel, aligned with the one in the plywood. Order the glass and mirror from a glazier to fit your measurements.

Step 3

A. Use mastic to attach the mirror panels to the plywood, leaving ¼-in. grooves between the side sections to hold the glass shelves.

B. Place silicone adhesive in the grooves and install the glass shelves.

C. Frame the niches with metal edging.

D. Wire and install the lights at the top of each niche.

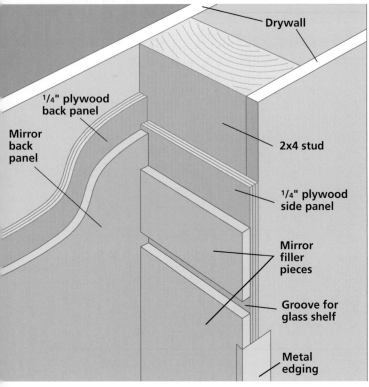

Drywall

¼" plywood back panel

Mirror back panel

2x4 stud

¼" plywood side panel

Mirror filler pieces

Groove for glass shelf

Metal edging

Tools
- wallboard saw
- utility knife
- hammer
- painting supplies

Materials
- nails
- blocking pieces
- ¼-in. plywood

- paint
- ¼-in. mirror, custom-cut
- ¼-in. glass shelves
- mirror mastic
- silicone adhesive
- metal edging
- "hockey-puck" halogen fixtures, ¾-in. deep x 2½-in. dia.

MIRRORED BACKSPLASH

This kitchen offers a striking combination of reflective surfaces: a mirrored and lighted backsplash set against black granite countertops.

Continuing the granite up the wall would have made the room look dark; the mirrored backsplash not only shows off the beauty of the countertops, but also reflects outdoor light and the light of the halogen fixtures under the upper cabinets. The mirrors actually double the brightness of the kitchen and make it appear larger.

Mirrors are inexpensive compared to other backsplash materials, such as stone and tile. They stand up well to heat, are easy to clean and are practically stainproof. Also, a mirrored backsplash allows you to keep an eye on activities elsewhere in the room while you cook.

The backsplash shown here was installed in three separate panels: two 15-in.-tall panels over the countertops and one 30-in.-tall panel over the stove. The mirrors were installed directly over the existing drywall surface.

For information on undercabinet lighting, see **Lighting a Wall Unit,** pages 126-127.

Step 1

A. Measure the mirror dimensions carefully, allowing for a ⅛-in. air-space between the bottom edge of the mirror and the countertop.

B. Order the mirrors from a glazier to fit your dimensions.

Step 2

A. Install J-channel on the wall along the base of the mirrors.

B. Insert neoprene-rubber setting blocks every 6 to 8 in. in the J-channel to lift the mirrors away from the moisture that may collect there. (This step isn't necessary for small mirrors if you can attach screw-in mirror holders to the wall.)

Step 3

A. Cover the back of the mirror with dollops of mirror mastic, spaced about 8 in. apart.

B. Position the mirrors and shim them into place until the mastic is fully cured.

Tools
• screwdriver

Materials
• ¼-in. mirror panels, custom-cut
• mirror mastic
• J-channel or
  screw-in mirror holders
• neoprene-rubber setting blocks

¼" mirror   Mirror mastic   Drywall

15"   30"   8"

Neoprene-rubber setting block   J-channel

Upgrading Floors & Ceilings

Give any room a
dramatic new look
with one of these
surprisingly easy
weekend makeovers.

*U*pgrading Floors & Ceilings

Floors and ceilings offer many interesting ways to update a room at a relatively low cost. In this chapter you'll find out how easy it can be to transform a worn-out floor with splashes of color, eye-catching patterns or convincing facsimiles of stone, marble and premium hardwoods. You'll also discover how to add distinction to a ceiling with traditional beadboard, reproduction tin ceilings or the clean, modern lines of easy-to-install drywall panels.

Although the projects in this chapter require some specialized skills, if you start with a small area and follow the instructions carefully, you'll be able to learn them as you go along. In addition, all of these projects will go easier (and faster) with two people.

Flooring

This section describes how to install four kinds of flooring—ceramic tile, resilient vinyl tile, resilient sheet vinyl and laminate. In general, all these floors can be installed over any smooth, sound surface and can transform a small room in one weekend.

A ceramic tile bathroom floor is a project that even a beginner can accomplish in a few days. It's relatively inexpensive and will result in an elegant, durable and watertight floor.

Vinyl tile is a good choice for any room where moisture isn't likely to be a factor. For a high-moisture area such as a bathroom or laundry room, choose sheet vinyl instead.

Laminate flooring is increasingly popular, due to its durability and ability to mimic more expensive flooring materials. Like the other flooring projects shown here, the difficulty of the task will depend largely on the size of the room and the complexity of the cuts involved.

The key to a successful flooring installation is planning ahead, making sure you have the right equipment and following the directions carefully. Taking shortcuts, especially in the preparation phase, can lead to problems later.

Ceilings

Although ceilings are the most visible single surface in a room, most are simply painted white and then ignored (unless they spring a leak). However, there are several easy-to-install materials that can help you turn a blank, boring ceiling into the focal point of a room.

Drywall panels are a modern way to add style to a ceiling and define the boundaries of a living area. They're especially effective when used in "open" home designs as a way to break up a large expanse of ceiling.

Beadboard and embossed metal panels are popular ceiling coverings that can provide a room with a warm, traditional look and feel. Here we show you how easy they can be to install yourself.

CERAMIC TILE FLOORING

When remodeling a bathroom, glazed ceramic tile is often the flooring of choice—it's durable, attractive, easy to clean, water-resistant, affordable and easy to install.

You can lay new ceramic tile right over an existing ceramic tile floor (as shown here), as long as the surface is sound and doesn't flex when you walk on it. However, if the existing flooring is rotted, or if more than 10 percent of the old tiles are loose, you will need to remove them all and level the floor.

Step 1

A. Check the existing floor for stability. Repair or reinforce the floor and subfloor, if necessary.

B. If the tile will be laid over existing tiles, pound them with a rubber mallet to detect any loose tiles. If you find any, remove them, apply tile adhesive and glue them back down.

C. Clean the floor thoroughly.

Step 2

A. Draw layout lines on the floor, as described in steps 1 and 2 of **Vinyl Tile Flooring**, pages 34-35.

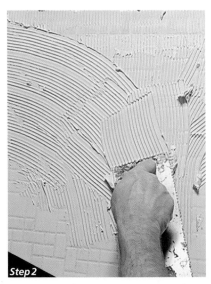

Spread thinset mortar onto the old floor with a notched trowel.

Tools
- tape measure
- chalkline
- 1/8-in. notched trowel
- rubber mallet
- 2x4 board
- handheld tile cutter
- tile nippers
- wet saw with diamond blade or jigsaw with tungsten-carbide blade
- circular saw with masonry abrasive blade
- needlenose pliers
- rubber grout float
- grout sponge
- soft cloth
- small brush or sponge

Materials
- glazed tile
- plastic tile spacers
- epoxy-based thin-set mortar
- marble threshold
- grout
- grout sealer

B. Starting in the center of the room, spread epoxy-based thinset mortar evenly against both reference lines of one quadrant, using a ⅛-in. notched trowel. Don't spread mortar over more than 2 sq. ft. at once; it will dry out before you're done.

Step 3

A. Set the first tile in the corner of the quadrant where the reference lines intersect. Press the tile into the adhesive with a slight twisting motion.

B. Ensure consistent spacing between tiles by placing plastic tile spacers at the corners of the set tile.

C. Position and set adjacent tiles into the adhesive along the reference lines. Make sure the tiles fit neatly against the spacers.

D. After setting several adjacent tiles, lay a straight 2×4 across them. Rap the 2×4 with a rubber mallet to ensure tiles are level with each other. Repeat this as you continue to lay the tile.

E. Lay the tiles in the remaining area of the quadrant, working in small sections until you've laid all the full tiles.

Step 4

A. Measure and mark the tiles that must be cut to fit, as described in step 5 of **Vinyl Tile Flooring,** pages 34-35.

B. Using a handheld tile cutter, score and snap the tiles that require only a straight cut.

C. For tiles that require notches, use a wet saw with a diamond blade or a jigsaw with a tungsten-carbide blade.

D. To cut curved lines, mark the cutting line on the tile, then use the scoring wheel of a handheld tile cutter to score several parallel lines, no more than ¼ in. apart, in the waste portion of the tile. Use tile nippers to gradually remove the scored part of the tile.

E. To cut a circular hole in a tile, score and cut the tile through the center of the hole, dividing the tile into two pieces. Use the curved method to cut each half of the hole.

Step 5

A. Apply mortar and fill in tiles in remaining quadrants. Complete each quadrant before beginning the next one.

B. Before the mortar dries completely, carefully remove the plastic spacers with needlenose pliers.

C. Cut marble threshold to fit the doorway, using a wet saw with a diamond blade or a circular saw with a masonry abrasive blade. Set the threshold so the top is even with the tile, keeping the same space between the threshold as between the tiles.

D. Let the mortar cure for 24 hours.

Step 6

A. Prepare a small batch of grout to fill the tile joints. Starting in a corner, pour the grout over the tile.

B. Use a rubber float to spread the grout outward from the corner, forcing it into the tile joints. Hold the float at a 60-degree angle and use a figure-eight motion.

C. Use the grout float to remove any excess grout from the tile surface. Continue applying grout and wiping off excess until about 25 sq. ft. of the floor has been grouted.

Step 7

A. To remove excess grout, wipe a damp grout sponge over about 2 sq. ft. of tile at a time. Wipe each area only once, to avoid pulling the grout out of the joints. Rinse the sponge in cool water between wipes.

B. Continue applying grout in this manner until the floor is completed.

Step 8

A. Allow the grout to dry for about four hours, then use a soft cloth to buff the tile surface.

B. Allow the grout to cure according to the manufacturer's instructions.

C. Apply grout sealer to all grout joints, using a small sponge or brush. Wipe any sealer from the tile surface immediately.

Step 3

Press each tile down into the mortar with a slight twisting motion.

Step 6

Hold the float at a 60-degree angle to force grout into the joints.

VINYL TILE FLOORING

Resilient vinyl tile is often designed to mimic ceramic tile, but it's much easier to install and far less expensive. It comes in both self-adhesive and dry-back styles.

Self-adhesive tile has a wax-paper backing that you peel off as you install the tiles. Dry-back tile is secured with adhesive that you spread onto the underlayment before installing the tiles.

In this project, the instructions for positioning and cutting the tiles are the same, regardless of which type you're using. However, step 3 only applies to dry-back tiles.

Step 1

A. To establish the layout lines (X and Y), divide the room (or the largest rectangular area in the room) into equal quadrants by snapping chalklines between the center points of opposite walls.

B. Check for squareness using the 3-4-5 triangle method. From the intersection of the chalklines, measure 3 ft. along one line and make a mark. Then measure 4 ft. along the perpendicular line and make another mark. The diagonal distance between the two marks should equal 5 ft. If it doesn't, adjust the reference lines until they're exactly perpendicular to each other.

Tools
- tape measure
- chalkline
- pencil
- linoleum or utility knife with extra blades
- straightedge
- tile cutter (for thick tiles)
- 1/16-in. notched trowel (for dry-back tile only)
- hammer

Materials
- resilient tile
- flooring adhesive (for dry-back tile only)
- metal threshold strip
- nails

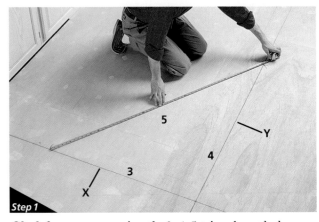

Check for squareness using the 3–4–5 triangle method.

Step 2

A. Dry-fit a row of full-size tiles along layout line Y, working from the center outward toward the walls.

B. Shift the tiles along the line as needed to make the layout look symmetrical or to reduce the number of edges that must be cut.

C. Using a different chalk color, draw a new line parallel to the original X line that runs through one of the tile joints in the Y line.

D. Keeping the first row of tiles in place, dry-fit a row of full-size tiles along the adjusted X line. Repeat step B for this line of tiles.

E. Using a different chalk color, draw a new line parallel to the original Y line that runs through one of the tile joints in the adjusted X line.

Step 3: For Dry-Back Tiles Only

A. For dry-back tile only, apply flooring adhesive around the intersection of the adjusted layout lines. Use a trowel with $1/16$-in. notches and hold it at a 45-degree angle.

B. Spread the flooring adhesive evenly over three of the quadrants in the installation area. Allow the adhesive to set according to the manufacturer's instructions.

C. To install the tile, proceed as described below, starting with step 4B. You can kneel on the tiles you've already installed to lay the new tiles.

D. When the first quadrant is completely tiled, spread the adhesive over the next quadrant, and finish setting the rest of the floor.

Step 4

A. For self-adhesive resilient tiles, peel off the paper backing as you proceed. Each time you lay a tile, rub the entire surface of the tile to bond it to the floor.

B. Install the first tile in one of the quadrants at the intersection of adjusted lines X and Y.

C. Set the tiles along the layout lines in the quadrant, keeping the joints between them tight.

D. Set all the full-size tiles tightly in the rest of that quadrant.

E. Set the full-size tiles in the other quadrants, as above—in the corner first, then on the layout lines, then in the rest of the quadrant.

Step 5

A. Mark the partial tiles in the first quadrant by laying the tile to be cut face-up on top of the last full tile you installed. Place a $1/8$-in. spacer against the wall. Set a marker tile against it, over the first tile.

B. Trace along the edge of the marker tile to draw a cutting line.

C. Cut the tile with a straightedge and a utility knife. To score and cut thick vinyl tiles, use a tile cutter.

D. Install the uncovered portion of the marked tile against the wall.

Step 6

A. Fit tiles around outside corners by making a cardboard template to match the space, allowing a $1/8$-in. gap along the walls. Cut the template and check to make sure it fits.

B. Trace the outline of the template on a tile and cut to fit. Install the cut tile against the walls.

Step 7

A. Continue installing edge tiles in the remaining quadrants, until the floor is completely covered.

B. Check the new floor; press down any loose tiles to bond them to the underfloor.

C. Install a metal threshold strip at the edges where the new floor joins another floor covering.

Install tiles along the layout lines of a quadrant first, then fill in the interior of that quadrant.

Mark the edge tiles to fit against walls. Here, the tile that will be cut is shown inverted for clarity; mark it facing up.

SHEET VINYL FLOORING

Resilient sheet vinyl offers a smooth, easy-to-clean floor at a low cost. It's available in either full-spread or perimeter-bond styles. Full-spread vinyl is secured with adhesive over the entire floor; perimeter-bond vinyl is secured only along the edges and seams. In both cases, the key to a successful floor is creating a smooth, level plywood underlayment and a perfectly cut flooring template.

Full-spread vinyl flooring bonds tightly to the floor and is unlikely to come loose. However, it's more difficult to install and requires a flawlessly smooth and clean underlayment. Perimeter-bond flooring is easier to install and will tolerate minor flaws in the underlayment, but it's also more likely to come loose.

Follow the instructions in steps 1 to 3 and step 5 for either type of sheet vinyl. In step 4, follow only the instructions for the kind of flooring you've chosen.

Step 1

A. To create a template, place sheets of heavy paper along the walls, leaving a consistent ⅛-in. gap against the wall. To secure the sheets, cut small triangular holes in them and tape them to the floor over the holes.

B. Follow the outline of the room, adding one sheet of paper at a time. Tape the edges of adjoining sheets, overlapping them by 2 in.

C. To fit the template around pipes, tape sheets of paper up to either side of the pipe. Measure the distance from the wall to the center and subtract ⅛ in.

D. Transfer the measurement to a separate piece of paper. Use a compass to draw the pipe diameter at the appropriate distance from the wall, then cut it out. Cut a slit from the edge of the paper to this hole.

Tools	Materials
• linoleum or utility knife with extra blades	• heavy butcher's or postal-wrap paper
• pencil compass	• masking tape
• scissors	• duct tape
• nonpermanent felt-tipped pen	• vinyl flooring
• ¼-in. notched trowel	• flooring adhesive
• J-roller or wallpaper seam roller (for perimeter-bond)	• ⅜-in. staples
	• metal threshold strip
• 100-lb. floor roller (for full-spread)	• nails
• staple gun	
• hammer	
• straightedge	

E. Fit the hole cutout around the pipe. Tape the hole template to the adjoining sheets.

F. When the template is done, roll or loosely fold it up.

Step 2

A. Sweep and vacuum the underlayment thoroughly.

B. Make sure the sheet vinyl is at room temperature. Carefully unroll it on a clean surface, taking care not to crease or fold it. Turn the sheet pattern-side up.

C. For two-piece installations, overlap the edges of the sheets by at least 2 in., matching the pattern lines. Duct-tape the sheets together.

D. Position the paper template over the flooring and tape it into place. Trace the outline of the template.

E. Remove the template. Cut the marked outlines, using a linoleum or utility knife, and a straightedge.

F. Cut the holes needed for pipes and other obstructions. Cut a slit from each hole to the edge of the flooring, cutting along a pattern line if possible.

Step 3

A. Roll up the flooring loosely and transfer it to the installation area. Unroll and position it carefully.

B. For two-piece installations, cut the seams. Hold a straightedge tightly against the flooring and cut along a pattern line through both pieces of flooring.

C. Remove both scraps. The pattern should now run continuously across the adjoining sheets.

Step 4: For Perimeter-Bond Vinyl Only

A. Fold back the seam edges of both sheets and apply a 3-in. band of adhesive to the underlayment, using a ¼-in. notched trowel.

B. Press the seam edges into the adhesive, one at a time. Make sure the seam is tight; press any gaps together with your fingers. Roll the seam edges with a J-roller. Clean any excess adhesive off immediately.

C. Apply adhesive under the cuts at the pipes and the perimeter of the room. Set the vinyl with the floor roller.

D. Fasten the outer edges of the vinyl with ⅜-in. staples driven every 3 in. Make sure the staples will be covered by the base molding.

Step 4: For Full-Spread Vinyl Only

A. Lay the flooring in place, then pull back half of the sheet and apply a layer of adhesive to the underlayment. Lay the flooring back on the adhesive.

B. Roll the flooring with the floor roller, moving from the center to the edges. Fold over the unbonded section of flooring, apply the adhesive, then lay and roll the flooring.

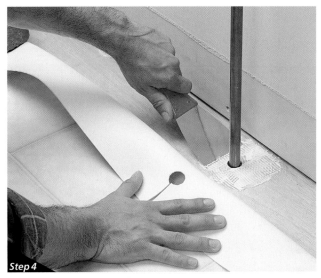

For perimeter-bond flooring, apply adhesive only around the perimeter of the room and under the cuts at pipes and seams.

C. Wipe up any adhesive that oozes up around the edges, using a damp rag.

Step 5

Measure and cut metal threshold strips to fit across the doorways and any other areas where the new floor joins another floor covering. Position each strip over the edge of the flooring and nail in place.

For full-spread flooring, lift half the sheet and apply adhesive under it. Replace the sheet and repeat on the other half.

LAMINATE FLOORING

Laminate flooring consists of a fiberboard core and a melamine surface encasing a printed photographic image that can depict almost anything. This unique material has the ability to mimic hardwoods, slate, marble, ceramic tile and other premium materials. Its versatility allows you to create custom design combinations that would ordinarily be prohibitively expensive—at a cost similar to that of simple oak strip flooring.

Laminate flooring also offers easy installation and versatility of use. For example, it can be installed over a heated floor or a basement slab. Once in place, it's durable, scratch-resistant and easy to maintain.

What to Buy

Most laminates are comparable in durability and strength, since the manufacturing process is similar. However, make sure that the floor you buy has:

- At least four layers (see **Laminate Layers** at right)
- A minimum thickness of $5/16$ in., to ensure strength and stability
- Edges sealed with water-resistant glue
- Clear installation and maintenance instructions
- A toll-free line to call with any questions
- A warranty of at least 15 years

Where to Put It

Laminate floors are floating floors; the planks or tiles aren't glued to the subfloor but to each other. This means they can go down with ease over existing floors, a plywood subfloor and even a concrete slab. Unlike solid wood, they can even be used over radiant-heat systems. However, since they have a wood-based core that will swell when wet, most aren't recommended for bathrooms, laundry rooms or other high-humidity areas.

You can choose tougher laminates for high-wear areas, such as a playroom, hallways and other heavily traveled areas, and save some money by using a less expensive flooring in the bedroom.

Installing a Laminate Floor

Installing laminate flooring in a small or average-size room is a manageable weekend project, especially if you have two people available for the gluing and assembly phase. However, unless you're quite experienced, a large room or one with a complex layout that requires significant cutting and trimming should be handled by a professional.

When installing a laminate floor, follow the manufacturer's instructions. Here are the major steps involved in laying a typical floating plank laminate floor.

Tools
- utility knife
- pencil
- chalkline
- tape measure
- flat bar
- handsaw, jigsaw or circular saw
- mallet
- plastic putty knife and spacers
- wet sponge, rag or towel

Materials
- laminate flooring planks
- wood glue
- foam backing
- masking tape

This striking floor pairs granite-look tiles with "oak" planks.

Laminate Layers

Good-quality laminate planks have at least four layers: a clear protective layer, a design image, a high-density fiberboard core and backing for added strength. Most are 7½ to 8 in. wide and 48 to 58 in. long.

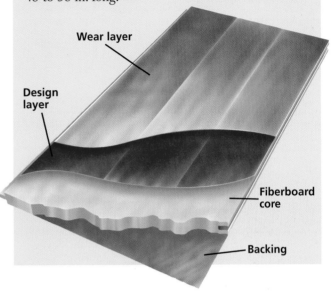

Wear layer

Design layer

Fiberboard core

Backing

Step 2

Roll out the foam backing and cut it to fit the room.

Step 1

Move the flooring, still in its original cartons, into the room where it will be installed at least 48 hours before you start working to allow the planks to adjust to the room's humidity level.

Step 2

A. If necessary, trim the bottom of the door casings with a handsaw. This will allow you to slip the flooring neatly beneath the casing.

B. Roll out the foam backing and cut it to fit the room. Don't overlap the seams.

C. Lay the backing in place, securing the seams with masking tape.

Step 3

A. Begin the installation along the longest wall. If there's a doorway or other opening across that wall, temporarily place a strip of wood or a plank across it to support the first row across the opening.

B. Place ¼-in. spacers along the wall to provide a gap in which the flooring can expand. (This gap will be covered by moldings.)

C. Dry-fit the first three rows of flooring, making sure the first row is straight. Stagger the seams in each row.

D. Cut the end pieces to fit, starting with the first three rows.

Step 4

Glue together the planks in the first three rows first, following the method described below. Allow them to cure for a few hours to provide a solid basis for the rest of the floor. Then complete the installation.

A. Apply a thin bead of wood glue to the matching grooves, tongues and end joints, according to the manufacturer's instructions. Apply the glue just before installation; it begins to set as soon as it's applied.

B. Quickly insert each tongue into the groove of the preceding row. Immediately tap the rows together tightly, using a mallet and a scrap of flooring to avoid flattening the tongue of the plank. Hold the plank tightly in place for a minute or two, until the glue sets.

C. As the glue oozes from the joints, remove it with a plastic putty knife, taking care not to scratch the flooring. Make a final pass with a clean, damp sponge, rag or towel.

Step 4

Secure the laminate planks with a thin bead of wood glue applied to the matching tongues and grooves just before you fit them together.

WHY CHOOSE LAMINATE FLOORING?

Affordable. The cost of laminate flooring is comparable to good-quality wood or vinyl flooring.

Many design options. The many designs and contrasting tiles available in laminate form make it easy to create a custom look.

Easy to install. Unless a room is large or complex, installing a laminate floor is a manageable do-it-yourself project.

Goes over existing flooring. Laminate flooring can go directly over most surfaces, including a concrete slab or a floor with a radiant-heat system.

Step 4

Tap the planks together, using a mallet and a scrap of flooring.

(Glue that's left on the floor will cause a haze on the surface.)

D. If a new plank rests higher than the previous one, weigh it down with an unopened carton of planks while the glue sets.

E. Make a cardboard template of any irregular areas, making allowances for the ¼-in. expansion gap. Trace the template onto a laminate plank and cut it to fit, using a jigsaw.

Step 5

Once the flooring is installed, extend its life by placing floor protectors under furniture, and mats at the front and back door. Use only a floor cleaner formulated for laminate floors and endorsed by the manufacturer.

Make a cardboard template to fit around irregular areas.

Manufacturers continue to develop new eye-fooling laminate designs. These ceramic-look tiles include realistic grout lines that hide the seams.

PROFESSIONAL TIPS

Here are some professional tips to consider for your laminate flooring project:

• Use your existing moldings to hide the expansion gap between the walls and the floor. Laminate companies do offer matching moldings, but they're expensive and they usually don't look as good as the existing moldings.

• The foam underlayment isn't a vapor barrier; it simply helps to reduce sound transmission. If you're installing the flooring over a concrete floor below grade, place a polyethylene vapor barrier down before you lay the foam.

• If you're installing flooring in the kitchen, use an elastomeric caulk around the edges. This flexible caulk will allow the flooring to expand and contract, while keeping spills away from the fiberboard core.

LAYERED CEILING

Tools
- hammer
- screwdriver
- straight 8-ft. 1x4 or ¼-in.-thick strip of hardboard or plywood
- drywall knife with extra blades
- paintbrush

Materials
- ½-in. drywall panels
- J-bead
- panel adhesive
- 1⅝-in. drywall screws
- joint compound
- sandpaper
- paint

Drywall can do far more than just cover wall studs and support paint, trim and wallpaper. One of the easiest and most interesting special drywall effects that you can achieve yourself is a layered ceiling. This allows you to visually define different living areas without blocking the light or the view.

In the wide-open interior shown at left, the drywall strips run in three directions from a central column, like beams. This provides a series of subtle yet effective boundaries between the living room, dining room and kitchen spaces. The added layer of drywall is edged with J-bead.

This is a simple improvement that you can install directly over an existing drywall ceiling. The J-bead is a sheet-metal molding shaped like a squared-off *J*, which you glue and screw to the edge of the drywall to provide a clean, finished edge. Here's how to do it:

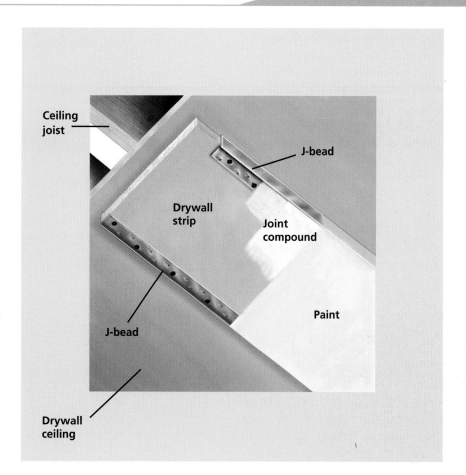

Step 1

Cut the drywall panels into 12-in.-wide strips.

A. Use a straight 8-ft.-long 1×4 (or a strip of ¼-in.-thick hardboard or plywood) as a straightedge to cut the drywall. Clamp the straightedge into position.

B. Score the line with a knife and snap the drywall. Use a utility knife to slice the paper from the back.

Step 2

A. Run a continuous bead of panel adhesive on the inside of the J-bead.

B. Press the J-bead into place on each side of one of the drywall strips.

Step 3

A. Apply two long, continuous beads of panel adhesive to the back of the first drywall strip.

B. Stick the strip in place on the ceiling.

C. Drive screws through the J-bead and the two layers of drywall, spacing the screws about 1 ft. apart. (Since the screws are only there to help secure the drywall strip, you don't need to drive them into ceiling joists.)

D. Follow steps 2A through 3C to install the rest of the drywall strips.

Step 4

A. Cover the drywall and J-bead with two or three applications of joint compound, to hide the screw heads and the lip of the J-bead, until you get a smooth finish.

B. After the joint compound is completely dry, lightly sand the surface and paint over it.

If you want the new layer to exactly match the color of the old ceiling, you'll probably need to repaint the entire ceiling.

TEXTURED CEILING

The most difficult ceiling texture to achieve is a smooth drywall finish, which requires meticulous finishing work. A textured finish is far more forgiving, and relatively easy to create on an existing drywall surface.

The variety of possible textures is limitless. Here are some of the more popular ones.

Veneer plaster allows you to give drywall ceilings and walls the solid, smooth look of old-fashioned plaster-and-lath surfaces. It goes over the drywall in one or two coats. Although it takes some practice to create a smooth trowel finish over a wide area, some people find this easier to do than conventional smooth drywall finishing.

Veneer plaster can be used to create a wide range of interesting textures. One of the most common is a skip-trowel finish, which leaves the surface roughly finished. To get a heavier finish, wait until the plaster is firm and then trowel on more plaster from the same batch. Here are some more texture ideas:

• For a rough, even texture, mix plaster with sand, and use a float to apply it over the first layer of plaster.

• For a fan or swirl pattern, arc a wallpaper brush or paintbrush across the plaster before it dries.

• To create lighter textures, use a sprayer. You can adjust it to create different effects, ranging from a splattered finish to a subtle orange-peel texture.

• To get a knockdown pattern, use a steel trowel to lightly "knock down" the peaks of a rough finish.

When it comes to creating textures, anything goes. Instead of sweeping with a brush, try a comb. Instead of floating with a trowel, try a heavy-nap roller or dab the wet plaster with anything you have on hand—a sponge, a rag or a crumpled-up plastic bag.

The easiest approach of all is to use a premixed texture finish. Roll it onto the ceiling and use a trowel or a brush to create textured effects.

SAND FLOAT

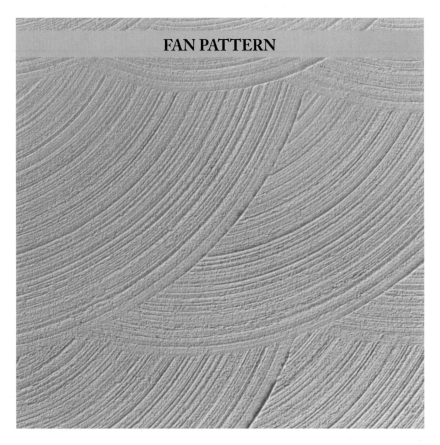

FAN PATTERN

EMBOSSED TIN CEILING

It's surprisingly easy to create a custom-designed tin ceiling that will add a striking touch to any room. You can order one from a catalog by selecting a pattern and sending in your ceiling dimensions. The company will send you back a layout that plots where each panel and plate will go.

Tin ceilings usually combine many elements (such as cornices, medallions and borders), which are actually 2 × 2-ft. or 2 × 4-ft. steel panels embossed in intricate designs. Since the nailheads are exposed, you need to use reproduction cone-head nails and half-round nailers to support the raised border designs.

Putting in a tin ceiling is a two-person job, since you're working overhead and the larger panels tend to flex. Here are the steps involved in the most common installation method.

Step 1

Nail or screw a layer of ⅜-in. plywood over the ceiling, securing it to the ceiling joists. This will provide a solid nailing surface for the ceiling panels, no matter where the seams fall.

Step 2

A. Measure the ceiling carefully and plan the layout of the panels.

B. Check the ceiling for squareness and adjust the layout accordingly.

C. Snap a grid of chalklines that mark the seams of the panels on the plywood. Measure carefully; the panels overlap less than ⅛ in., so there's little room for error.

Step 3

A. Secure the metal panels in place by nailing them to the plywood through the prepunched holes in the panels.

B. Working from the center of the room, tack up the first panel loosely.

C. Remove the nails from one side, overlap the next panel and firmly nail both panels in place.

D. Where the different patterns overlap, you may need to flatten some parts of the edges to bring the seams together. To do this, use a hammer and the head of a large nailset laid flat along the seam.

E. Follow the same procedure for all the remaining

Tools	Materials
• chalkline	• embossed ceiling panels
• hammer	• half-round nailers
• screwdriver	• cone-head nails
• large nailset	• ⅜-in. plywood
	• screws
	• paint or polyurethane varnish

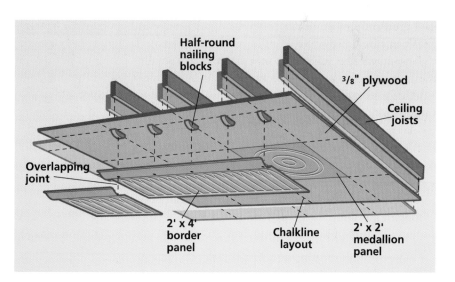

ceiling panels.

Step 4

A. Paint the ceiling. For a one-color look, use a deep-nap roller. For a polychrome ceiling, roll on the primary color, then brush on the accents.

BEADBOARD CEILING

One of the most popular do-it-yourself ceiling finishes is tongue-and-groove beadboard paneling. A beadboard finish creates a distinctive, traditional look and draws the eye upward, which can be very effective in a small room, such as the bathroom shown here.

Before starting this project, find out which way the ceiling joists run; the boards must be installed perpendicular to them. If the ceiling is accessible from above, check the joists from the attic. From below, use an electronic stud finder, or lightly tap the ceiling with a hammer until you hear the dull thud that indicates a joist. Once you know which way the joists run, you can proceed with installing the beadboard.

Tools	Materials
• paintbrush	• beadboard
• measuring tape	• primer or stain
• chalkline	• 4d (1½-in.) finishing
• hammer	nails
• drill	• putty
• jigsaw or	• decorative molding
portable circular saw	• paint
• nailset	

Step 1

Prime or stain all the surfaces (front, back and edges) of the boards. This is critical, as it prevents moisture from passing through them and blistering the finish.

Step 2

A. Find the center of one of the ceiling joists by tapping nails into the ceiling.

B. Once you find the center, mark it and measure 16 in. over to find the next joist. (Don't worry about the marks or holes you're making in the ceiling; they'll be covered by the new paneling.)

C. Once you've located and marked all the joists, snap chalklines along the marks that indicate the center of each joist.

Step 3

A. Remove all light fixtures and turn off the electrical circuit to the work area.

B. Hold the first board up to the ceiling, perpendicular to the chalklines, with the grooved edge against the wall. If the room is wider than 8 ft., span the distance with two or more boards, placing the joints on the centerline of a joist.

C. While you're holding the first row of boards in place, have someone else measure from one end of the boards across the room to the opposite wall, and then from the other end to the opposite wall.

D. If the two measurements aren't exactly the same, adjust the position of the boards until they are. Don't worry if there's a slight gap between the first board and the wall; it will allow room for expansion and will be hidden by the molding.

Step 4

A. Holding the first board in position, drive finishing nails through the tongue and into the joist centerlines.

B. Secure the edge along the wall by face-nailing—nailing straight in through the face of the board. Only the first and last boards are face-nailed.

C. Before nailing the ends, drill pilot holes to keep the thin wood from splitting.

D. Set the nailheads.

Step 5

A. Install the second board by pressing its grooved edge over the exposed tongue of the first board. Make sure it fits tightly; hold a scrap of beadboard against the edge and tap it lightly with a hammer, taking care not to damage the tongue.

B. Secure the board by toenailing—driving nails at an angle through the tongue and into the joists. Drill pilot holes before nailing the board ends.

C. Set the nailheads below the surface, being careful not to split the tongue.

D. Install the rest of the boards, except the last one, the same way. Be sure all the joints between the boards are tight.

Secure the first board by toenailing into the tongue, then nailing through the face of the board along the wall.

Step 6

To work around light fixtures, electrical wires or other obstructions, make a paper template of the area. Transfer the markings to the boards and use a jigsaw to cut them to fit around the obstruction.

For recessed light fixtures, use the circular cover to trace the cutting lines. Cut the boards to fit and nail them in place.

Step 7

A. Using a circular saw or jigsaw, rip the last board lengthwise to fit along the wall. Don't fit it tightly to the wall; the beadboard needs room to expand.

Bore small pilot holes near the ends of the boards so the finishing nails don't split the thin wood.

B. Slip the last board into place and face-nail it to the joists.

C. Set all the nailheads just below the surface.

D. Fill the nailheads with putty.

Step 8

A. Install a decorative molding to hide the gaps around the edges of the ceiling.

Flat moldings, such as doorstop, base cap and cove, are easy to install but don't look as elegant as a classic crown molding. (However, see pages 18-19 for a simple, do-it-yourself crown molding project.)

B. Apply a final coat of paint to the beadboard and the molding.

Finish by installing crown (shown) or other molding. Apply a final coat of paint.

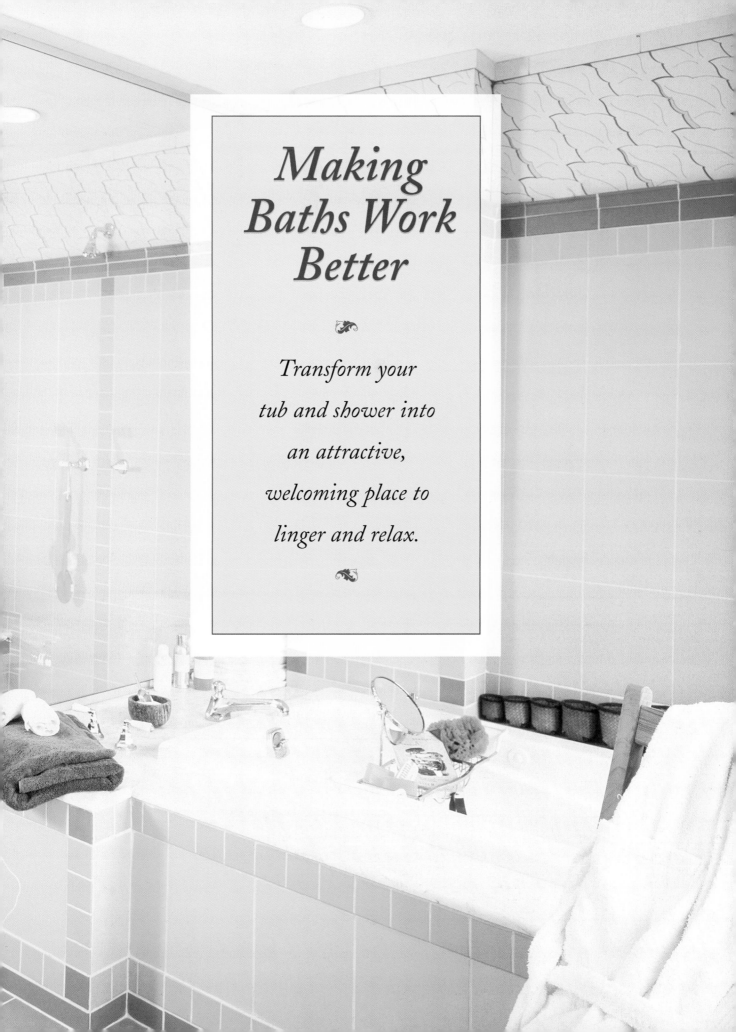

Making Baths Work Better

❧

Transform your
tub and shower into
an attractive,
welcoming place to
linger and relax.

❧

$\mathcal{M}$aking Baths Work Better

Improving a bathroom doesn't need to be expensive or complicated. You can easily upgrade your existing tub or shower by adding a few extra details that will enhance its safety, practicality and attractiveness.

The suggestions in this chapter require only a modest investment of time and money, but they do call for a range of skill levels. While installing a porcelain soap dish is a good project for a beginner, installing a tiled shower seat requires more advanced skills.

While none of these projects is particularly difficult, it's advisable to develop a modest level of carpentry skill before you tackle them. If you haven't worked with caulk before, it's also a good idea to practice first, until you have complete confidence in your ability to create watertight seals.

The most important factor for success with the projects in this chapter is making sure you have the correct materials. If you start with the right tools and supplies, the work should go smoothly.

Regardless of your skills and experience, it's a good idea to have a partner assist you with installing the larger projects—the pieces involved are bulky and may be difficult to handle alone.

Showers

When positioned properly—out of range of the shower spray—a porcelain soap dish can be a handy addition to a shower. In the first project you'll see that installing a soap dish can be as simple as replacing a tile.

The slide-bar showerhead featured next combines the convenience and flexibility of a fixed and a handheld showerhead, and can be adjusted to any height. If you have some basic plumbing knowledge, installing this fixture should be quite easy.

A shower seat provides a sturdy place to sit while bathing, which is especially helpful for an elderly bather. Here, we show you how to simplify the installation of a shower seat with a kit that's available at specialty tile shops. It includes a triangular pan that's attached directly to the wall, filled with mortar and then covered to match the existing wall tiles.

Probably the most difficult of this trio of projects, the shower seat requires moderate construction skills and some experience with installing ceramic tile.

Bathtubs

The glass tub and shower enclosure featured here offers total access to the tub, because it has no horizontal rails. Its unique panels slide and pivot independently, providing a variety of ways to access the tub.

Solid surfacing, a popular choice for kitchen countertops, is also useful in the bathroom. In the last project in this chapter, we show you how to install vertical-grade solid surfacing over your existing tub and shower walls and use matching moldings to create a finished look.

PORCELAIN SOAP DISH

A porcelain soap dish installed on the shower wall is a good way to keep your soap from getting soggy—as long as the dish is in the right position. Place the dish high on the wall to keep the soap safe from shower spray.

Pick a dish that matches the color and finish of your existing wall tile. If your shower walls are covered with a fiberglass or acrylic surround, buy a soap dish that can be glued right to the wall. Be sure to use the recommended adhesive, or you may permanently damage the shower surround.

Tools
- eye protection
- grout saw or awl
- hammer
- nailset
- drill
- ¼-in.-dia. masonry drill bit
- cold chisel
- putty knife or notched trowel

Materials
- 4x4-in. or 4x6-in. porcelain soap dish
- tile adhesive
- tile grout
- masking tape

Bore a series of holes through the tile but not into the wall surface behind it.

Crack the tile by striking the edge of each hole with a chisel and hammer.

Spread the tile adhesive onto the wall and scratch in a series of ridges.

Step 1
A. First, choose the best place on the wall to put the soap dish.

Choose a spot that's four or five tiles below the showerhead (about 16 to 20 in.) and two or three tiles to the right or left of it (about 8 to 10 in.).

B. Identify the tile that you will replace with the soap dish.

A 4×4-in. soap dish requires one tile space; a 4×6-in. dish requires 1½ tile spaces.

Step 2
A. Wearing eye protection, scratch out the grout from around the tile, using a grout saw or awl.

B. Use a hammer and nailset to punch a series of divots across the face of the tile in an X pattern.

C. Using the divots as starting points, bore through the tile, but not the wall behind it, with a ¼-in.-dia. masonry drill bit.

Step 3
A. Crack the tile into smaller pieces by striking the edge of each hole with a ¼-in.-wide cold chisel and a hammer.

B. Pry out the fractured shards of tile. Scrape the wall surface clean of any old mortar or leftover adhesive.

Step 4
A. Spread a thin coat of tile adhesive onto the wall and the back of the soap dish, using a putty knife or notched trowel. If you're using a putty knife, scratch ridges into the adhesive.

B. Firmly press the dish into place and secure it with two or three strips of masking tape. Check to make sure the dish is level.

Step 5
A. Wait 24 hours, then fill all the joints around the soap dish with grout.

B. Allow the grout to dry overnight before using the shower.

SLIDE-BAR SHOWERHEAD

A sliding showerhead is an attractive and practical shower addition, since it combines the convenience of a fixed showerhead with the flexibility of a handheld sprayer.

The model shown here has a 2-ft.-long vertical bar with an adjustable slide-lock mechanism. The showerhead can be positioned anywhere on the bar, or lifted off and used as a handheld sprayer.

Step 1

A. Select a slide-bar showerhead that matches your bath fixtures.

B. Remove the existing showerhead with a pipe wrench. If you plan to reuse it, protect its finish by wrapping it in a cloth.

Step 2

A. Wrap the threads of the brass nipple with Teflon tape.

B. Thread it into the stub-out in the wall. Leave about $9/16$ in. of the nipple protruding from the wall.

C. Carefully thread the chrome wall supply elbow onto the nipple.

D. Cover the elbow with a soft cloth and tighten it with a pipe wrench (or use a strap wrench).

Step 3

A. Press a mounting bracket onto each end of the slide bar.

Tools
- pipe wrench or strap wrench
- soft cloth
- $3/16$-in.-dia. masonry drill bit
- $1/2$-in.-dia. masonry drill bit
- screwdriver
- level
- nailset
- hammer
- drill

Materials
- slide-bar showerhead kit
- $1/2$-in.-dia. x $1\frac{1}{2}$-in.-long brass nipple
- Teflon tape
- hollow-wall anchor or toggle bolt
- $1/4$-20 machine screws

B. Place the bar 4 to 6 in. to the side of the wall supply elbow; the lowest end of the bar should be about 52 in. above the bottom of the tub or shower.

C. Hold the bar against the wall and check it for plumb with a level.

Step 4

A. Outline the screw holes in the brackets on the wall.

B. Use a hammer and nailset to start the screw holes. Drill the holes with a $3/16$-in.-dia. masonry drill bit.

C. If you hit a stud, attach the slide bar directly to the wall.

D. If you don't hit a stud, use a $1/2$-in. masonry drill bit to enlarge the hole. Insert a hollow-wall anchor or toggle bolt into the hole.

E. Slide the retainer ring forward to hold the fastener against the back of the wall. Snap off the plastic straps.

Step 5

A. Attach the slide bar to the wall with screws driven through the mounting brackets and into the wall. If you're fastening the bar to a stud, use the screws provided with the kit. If you're using toggle bolts, attach it with $1/4$-20 machine screws.

B. Conceal the screws by sliding chrome-finished end caps onto the upper and lower mounting brackets.

C. Thread the flexible steel hose onto the wall supply elbow. Clip the showerhead into the slide-lock mechanism.

Thread the chrome-plated wall supply elbow onto the nipple and tighten.

Insert the toggle bolt into the hole and slide the retainer ring forward.

SHOWER SEAT

This attractive shower seat is built with a kit that greatly simplifies the installation. It provides an attractive, secure place to sit during a shower, and can also serve as a handy shelf.

Because of the kit, you don't have to tear open the wall, break up any tile or build a wooden frame. The kit includes a triangular aluminum pan that's fastened directly to the existing wall, then filled with mortar and covered with ceramic tile. Ask for it at specialty tile shops.

Tools
- tape measure
- masking tape
- felt-tip marker
- drill
- ⅜-in.-dia. carbide-tip masonry drill bit
- screwdriver
- mortar trowel
- tile cutter
- trowel with ⅛-in. notches
- rubber float

Materials
- shower seat kit
- masonry mortar mix
- tiles
- thin-set mortar or latex mastic
- grout
- sponge
- soft cloth
- silicone caulk

Step 1
Determine where you want to install the shower seat and how high you want to put it on the wall. For most adults, the most comfortable position will be about 16 to 20 in. above the shower floor.

Step 2
A. Hold the metal pan in position on the wall. Place a strip of masking tape on the wall at the locations of the six screw holes. (The tape will make marking the holes easier and will help keep the drill bit from spinning off the marks.)

B. Using a felt-tip marker, outline the screw holes on the tape.

C. Drill through the wall at each mark, using a ⅜-in.-dia. carbide-tip masonry bit. Remove the tape.

D. Insert the hollow-wall screw anchors provided with the kit partway into the holes.

(The anchors open as the screws are tightened, attaching the seat securely to the wall. If you hit a stud while boring the anchor holes, use a 2½-in. wood screw instead.)

E. Place a dab of silicone caulk around each anchor head, to seal out water, then press the anchors all the way in.

Tighten the screws in the wall anchors to secure the pan to the wall.

Step 3

A. Hold the metal pan in position on the wall.

B. Insert the screws through the holes and into the wall anchors. Tighten the screws until the bench is securely fastened to the wall.

C. Apply a thin bead of silicone caulk along the top edge of the bench.

Step 4

A. Mix the masonry mortar according to the manufacturer's instructions.

B. Use a trowel to pack the mortar tightly into all three corners, until it comes out of the holes in the front. Smooth the top surface.

C. Trowel a thin, wetter coat of mortar onto the front edge of the bench.

D. Let the mortar cure for at least 24 hours.

Step 5

Cover the top of the bench with tile that matches the shower walls (you can also use a slab of stone or solid-surface material). If you like, you can trim the front edge with smaller tiles.

A. Dry-lay a full tile in the center of the bench, allowing it to overhang the front edge by about ¼ in.

B. Dry-lay the remaining full tiles, working out in both directions and back to the corner.

C. Use a tile cutter to trim the tiles that abut the walls. Dry-lay the cut tiles around the full tiles.

Step 6

A. Remove all the tiles. Spread thin-set mortar or premixed latex mastic over the top and front edges of the bench, using a trowel with ⅛-in. notches.

B. Lay the top-surface tiles first, then the edge tiles. Firmly press down on each tile to set it. Allow to cure overnight.

Step 7

A. Press grout into the joints between tiles with a rubber float, spreading the grout over the entire surface of the tile. To completely seal out moisture, you need to force the grout into every crack.

B. Let the grout set for about 20 minutes, then wipe off the excess with a damp sponge.

C. Once the grout is dry and hard, buff the tile with a soft, dry cloth.

D. Allow the grout to cure for at least 24 hours.

Step 8

A. Run a thin bead of silicone caulk around the perimeter of the bench, to seal out water.

B. Let the caulk set for six to eight hours before you use the shower.

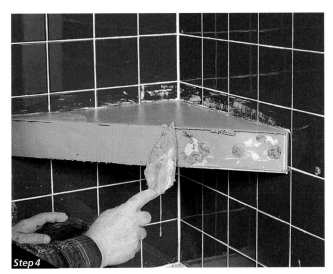

Fill the pan with mortar, smooth it with a trowel, and apply a thinner coat to the front edge of the bench.

Lay the top-surface tiles first, then the edge tiles. Press down firmly on each tile to set it into the mortar or mastic.

GLASS TUB ENCLOSURE

This attractive glass-and-aluminum tub enclosure has four narrow tempered glass panels that slide or pivot independently, allowing you to access the tub and shower in a variety of convenient ways.

For a small opening, you simply slide open the two center panels. To access the whole tub at once, slide open the center panels and pull the doubled-up panels outward into the room.

The panels will also pivot inward, which comes in handy in tiny bathrooms or when you're cleaning the tub or shower. Since the glass panels are supported by vertical jambs mounted to the side walls, there are no horizontal rails to clean around or duck under.

Step 2

At each screw location, bore a hole through the tile and wallboard, then tap in a screw anchor.

Tools
- level
- hammer
- nailset
- drill
- ¼-in.-dia. masonry drill bit
- screwdriver

Materials
- glass tub enclosure
- plastic wall anchors
- 1¼-in. screws
- ½-in. screws
- clear silicone caulk

Step 1

A. Hold one of the aluminum wall jambs against the wall to which it will be attached. Use a level to make sure it's plumb.

B. Mark the six screw holes onto the wall.

C. Repeat for the other jamb.

Step 2

A. If the wall is tiled, use a hammer and a nailset to make a small divot at each screw hole.

B. Bore a ¼-in.-dia. hole through the wall at each divot.

C. Insert plastic wall anchors into the holes. Gently tap them in with a hammer. (If you hit a stud, use 2½-in. wood screws instead of wall anchors.)

Step 3

A. Hold the jamb in place and secure it with six 1¼-in. screws driven into the anchors.

B. Repeat for the other jamb.

C. Check to make sure the jambs are plumb. If they aren't, loosen the screws, tap the jambs into alignment and retighten the screws.

Step 4

A. Lay one of the panel assemblies on its side.

B. Apply clear silicone caulk to the underside of the pivot block that sits on the tub ledge. Be careful not to get any caulk on the glass panels.

Step 5

A. Hold the panel assembly a few inches above the tub ledge and push the pivot block down over the wall jamb.

B. Carefully lower the entire panel assembly down onto the tub ledge.

C. Secure the panels by driving two ½-in. screws through the pre-bored holes in the panel frame and into the wall jamb.

D. Repeat the above steps to prepare and install the other panel assembly.

Step 6

A. Test the glass panels to see how smoothly they slide and pivot.

B. If necessary, raise or lower them by turning the top roller bracket screws.

C. Apply a bead of clear silicone caulk along the vertical joints where the frame meets the wall.

D. Apply a bead of clear silicone caulk along the inside and outside of the frame.

Hold the panel assembly above the tub ledge, press it to the wall, and lower it.

If the glass panels don't slide smoothly, adjust the screws in the top roller bracket.

SOLID-SURFACE TUB SURROUND

Durable solid surfacing has long been popular for kitchen counter-tops—and it works just as well as a tub surround. Here we demonstrate how it can give a shower enclosure a facelift in one weekend.

This project uses ⅛-in. solid-surface veneer to cover the tile walls around a 5-ft. tub. It comes in a kit that includes two 30×60-in. wall panels, one 60×60-in. wall panel and matching trim molding.

Although these wall panels extend all the way to the ceiling, that isn't typical; they usually stop 18 to 22 in. short of it. However, you can use the installation method shown here for any wall.

Step 1

Inspect the existing wall. Solid-surface panels can be glued to almost any surface that's flat, structurally sound and completely clean. If there are any loose tiles, pry them off and reinstall them with ceramic-tile adhesive. If more than 10 percent of the tiles are loose, remove them all and cover the wall with cement backerboard or water-resistant drywall.

Step 2

A. Lay cardboard or an old blanket on the tub bottom to protect it.

B. Remove the showerhead, tub spout and faucet handles. Use a cold chisel and a hammer to knock off any wall-mounted towel racks and soap dishes.

C. Wearing eye protection and a dust mask or respirator, remove caked-on dirt and soap scum from the tiles by scuff-sanding them with a random-orbit sander fitted with 80-grit sandpaper.

D. Use a damp rag to wipe away the sanding dust.

Tools
- cold chisel
- hammer
- random-orbit sander fitted with 80-grit sandpaper
- portable circular saw, or router & carbide-tipped straight bit with top-mounted ball-bearing pilot & straight-edge guide
- caulk gun
- J-roller
- drill
- hole saw
- scissors
- plastic trowel with ⅛-in. notches

Materials
- solid-surface tub-surround kit to fit the size of your tub
- cardboard or blanket (tub liner)
- cardboard (template)
- silicone adhesive
- ¹⁄₁₆-in. shims

Test-fit the cardboard template over the holes in the plumbing-end wall.

Step 3

A. Measure the three walls.

B. If necessary, trim the wall panels to fit. Cut them about ⅛ in. less than the width and height of the existing wall.

To trim the panels, you can use a circular saw, but a router and a carbide-tipped straight bit with a top-mounted ball-bearing pilot will give you quicker, cleaner cuts. Clamp a straightedge guide to the panel and move the router from left to right. The ball-bearing pilot will ride against the straightedge guide and produce a perfectly straight cut.

Step 4

A. Make a cardboard template of the plumbing, indicating the exact position of the showerhead pipe, tub spout and faucet handle stems. Transfer these marks to the cardboard and cut out the holes.

B. Test-fit the cardboard template to make sure the holes align exactly with the pipes in the wall.

Step 5

Install the large panel to the back wall of the tub.

A. Using a caulk gun, apply a continuous ¼-in. bead of silicone adhe-sive to the entire wall in a grid of horizontal and vertical lines, spaced about 6 in. apart.

B. Apply a double bead of adhe-sive along the top and bottom of the wall for extra holding power.

C. Spread the adhesive across the wall, using a plastic trowel with ⅛-in.-wide notches.

D. Immediately press the panel into the wall. Place 1/16-in.-thick shims under the panel to hold it above the top of the tub.

E. Go over the entire surface firm-ly with a J-roller to set the panel into the adhesive.

Step 6

A. To cut the plumbing-end panel, place the cardboard template over the panel and mark all the holes.

B. Remove the template; drill out the holes, using a hole saw for smaller holes and a router and straight bit for larger holes.

C. Test-fit the panel to make sure that it fits over the pipes.

D. Spread adhesive on the wall, as in steps 5A to 5C.

E. Press the panel into place, mak-ing sure the holes line up properly. Go over it firmly with a J-roller.

F. Repeat steps 6D and 6E for the opposite end panel.

Step 7

A. Measure the back wall.

B. Cut a piece of molding ⅛ in. less than that length to allow the trim to expand without buckling.

C. Apply adhesive to the back of the molding and press it to the wall. Use several strips of masking tape to hold it in place.

D. Repeat steps 7A to 7C for the two end walls.

E. Cut and install the vertical cor-ner trim in the same way. Again, hold it in place with masking tape.

Press the plumbing-end panel in place, making sure the holes align correctly with the showerhead, the tub spout and the faucet.

Step 8

A. On some tub surrounds, the tile extends an inch or so beyond the end panels. To conceal it, form a corner trim from two flat pieces of solid-surface molding joined at a 90-degree angle.

B. Glue the molding to the tile with silicone adhesive.

C. Allow the adhesive to dry for 24 hours before removing the tape or using the tub.

Conceal the outer rim of the wall tile with two molding pieces joined togeth-er at a 90-degree angle.

Lighting Up Your Home

Brighten your home
with this resourceful
collection of
lighting, window and
skylight projects.

Lighting Up Your Home

Light is perhaps the one element of a room that's essential to both its visual appeal and its function as a living space. The play of natural and artificial light in a room can be multiplied indirectly by using mirrors (see **Mirrors**, pages 22-27). However, the most direct way to enhance the light in a room is to add or improve light fixtures, windows and skylights.

Lighting

This section describes three kinds of projects: installing new switches, replacing a recessed light fixture and converting an overhead fixture to a fan-light.

There are many different kinds of dimmer and specialty switches on the market. Here we show how easy it is to install new switches that can make it more convenient to control your light fixtures.

These projects are very simple, even if you've never worked with electrical circuits before. Just follow the safety steps that are described for each project.

Replacing a recessed light fixture and installing a ceiling fan-light are somewhat more challenging projects, but they won't present any serious difficulties if you've done electrical work before.

The ceiling fan-light installation is the most difficult project in this section, and if you need to build a ceiling brace to secure the fixture, it will also require solid carpentry skills.

Windows

Windows are our link with the outside world; they let in the air and light that brighten our homes. Adding, remodeling or upgrading a window can do wonders for a room.

This section includes four projects: weatherizing windows, replacing sashes, installing interior shutters and installing a glass block window.

If you're comfortable with power tools and familiar with do-it-yourself carpentry techniques, you'll enjoy improving your home with these projects.

Skylights

Skylights are a wonderful way to brighten a dark room, but they do have some drawbacks—they tend to be energy-inefficient and difficult to install. However, there's a new kind of skylight that comes preassembled in a tube and minimizes both of these problems.

Tubular skylights are far more energy-efficient than regular skylights and can be installed in one weekend. Since the flexible tube channels light into the house through a reflective interior coating, the tube doesn't need to travel in a straight line, and you can maneuver it to get around obstructions and tight spaces in the attic. Also, since you don't need to build a shaft, you don't have to do any of the drywall or painting work required for a regular skylight.

Dimmer Switches

Dimmer Switches

A dimmer switch allows you to adjust the brightness of the light fixture to any level you wish—and replacing a regular switch with a dimmer is a very easy electrical project. You can replace any standard single-pole switch with a dimmer, as long as the switch box is big enough.

Here are the general instructions for this project; however, if the manufacturer's instructions for your dimmer switch differ from these, follow them instead.

Tools
- screwdriver
- neon circuit tester
- combination tool

Materials
- twist-on wire connectors
- fine sandpaper
- dimmer switches

Step 1
A. Turn off the power to the switch at the service panel.

B. Remove the switch coverplate and the mounting screws. Pull the switch from the box, holding it by the mounting straps. Don't touch the bare wires or screw terminals.

Step 2
A. Touch one probe of a neon circuit tester to the grounded metal box or the bare copper grounding wires. Touch the other probe to each screw terminal.

If you're replacing an existing dimmer, insert the second probe into each of the wire connectors, in turn.

B. If the tester glows, it means there's still power running to the switch. Return to the service panel and shut off the correct circuit.

Step 3
A. Once you've confirmed that the power is off, disconnect the circuit wires and remove the switch.

B. Straighten the circuit wires and check them. If the ends are darkened or dirty, clean them with fine sandpaper. If they're nicked, clip them with a combination tool.

C. Use the combination tool to strip about ½ in. of clean bare wire.

Step 4
A. Connect the wire leads on the dimmer switch to either of the circuit wires, using wire connectors.

B. If you're installing a three-way dimmer, it will also have an additional wire lead, called a common wire. Attach it to the darkest screw terminal.

Step 5
A. Mount the switch in the electrical box, tucking the wires in carefully.

B. Reattach the switch coverplate.

C. Restore the power to the switch at the main service panel.

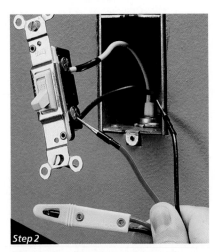

Use a neon circuit tester to test the connection to make sure the power is off.

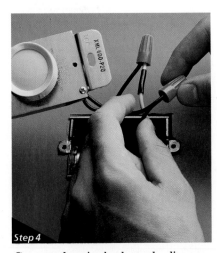

Connect the wire leads on the dimmer to the circuit wires.

SPECIALTY SWITCHES

Automatic Switches

Automatic switches are especially convenient for children, the elderly and those with physical disabilities. They have an infrared beam that detects nearby movement—such as a passing hand—and signals the switch to turn on or off. Some also include a manual dimmer.

Step 1

Follow steps 1 to 3 under **Dimmer Switches**, page 64.

Step 2

Connect the black wire leads on the specialty switch to the black (hot) circuit wires. If the box also has white neutral wires, connect them to each other with a wire connector. Connect the bare copper grounding wires to the grounding wire from the metal box, as shown.

Step 3

Follow step 5 under **Dimmer Switches**, page 64.

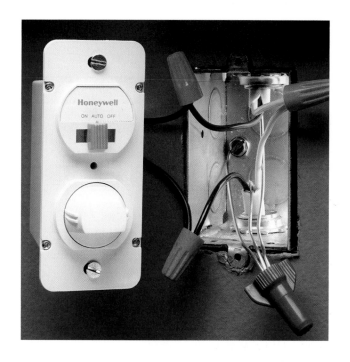

Motion-Sensing Switches

Motion-sensing switches have a wide-angle infrared beam that turns on a light fixture whenever it detects movement in the room. Most have a manual override, and some have a sensitivity control and a time-delay shutoff.

Step 1

Follow steps 1 to 3 under **Dimmer Switches**, page 64.

Step 2

Follow step 2 under **Automatic Switches,** above.

Step 3

Follow step 5 under **Dimmer Switches**, page 64.

Programmable Switches

Programmable switches are a good idea whenever you have to leave your home unoccupied. They can recall up to four on-off cycles a day. To make a home look active, they should ideally be set in a random on-off pattern.

Step 1

Follow steps 1 to 3 under **Dimmer Switches**, page 64.

Step 2

Follow step 2 under **Automatic Switches,** above.

Step 3

Follow step 5 under **Dimmer Switches**, page 64.

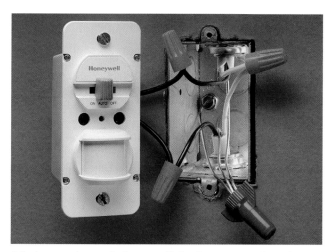

Motion-sensing switches turn light fixtures on when they detect any movement in the room.

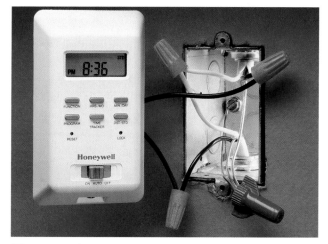

The automatic controls of a programmable switch offer an invaluable safety feature when you're away from home.

RECESSED LIGHTING

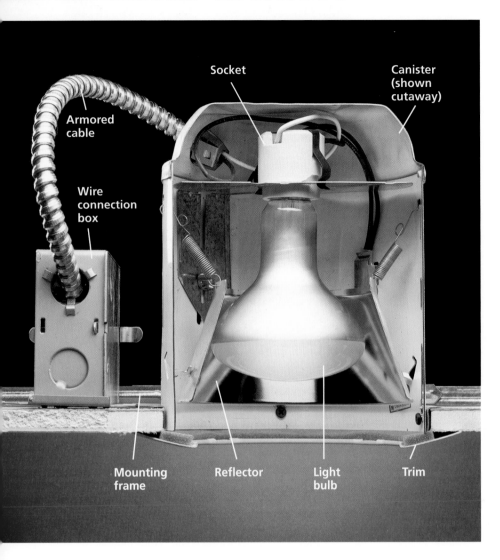

Armored cable

Socket

Canister (shown cutaway)

Wire connection box

Mounting frame

Reflector

Light bulb

Trim

Step 1
Step 1

Turn off the power to the recessed light fixture at the service panel. Don't just turn off the switch—voltage may continue to leak through the wires and cause a shock. Instead, turn the light on and follow these steps:

If your electrical circuits are labeled, locate the breaker or fuse in the service panel that controls the fixture's circuit, and turn it off. The light should go out.

If your circuits aren't labeled, go to the circuit box and turn off each circuit in turn until the light goes out.

Don't touch any bare wires until you've confirmed that there is no power to the circuit (step 3).

Step 2

A. Remove the trim, the bulb and the reflector, which is held in place by springs or mounting clips.

B. Loosen the screws or clips that hold the canister to the mounting frame. Carefully raise the canister and set it aside inside the ceiling cavity.

C. Remove the coverplate on the

Light fixtures that are recessed into the ceiling can provide a range of lighting effects, from subtle to dramatic, to complement the decor of your home. However, replacing a recessed light fixture is somewhat more complicated than replacing a standard ceiling-mounted fixture.

It's easiest to replace a recessed light if you get a new fixture that's the same model as the old one, because this means that you'll be able to install the new one in the existing metal canister.

Recessed fixtures that are marked "I.C." can be placed right up against the attic insulation. All other recessed lighting canisters must be kept at least 3 in. away from any insulation—if they get any closer, they'll trap heat, which can melt the insulation on the socket wires and cause the fixture to fail or even catch fire.

As with any electrical repair, follow the manufacturer's instructions and commonsense rules of electrical safety. Here are the steps involved in safely evaluating and replacing a recessed light fixture.

Tools
- screwdriver
- neon circuit tester
- continuity tester

Materials
- recessed light fixture
- twist-on wire connectors

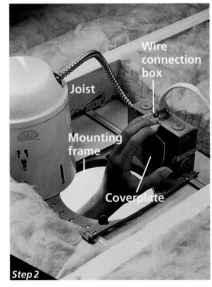

Wire connection box

Joist

Mounting frame

Coverplate

Step 2

Remove the coverplate on the wire connection box.

wire connection box, which is attached to the mounting frame between the ceiling joists. Be careful not to touch any bare wires.

Step 3

A. Test to make sure the power is off: touch one probe of the circuit tester to the grounded wire connection box and insert the other probe into each wire connector. If the tester doesn't light, it's safe to continue working and touch the bare wires.

B. If the tester glows at any point during the test, it means that power is still reaching the fixture. Return to the service panel and shut off circuits until the tester no longer lights.

Step 4

A. Once you're sure that the power is off, disconnect the black and white circuit wires by twisting off the wire connectors holding the matched pairs together.

B. Pull the armored cable from the wire connection box.

C. Remove the canister through the frame opening.

D. Lift out the socket.

E. Adjust the metal tab at the bottom of the fixture by prying it up slightly with a small screwdriver. This will improve its contact with the light bulb.

Step 5

Test the socket with a continuity tester to make sure it's operating correctly.

A. Place the clip of the continuity tester on the exposed end of the black wire while touching its metal probe to the metal tab.

B. Place the clip of the continuity tester on the exposed end of the white wire while touching its metal probe to the threaded metal socket.

C. The tester should glow during both tests. If it doesn't, it means that the socket is defective and needs to be replaced.

Step 6

A. Set the new canister inside the hole in the ceiling.

B. Thread its wires through the hole in the wire connection box.

C. Push the armored cable into

the wire connection box to secure it (it should snap into place).

Step 7

A. Connect the white fixture wire to the white circuit wire, using a twist-on wire connector.

B. Connect the black fixture wire to the black circuit wire, using a twist-on wire connector.

C. Attach the coverplate to the wire connection box.

D. Unless the fixture is marked "I.C.," take care to keep any insulation at least 3 in. away from the canister and the connection box.

Step 8

A. Position the canister inside the mounting frame.

B. Attach the mounting screws or clips. Attach the reflector and trim.

C. Install a light bulb of the proper wattage.

D. Restore power to the fixture at the main service panel.

E. Check to make sure that the new fixture is working properly.

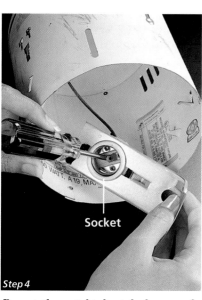

Pry up the metal tab at the bottom of the fixture with a screwdriver.

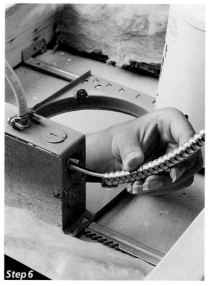

Push the armored cable into the wire connection box.

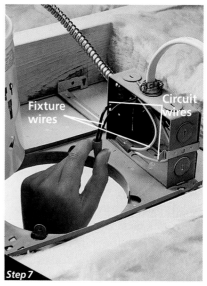

Connect the fixture wires to the circuit wires with twist-on wire connectors.

CEILING FAN-LIGHT

In addition to adding a touch of elegance, an investment in a ceiling fan-light will pay off year-round by cooling the room in the summer and circulating trapped heat downward in the winter. Some models, such as this one, also have a remote control feature. You can install the fan-light yourself if you use the wiring for an existing ceiling fixture, as shown here.

Tools
- neon circuit tester
- screwdriver
- drill
- 5/16-in.-dia. drill bit

Materials
- ceiling fan-light fixture
- 2x6 brace or expandable ceiling fan brace
- 3-in. screws
- 1/4-in.-dia. x 4-in.-long lag screws
- twist-on wire connectors
- electrical tape
- 40W light bulbs (2)
- 9V battery

Step 1
Leave the existing light on and turn off the power to the fixture at the service panel. Don't just turn off the switch—voltage may still leak through. When you turn off the correct circuit, the light will go out.

Step 2
A. If the old fixture has a glass globe, remove it and take out the light bulbs.

B. Unscrew the fixture from the electrical box; support it carefully while you disconnect it by twisting off the wire connectors. Don't touch any bare wires.

C. Touch the bare wires with the probe of a neon circuit tester.

D. If the tester doesn't light, it's safe to begin working. If the tester lights, power is still running to the fixture. Return to the service panel and shut off the correct circuit.

Step 3
A. Determine whether the electrical box is firmly attached to a support brace that's secured to the joists. Never hang a fan from an unbraced box—it can pull out of the ceiling.

B. If there's no support brace in place, install one above the electrical box by cutting a piece of 2×6 lumber to fit between the joists.

C. If the ceiling is accessible from above, push the brace down over the electrical box. Secure it by driving 3-in. screws through the joists and into the ends of the brace.

D. If the ceiling isn't accessible from above, you have two options. You can cut out a section of the ceiling, screw a support brace in place above the electrical box and then patch and paint the ceiling. Or you can install an expandable metal brace through the hole for the electrical box.

Step 4
A. Drill two 5/16-in.-dia. holes through the electrical box only. Continue by drilling 3/16-in.-dia. pilot holes into the support brace.

B. Attach the plate with two lag screws driven through the hole in the box and into the brace.

Secure the ceiling plate to the support brace with two lag screws.

Step 5

A. Gather the six wire leads from the fan motor.

B. Feed them through the holes in the brass-plated canopy and the pipe nipple.

C. Thread the nipple into the motor housing and tighten the setscrew to lock it in place.

D. Lift the fan motor and hang it onto the hook that protrudes from the ceiling plate.

Step 6

A. Place the receiver for the remote control inside the canopy.

B. Begin connecting the wires as shown in the instructions, joining pairs of same-color wires with twist-on wire connectors. Wrap each connection with electrical tape.

C. The one remaining wire, a thin white strand, is the remote antenna. Pull it out through the slot in the ceiling plate and let it hang out.

Step 7

A. Tuck the wires into the electrical box. Wind up any excess wires and place them on top of the receiver.

B. Lift the fan motor by the canopy and slide it onto the mounting screws protruding from the side of the ceiling plate. Don't let any

Thread the wire leads through the canopy and the pipe nipple.

wires stick out from the canopy.

C. Tighten the mounting screw.

Step 8

A. Install the fan blades by sliding them one by one through the slots in the rotating ring, or belly band.

B. Secure each blade, using the hardware provided.

C. Attach the fan-light fixture by snapping together the electrical fitting.

D. Screw in two 40W light bulbs. Install the glass globe.

E. Put a 9V battery in the hand-held remote-control transmitter.

Step 9

A. Restore the electrical power at the service panel.

B. Test to make sure that the fan and the light are operating properly.

C. Secure the wall-mounted remote holder in place with screws.

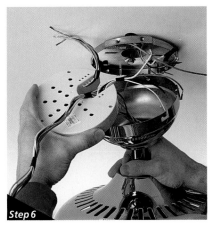

Slip the receiver for the remote control into the canopy.

Let the white antenna wire hang out to receive the transmitter signal.

Insert the fan blades through the rotating ring below the motor housing.

Sealing the heat loss areas around a window can increase its energy efficiency by 100 percent by creating a dead air space between the inner and outer panes. Modern double- and triple-paned windows contain inert gases between the panes to help create such air spaces. You can create a similar effect in older windows by adding weatherstripping and a good storm window (or plastic window sheeting) to block the movement of air. This keeps warm, moist air inside the window, minimizing condensation and frost buildup between the window and the storm. Here's how to do it properly.

Weatherizing Double-Hung Windows

Step 1

A. Cut V-channel (metal tension) weatherstripping to fit in the sliding sash channels. Cut it so that it extends at least 2 in. past the closed position but doesn't cover the sash-closing mechanisms.

B. Attach the V-channel by driving wire brads (which usually come with it) through it and into the sash channel with a tack hammer. Drive the fasteners flush with the surface, so the sliding sash won't catch on them.

C. Flare out the open ends of the V-channel with a putty knife, so the channel is slightly wider than the gap between the sash and the track it fits into. Don't flare too much at one time—pressing the channel back together may cause buckling.

Step 1

Double-hung windows: Cut a metal V-channel to fit in the channels for the sliding sash.

Tools	Materials
• tack hammer	• V-channel (metal tension) weatherstripping
• putty knife	• compressible foam weatherstripping
• hair dryer	• tubular gasket strips
• staple gun	• reinforced felt strips
	• wire brads
	• self-adhesive foam
	• caulk backer rope

Double-hung windows: Use a putty knife to flare out the open ends of the V-channel.

Step 2

A. Wipe down the underside of the bottom window sash with a damp rag and allow it to dry.

B. Attach self-adhesive compressible foam or rubber to the underside of the sash. If possible, use hollow tubular gasket strips, which create an airtight seal when the window is locked into position.

Step 3

A. To seal the gap between the top sash and the bottom sash, start by lifting the bottom sash and lowering the top sash. Tack metal V-channel to the bottom rail of the top sash, using wire brads. Be sure to point the open end of the "V" downward, so moisture won't be able to collect in the channel.

B. Flare out the V-channel with a putty knife to fit the gap between the sashes.

Weatherizing Storm Windows

After installing a storm window, fill any gaps between the exterior window trim and the storm window with caulk backer rope. Create a tight seal by attaching foam compression strips to the outside of the storm window stops.

During cold weather, check the inside surface of the storm window for condensation or frost buildup, which are caused by moisture trapped between the storm window and the permanent window. To allow the trapped moisture to escape, drill one or two small holes at a slight upward angle through the bottom rail of the storm window.

Double-hung windows: Attach self-adhesive compressible foam or rubber to the underside of the sash.

Weatherizing Sliding Windows

Treat side-by-side sliding windows as if they were double-hung windows turned 90 degrees, and follow the steps for double-hung windows. However, use metal tension strips instead of self-adhesive foam in the sash track that fits against the sash when the window is shut.

Weatherizing Casement Windows

Attach self-adhesive foam or rubber compression strips on the outside edges of the window stops.

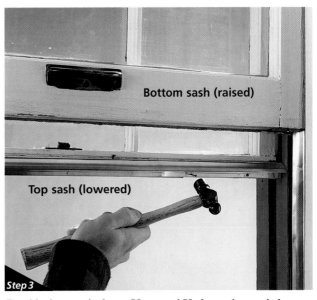

Double-hung windows: Use metal V-channel to seal the gap between the top and the bottom sash.

REPLACING SASHES

Replacing a sash is an easy, inexpensive alternative to replacing the entire window. For example, we upgraded the lovely cottage-style window shown here with a sash-replacement kit at half the cost and a fraction of the effort required to install a new window.

Most window manufacturers offer sash replacement kits sized to fit existing windows. These kits are designed to fit existing window frames; all you need to do is remove the window stops, pull out the old sash and install the new one.

Replacement sashes are made of primed wood or wood with a low-maintenance exterior cladding of aluminum or vinyl. Glazing options include single-pane, insulated double-pane and energy-efficient low-e or argon gas-filled panes.

Although most sash-replacement kits are installed in a similar manner, be sure to follow the instructions included with your model. Here are the basic steps involved:

Step 1

A. Before choosing a sash kit, measure the width of the existing window frame between the inside surfaces of the left and right side jambs. Be sure the measuring tape hook is against the jamb, not sitting on the stop molding.

B. Measure the height of the frame from the underside of the head jamb down to the top of the sill.

C. Buy a sash kit to fit these dimensions.

Tools	Materials
• pry bar	• sash-replacement kit
• pliers	• 4d (1½-in.) finishing nails
• putty knife	• wood putty
• hammer	
• nailset	

Step 2

Use a thin pry bar to remove the interior stops from the jambs. If you plan to reuse the stops, work carefully.

Step 3

A. If the sash operates on a rope-and-pulley system, cut the ropes on the bottom sash and let the counterbalance weights drop down inside the wall.

B. Lift out the bottom sash. Pry out the parting stop from the side jambs.

C. Cut the ropes holding the upper sash and lift it out. Remove the pulleys from the jambs.

D. If the sash rides in aluminum tracks, raise the bottom sash and lower the upper sash. Carefully slip the pry bar behind the aluminum window tracks at the top and bottom and lever them away from the jambs.

E. Grab both sashes and tug; they will slip out with the two aluminum side tracks intact.

Lever the aluminum window tracks away from the jambs and pull the sashes out of the window frame.

Step 4

A. With a pair of pliers, pull the wooden parting stop from the head jamb.

B. Scrape the jamb smooth with a putty knife.

C. Nail the metal mounting clips to each side jamb. Space the clips as specified in the instructions.

D. Install the new jamb liners by holding them in position, then firmly pushing them onto the clips until they snap into place.

E. Nail the new wood parting strip to the head jamb.

Hold the new jamb liner in position and firmly press it onto the metal mounting clips.

Step 5

A. Set the bottom edge of the upper sash between the jamb liners. Insert its pivot pins into the grooves nearest the exterior of the house; be sure the pins are above the clutch assemblies.

After installing the upper sash, slip the bottom sash between the two vinyl jamb liners and tilt it into place.

B. Swing up the top of the sash, depress the jamb liners and press the sash into place. Slide the sash down until the pivot pins engage the clutches.

C. Slip the bottom sash between the jamb liners. Set its pivot pins into the grooves nearest the interior. Tilt it into place.

Step 6

A. Refasten the interior stops to the side jambs with finishing nails. Set the nails and fill the holes with putty.

B. Test the sashes to make sure they slide smoothly and lock securely.

Before plastic miniblinds, windows were often covered by handsome wooden shutters that could be opened for light and an outside view or closed for privacy. Today, wooden shutters have been rediscovered by people who are looking for traditional and practical window treatments.

Ready-made hinge-mounted shutters are inexpensive, available with either fixed or movable slats and easy to install on virtually any window.

Step 1

A. Measure the window dimensions and purchase a pair of ready-made shutters. If the exact size isn't available, select shutters that are slightly larger. The shutters should cover half the height of the window. On double-hung windows, they should reach (but not extend past) the top of the lower sash.

Tools
- tape measure
- power miter saw, radial arm saw or table saw
- jointer, belt sander or hand plane
- pencil compass
- screwdriver
- narrow paintbrush

Materials
- 2 pairs ready-made operable-louver shutters
- tape
- 1/8-in. shims
- 120-grit sandpaper
- 2 1/2-in. nonmortising hinges (8)
- screws
- paint or varnish
- decorative brass latch

B. Trim the shutters to the correct height with a power miter saw, radial arm saw or table saw. If you're removing ¾ in. or less, take it all off the bottom of the shutters. If you need to remove more, take half off the top and half off the bottom.

Step 2

A. Make sure the window frame is square before installing the shutters. Tape two shutters together and stand them in the window opening with the left-hand shutter touching the left jamb. Be sure the bottoms of the shutters are flat on the window stool (the flat horizontal molding that rests on the sill).

B. If there's no gap between the jamb and the shutter, that side is square. Tape the other two shutters together and check the right side the same way.

C. If the window is out of square, taper the shutters to accommodate the variance. Adjust a pencil compass to the widest part of the gap. Hold the pivot point against the jamb and slide the compass down from top to bottom of the shutter, marking a corresponding line.

D. Use a jointer, belt sander or hand plane to trim the shutter to the pencil line. Test-fit the shutter in the window opening.

E. If necessary, trim the shutter again until it fits properly.

F. Repeat step 2 for the shutter on the other side, if necessary.

Step 3

A. Position all four shutters in the window and create clearance spaces by putting ⅛-in.-thick shims beneath them and along both sides.

B. Check for uniform ⅛-in. spaces. If necessary, trim the shutters to fit.

C. Lightly sand each shutter with 120-grit sandpaper.

D. Paint, stain or varnish the shutters. Use a narrow brush to reach between the louvers.

Step 4

A. Join each pair of shutters with two 2½-in. nonmortising hinges, screwing them directly to the edges of the shutters. Position each hinge so that its barrel (the part that holds the pin) is on the inside of the shutters facing the window. The shutters should fold outward and swing away from the sash.

B. Attach two hinges to the shutter edges that abut the side jambs. Position the hinge barrels to face out into the room. Hold one pair of shutters in the window opening and drive screws into the side jamb to fasten them. Hang the remaining pair the same way.

C. Close both shutters and check for an even gap where they join in the middle. If necessary, shim behind the jamb hinge to create a uniform gap.

D. Attach a small brass latch to the two middle shutters to hold them closed and add visual interest.

Step 2

Scribe the shutters and trim along the line to fit out-of-square window frames.

Step 3

Stand the shutters in position, shim them, and check for uniform spacing.

Step 4

With the shutter resting on a shim, screw the hinges to the side jamb.

GLASS BLOCK WINDOW

Tools
- reciprocating saw fitted with a metal-cutting blade
- flat pry bar
- hacksaw
- caulking gun

Materials
- 30 8 x 8 glass blocks
- 2 glass block installation kits
- 1½-in. drywall screws
- rubbing alcohol
- silicone adhesive

Glass block offers a stylish way to create windows or partitions that add the right amount of light and privacy to any room. Today this classic look is experiencing a renaissance, and innovative new methods are making glass block quicker and easier than ever to install.

Glass block is durable, energy-efficient, easy to clean and versatile enough to look great on both exterior and interior walls. It also comes in a variety of styles that can provide just the right amount of light transmission and visibility. Clear glass blocks transmit the most light, while translucent frosted blocks offer maximum privacy. In addition to the familiar 4-in.-thick, 8 × 8 size, glass blocks are also available in 6 × 6 in. and 12 × 12 in. dimensions, and a 3-in. thickness.

For this window replacement project we selected a glass block pattern with crisscrossing horizontal and vertical flutes that offer privacy, yet still allow plenty of natural light to shine through—an important consideration in this small bathroom. (If you're replacing a window that's the only source of ventilation in a bathroom, you'll also need to install a ceiling vent fan to prevent moisture and mildew accumulation.)

We also used a mortarless glass block installation kit here. With the kit, we simply set the blocks in a plastic channel, separate them with vertical and horizontal spacer strips and seal the joints with silicone adhesive. Each kit has enough material to install twenty 8 × 8-in. glass blocks.

Use a reciprocating saw with a metal-cutting blade to slice through any nails driven between the jambs and the studs.

Wearing gloves and eye protection, go outside and use a flat pry bar to detach the old window from the side of the house.

Step 1

A. Inside the house, pry off the interior casing from around the old window.

B. Use a reciprocating saw fitted with a metal-cutting blade to slice through any nails that have been driven through the jambs and into the studs.

C. Wearing gloves and eye protection, go outside and pry the window from the house, using a flat pry bar.

Once you've detached it from the house, pass the window through to an assistant inside the house.

Step 2

A. Measure the rough opening to determine if its dimensions are the right size for a course of whole blocks, both vertically and horizontally. (You can't cut glass block to fit the opening.) Calculate the room

Step 3

Cut the four plastic channel pieces to fit the rough opening. Screw them into place, then bore weep holes in the lower outside flange.

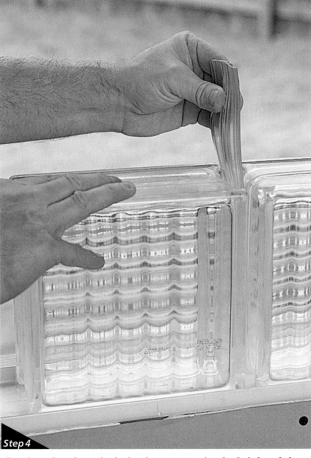

Step 4

Cut lengths of vertical plastic spacer strip the height of the blocks. Hold a strip next to the last block you laid, then slide a new block into place and push the two blocks together.

needed for the spacer strips and plastic channel, as well as the blocks.

B. If the opening can't accommodate a whole course of blocks, reduce it by adding framing to the sides, top or bottom, as needed. (Reducing the opening is almost always easier than enlarging it, which often requires installing a new header and rough sill.)

Step 3

A. Use a hacksaw to cut the plastic channel so it will fit around the inside of the rough opening.

B. Cut out a section of the upper part of the plastic channel so you'll be able to slide in the last row of blocks. Save the cut-off piece of the channel

(you'll glue it back in place in the last step).

C. Attach the four channel pieces to the rough opening, using 1½-in. drywall screws.

D. Bore ⅛-in.-dia. weep holes in the lower, outer flange.

Step 4

A. To set the first block, press it down into the sill channel and slide it toward the corner until it fits tightly into the side-jamb channel.

B. Cut a vertical length of flexible spacer strip, hold it beside the first block, and slide the second block into position. Push the two blocks together.

C. Repeat this procedure for the

remaining blocks in the first course, inserting a vertical spacer strip between each block. Don't use spacers between the blocks and the channel.

Step 5

A. Lay a flexible spacer strip along the top of the first course. If it won't lie flat, soften it with a heat gun or blow-dryer.

B. Install the second course the same way as the first.

C. Continue in this manner until you reach the top course.

D. Insert the top course of blocks through the notch you cut in the head channel and slide them into position.

E. Insert the vertical spacer strips between the blocks, as in the previous rows.

F. Once all the blocks are installed, carefully check each spacer strip. If any are wrinkled or out of alignment, force them into place with a putty knife.

Step 6

A. Clean both sides of the blocks thoroughly with rubbing alcohol.

B. Place the cartridge of silicone adhesive into a caulking gun. Use the caulking gun to fill all the horizontal joints on the outside of the window with silicone adhesive.

C. Continue by filling all the vertical joints on the outside of the window.

D. Use the spoonlike smoothing tool that comes with the kit to force the silicone into the joints.

E. Immediately remove any excess adhesive.

Set a horizontal length of spacer strip across the top of the first course of blocks. Press it flat, softening it with a heat gun or a blow-dryer, if necessary.

Step 7

A. Fill and smooth the joints on the inside of the window, as above.

B. Use silicone adhesive to secure the piece of flange that you cut off the head channel (in Step 3) back into place.

Insert the top course of blocks through the notch you cut in the head channel. Slide the blocks into place, separating them with the vertical spacer strips. Once all the blocks are in place, check each spacer strip and correct any misalignments.

Fill all the joints between the glass blocks on the inside of the window with silicone adhesive.

TUBULAR SKYLIGHT

Until recently, if you wanted to add natural light to a dark room, your only option was a conventional skylight, but these units are energy-inefficient, expensive and difficult to install. However, now there are new tubular skylights that literally "pipe" in the sun, while minimizing the effort, expense and energy loss associated with conventional skylights.

A tubular skylight has a clear rooftop collector dome that captures light and channels it down a ductlike tube. The highly reflective interior of the tube directs the light through the attic to a diffuser lens mounted on the ceiling of the living area below.

Because the tube fits between the joists and rafters, you don't have to cut into the structural members of the house. And since it can make turns without losing any light, it's easy to avoid vents, ducts and rafter supports. Finally, there's no drywall or painting work required.

All this makes installing a tubular skylight kit a manageable weekend project—in fact, it may take as little as half a day, depending on your skill level.

Before you buy a tubular skylight, you'll need some information. Check the distance between the ceiling and the roof, and determine whether any turns or offsets will be required in the pipe's path. Some models are able to "grab" sunlight even when their dome isn't facing the sun; this comes in handy if you need to place the dome on the shady side of the roof. When planning the location of the diffuser, check whether your ceiling joists and rafters are 16 or 24 in. apart, and choose a spot that falls halfway between two joists.

Although the instructions vary by model, there are three basic tasks involved in installing a tubular skylight: 1) cutting holes in the roof and the ceiling; 2) slipping the pipe in; and 3) installing the collector dome and the diffuser lens. The hardest part is actually shuttling between the attic and the roof. Although you can do most of the work yourself, you'll need a helper to handle the pipe itself. Also, before starting, check the weather forecast—if it starts to rain, you don't want to be caught with a hole in your roof.

Tools
- electric drill
- reciprocating saw or jigsaw
- plumb bob
- screwdriver

Materials
- tubular skylight with installation kit

Step 1

A. Shut off all the electrical circuits in the work area.

B. Mark the center of the diffuser on the ceiling and drill a small hole there. Push a straightened wire clothes hanger into the hole and poke it up through the attic insulation to mark its location.

C. Locate the wire hanger in the attic floor and remove the insulation around it. If the wire isn't centered between two ceiling joists, reposition the center mark and redrill down from the attic.

D. Using a plumb bob, transfer the center mark to the underside of the roof sheathing. Mark and drill a small center hole through the roof.

Step 2

A. Using the adjusted drill hole in the ceiling as the center, measure and mark a hole to fit the outline of the diffuser. Use a reciprocating saw or a jigsaw to cut the hole.

B. On the roof, cut a hole to fit the collector dome.

C. Pry loose the surrounding shingles and center the boot (the one-piece flashing and sleeve that holds the pipe in place) over the hole.

Step 3

A. Push the tube up the ceiling hole from below.

B. In the attic, use screws to secure the bottom of the tube to the adjoining joists.

C. On the roof, fit the white pipe through the metal sleeve. Make sure it fits through the boot snugly.

Step 4

A. Remove the protective film from the reflective surface inside the pipe.

B. Attach the collector dome.

C. Carefully seal the shingles to the boot on the roof, following the manufacturer's instructions.

D. Inside the house, attach the diffuser to the ceiling.

Cut a hole in the ceiling from below to fit the diffuser.

Cut a hole through the roof to fit the collector dome.

Inside the house, push the pipe up through the ceiling.

On the roof, top the pipe with the clear light-collector dome.

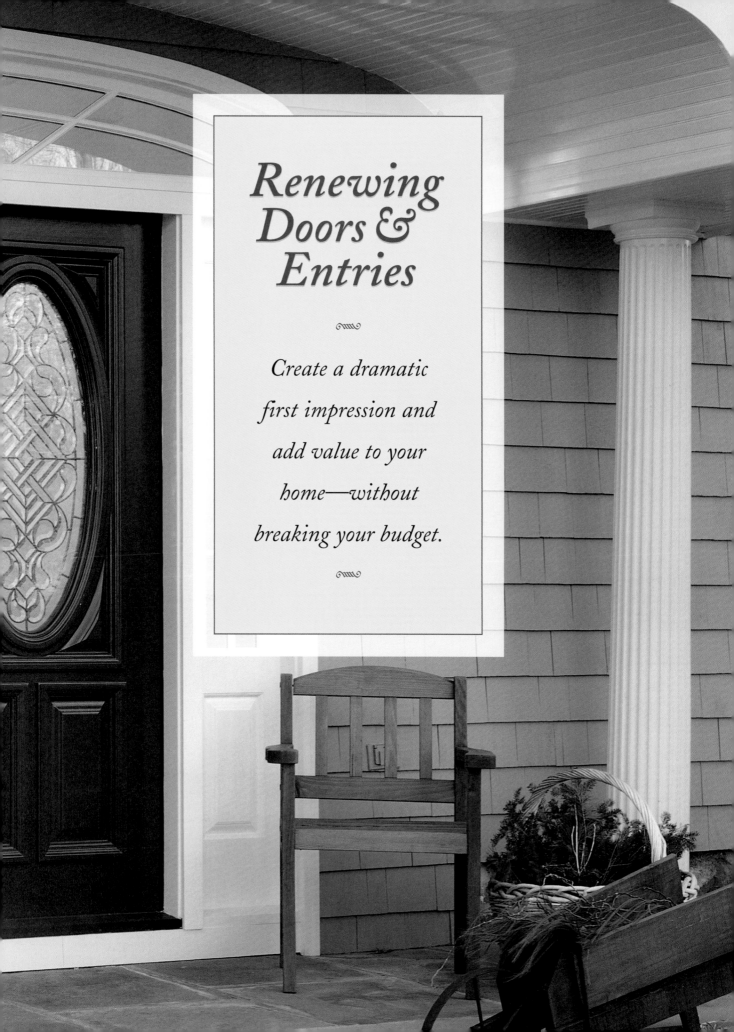

Renewing Doors & Entries

Create a dramatic first impression and add value to your home—without breaking your budget.

Renewing Doors & Entries

When it comes to doors, first impressions mean a lot. Updating a door, whether by replacing it completely or simply by upgrading it, can not only improve the appearance of your home, but also make it considerably safer and more energy efficient, as well.

The projects in this chapter present a range of ways to update your doors in just one weekend. They include installing storm and screen doors, upgrading and weatherizing doors and installing bifold closet doors.

Door installation projects require familiarity with relatively advanced carpentry skills and construction techniques. Before starting a project, read the instructions through to ensure that you have all the tools, materials and skills you'll need for the job. If necessary, ask a friend or neighbor to lend a hand with positioning and installing new doors.

Door Upgrades

Entry doors are designed to last for many years, so before you decide to replace an old entry door, consider how you might improve its performance by weatherizing it or upgrading its security features.

Weatherstripping, caulking and replacing a threshold can greatly improve the energy efficiency of an older exterior door. Although these upgrades require only a small amount of time and minimal carpentry skills, they can have a big payoff: fewer drafts and far lower utility bills.

The other simple door improvements shown here—installing a security lock and securing a door frame—are effective ways to make your home safer and to help prevent break-ins.

New Doors

The first project in this section shows how you can dramatically improve the appearance of an ordinary entrance with a new door and lightweight architectural millwork. This project requires some precision, good carpentry skills and familiarity with power tools.

The next project—replacing a drafty old storm door with a new model—can make a big difference in your heating bill and give your entryway a fresh look as well. Today's storm doors are far more energy-efficient than older models and are available in a wide range of styles.

If you have a vintage house and would like your entry to have the same classic look, consider the next project—a reproduction antique wood screen door. Many antique door designs are now available in kits that offer a rewarding weekend project for an experienced do-it-yourselfer.

Although they're more likely to be overlooked, interior doors can also benefit from an upgrade. For example, bifold doors are a stylish and practical replacement for an old set of sliding closet doors. The two-paneled doors shown here swing open on a pivot, doubling your access to the closet.

WEATHERIZING DOORS

In most homes, a primary area of heat loss is around the entry door—and the weatherstripping around it requires regular maintenance, because it's under constant stress.

Weatherizing an entry door involves adding weatherstripping around the jambs and replacing the threshold. If possible, use only metal weatherstripping products, especially around the jambs—they're more durable than self-adhesive products. If you need a flexible weatherstripping, select a product made of neoprene rubber, rather than foam. A new threshold is one way to further weatherize your door and cut down on drafts. As a rule, you should replace door thresholds or threshold inserts as soon as they begin to show signs of wear.

Weatherstripping a Door
Step 1
A. Cut two pieces of V-channel (metal tension) weatherstripping, one the full height of the door and the other the full width at the top.

B. Use wire brads to tack the weatherstripping to the door jambs and the header on the interior side of the door stops. Attach them from the top down to prevent buckling.

C. Flare out the tension strips with a putty knife to fill the gaps between the jambs and the door when the door is closed (pry gently and slowly).

Tools
- putty knife
- tack hammer
- screwdriver
- backsaw
- flat pry bar
- chisel
- mallet
- tape measure
- drill

Materials
- V-channel (metal tension) weatherstripping
- reinforced felt strips
- door sweep
- nails or brads
- caulk
- new threshold & insert

Weatherstripping: Attach reinforced felt strips to the door stop.

Weatherstripping: Attach a new door sweep.

Step 2

A. Use nails or brads to attach reinforced felt strips to the edge of the door stop on the exterior side. (When the door is closed, the felt edge should create a tight-fitting seal.)

B. Drive the fasteners only until they're flush with the surface of the reinforcing spine—driving them too far may lead to damage and buckling.

Step 3

A. Attach a new door sweep to the bottom of the door on the interior side. If the floor in your entry area is uneven, a felt or bristle door sweep is the best choice.

B. Lightly screw the door sweep into place; test the door swing to make sure there's enough clearance, then permanently tighten the screws.

Replacing a Threshold

Step 1

A. Cut the old wood threshold in two, using a backsaw. Pry out the pieces and clean the debris from the sill area below the threshold.

B. Note which edge of the threshold is more steeply beveled. Install the new threshold in the same way.

Step 2

A. Measure the opening for the new threshold. Trim it to fit, using the old threshold as a template.

B. If the profile of the new threshold is different from the old one, trace the new profile onto the bottoms of the door jamb and stops. Chisel the jamb to fit.

Step 3

A. Apply caulk to the sill.

B. Position the new threshold, pressing it into the caulk.

C. Drive the screws provided with the threshold through the pre-drilled holes in the center channel and into the sill.

D. Install the threshold insert according to the instructions.

Patio Doors

Use rubber compression strips to seal the channels in the patio door jambs, where the movable panels fit when closed.

Install a patio door insulator kit (similar to the plastic sheeting kits used for windows) on the interior side of the door.

Garage Doors

If the old door sweep is in poor condition, attach a new rubber sweep to the lower outside edge of the garage door.

Check the door jambs for drafts and add weatherstripping, if needed.

SECURITY LOCK

Deadbolt security locks have long bolts that extend into the door jamb. Because they're an effective deterrent against intruders, installing one on an entry door may qualify you for a reduction in your homeowner's insurance rate.

At one time, double-cylinder deadbolt locks keyed on both sides were often used in doors with sidelights or other glass elements to prevent break-ins through the glass. However, these locks are no longer allowed by code and should be replaced. In an emergency, such as a house fire, double-cylinder keyed locks can trap people inside the house if they can't find the key.

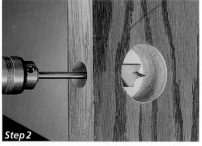

Bore a cylinder hole through the door, then a latchbolt hole into the side edge.

Step 1

A. Measure the door to determine the proper height of the lock on the door. Tape the cardboard template that comes with the lockset onto the door at that height.

B. Use a nail or an awl to mark the centerpoints of the cylinder and the latchbolt holes on the door, placing them according to the lock template.

Step 2

A. Use a hole saw and drill to bore the cylinder hole into the door. To avoid splintering the wood, drill through one side until the hole saw pilot bit (the mandrel) just comes out the other side. Remove the hole saw and complete the hole from the opposite side of the door.

B. Use a spade bit and drill to bore the latchbolt hole from the edge of the door into the cylinder hole. Keep the drill perpendicular to the door edge while drilling.

Step 3

A. Insert the latchbolt into the edge hole.

B. Insert the lock tailpiece and the connecting screws through the latchbolt mechanism and screw the cylinders together.

Step 4

A. Close the door to find the point where the latchbolt meets the door jamb; this is the position of the strike plate. Score the outline of the strike plate on the door frame with a utility knife, using the hardware as a template.

B. Chisel around the outline of the mortise, holding the tool bevel-side in. Tap the butt end lightly with a mallet until the chisel reaches the right depth.

C. Chisel a series of parallel cuts ¼-in. apart over the mortise, hold-

Insert the latchbolt, then insert the lock pieces and screw them together.

ing the tool at a 45-degree angle. Lever out the waste, pointing the tool downward at a low angle, with the beveled edge toward the wood.

D. Use a spade bit to bore the latchbolt hole into the center of the mortise.

E. Secure the strike plate to the mortise, using the retainer screws provided with the lockset. The screws should be at least 3 in. long so they extend through the jamb and into the trimmer stud.

Tools
- tape measure
- awl
- utility knife
- mallet
- lockset drill kit with hole saw & spade bit
- drill
- chisel

Materials
- security lock (deadbolt) kit

SECURING A DOOR

Drafts aren't the only thing that can sneak in through an unsecured door frame—a loose frame also allows intruders to pry their way in more easily. However, a few simple steps can ensure that your door is not only weatherized, but securely attached to the house.

Step 1

A. First, test the frame to find out if it needs additional support. Cut a 2×4 about 1 in. longer than the width of the door. Wedge the board between the jambs near the lockset.

B. Check the door frame. If it flexes more than ¼ in., it should be secured more tightly—proceed to step 2.

Step 2

A. Remove the interior jamb casing to reveal the shims between the jambs and the framing members.

Measure the gap between them.

B. Cut plywood shims to the thickness of the gap between the jambs and the framing members. Insert the plywood between the existing shims.

Step 3

A. Drive casing nails through the jambs and the shims into the framing members.

B. Set the nailheads and reattach the door casing.

More Tips for Securing Doors

For added security, you can also incorporate these security measures into your entry door:

• Add metal sleeves to the edges of the door around the lockset and the deadbolt. This will help keep anyone from kicking the door in. Make sure the sleeves are the correct thickness for your door.

• Add heavy-duty strike plates to reinforce the door and the locks. This will help prevent kick-ins, jimmying and prying. Select a strike plate that has a flange that protects the lockset from being pried loose.

• Install a wide-angle viewer in entry doors. To do this, drill an eye-level hole through the door, the same diameter as the shaft of the viewer. Insert the shaft so that the attached eyepiece is flush against the door. Screw the exterior eyepiece onto the shaft.

Tools
• tape measure
• circular saw
• hammer
• nailset

Materials
• 2x4
• plywood shims
• 10d (3-in.) casing nails

Step 1

Wedge a 2×4 between the door jambs and check the frame.

Step 3

Nail through the jambs, the new shims and the door frame.

GRAND ENTRANCE

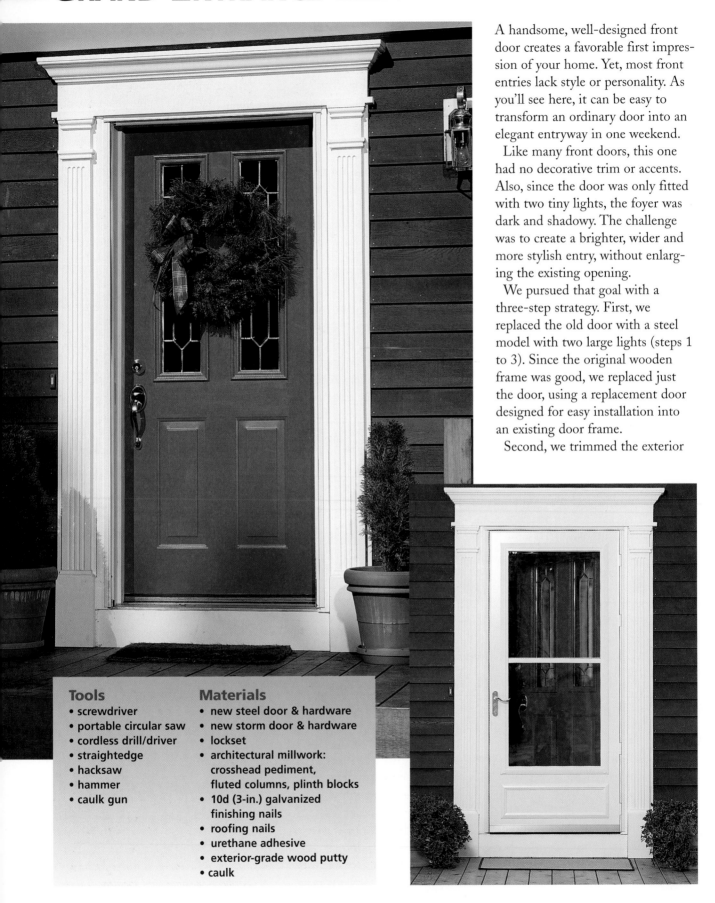

A handsome, well-designed front door creates a favorable first impression of your home. Yet, most front entries lack style or personality. As you'll see here, it can be easy to transform an ordinary door into an elegant entryway in one weekend.

Like many front doors, this one had no decorative trim or accents. Also, since the door was only fitted with two tiny lights, the foyer was dark and shadowy. The challenge was to create a brighter, wider and more stylish entry, without enlarging the existing opening.

We pursued that goal with a three-step strategy. First, we replaced the old door with a steel model with two large lights (steps 1 to 3). Since the original wooden frame was good, we replaced just the door, using a replacement door designed for easy installation into an existing door frame.

Second, we trimmed the exterior

Tools
- screwdriver
- portable circular saw
- cordless drill/driver
- straightedge
- hacksaw
- hammer
- caulk gun

Materials
- new steel door & hardware
- new storm door & hardware
- lockset
- architectural millwork: crosshead pediment, fluted columns, plinth blocks
- 10d (3-in.) galvanized finishing nails
- roofing nails
- urethane adhesive
- exterior-grade wood putty
- caulk

of the door with a pair of fluted columns and a crosshead pediment (steps 4 and 5). The new trim visually extended the doorway from 3 ft. to 5 ft. wide.

Instead of wood trim, which requires regular upkeep, we used architectural millwork—a high-quality, low-maintenance alternative. Molded from durable high-density urethane foam, it comes primed white and is impervious to rot, insects, moisture, cracking and splitting. Best of all, it's easy to install and looks like handcrafted wood molding, even up close.

Third, we finished the entryway by adding an attractive aluminum storm door to protect the entry door and increase its energy efficiency (step 6). This is the easiest part of the job; it took us about an hour.

Remove the wood threshold from the sill to create a flush surface for the new door.

Step 1

Select a replacement door that comes prehung in a steel frame and has a threshold designed to fit into the existing wood frame.

A. Carefully pry off the casing from around the inside of the door.

B. Unscrew the hinges from the side jambs and remove the old door—have a helper hold the unit as you remove the last few screws.

C. Unscrew the old strike plate from the side jamb.

Step 2

A. Remove the adjustable wood strip from the original threshold to create a flush surface for installing the new door. If there's no adjustable part, chisel the surface flush or cut out the whole sill.

B. Sweep the sill clean and apply two thick beads of caulk where the new threshold will go.

Step 3

A. Set the threshold of the new door onto the sill and tilt the door into the opening. Make sure its steel frame fits snugly around the doorway opening.

B. Make sure the frame is square and the door is plumb.

C. Temporarily secure the door by driving roofing nails through the predrilled holes in the steel frame and into the trimmer studs on each side of the opening.

D. Swing open the door. Use a cordless drill/driver to drive long "security" screws through the sides and top of the steel door frame. Don't overtighten these screws; this could distort the frame.

E. Install a lockset (see **Security Lock,** page 88).

Tilt the prehung replacement door into position. Make sure its frame fits snugly around the doorway opening.

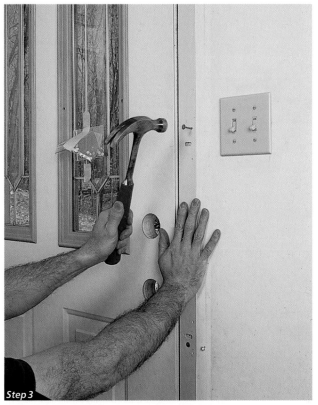

Drive roofing nails through the holes in the frame and into the trimmer studs on each side of the opening.

Cut the fluted columns to length; place one under each end of the pediment. Nail in place.

Attach a plinth block to the base of each fluted column, using urethane adhesive and nails.

F. Nail on the magnetic weatherstripping that comes with the door.

Step 4

The easiest way to install the columns and pediment is to nail them over the siding. However, if you cut back the siding and nail the trim to the sheathing, it will appear to be original. Here's how to do it:

A. Tack a straightedge board to the house to use as a guide.

B. Run a circular saw along the guide, cutting only through the siding.

C. Pry off the severed siding pieces and strip away the housewrap or building felt to expose the sheathing.

Step 5

A. Apply a bead of urethane adhesive to the back of the pediment.

B. Press the pediment into position above the door. Fasten it with eight 10d galvanized finishing nails.

C. Cut the fluted columns to size and install them in the same manner.

Use a hacksaw to trim off the bottom end of the combination hinge/mounting flange on the door.

Press the door sweep onto the bottom of the door. Tighten it against the threshold after installing the door.

D. Apply urethane adhesive to the back of the plinth blocks. Nail one to the bottom of each column.

E. Set all the nailheads and fill the holes with exterior-grade putty.

Step 6

A. Screw the combination hinge/mounting flange to the storm door.

B. Use a hacksaw to trim the flange to fit the bottom of the storm door.

C. Insert the flexible rubber fin into the slot in the expander door sweep, and slip the sweep onto the bottom of the storm door.

D. Set the storm door into the opening; have a helper hold it while you drive screws through the mounting flange and into the existing wood brick mold.

E. Install the latch-side and head-mounting flanges the same way. You can hide the mounting screws by snapping on the plastic cover strips.

F. Finish by installing the door closer and the lockset included with the storm door.

Secure the storm door by driving screws through the mounting flange and into the wood brick mold.

STORM DOOR

One of the most effective ways to immediately improve both the appearance and the performance of an entry door is to replace the storm door.

Today's storm doors are attractive, solidly constructed designs that offer both beauty and utility. The new models come in a wide range of styles and offer excellent energy efficiency.

When buying a storm door, look for a unit that has a solid inner core and seamless outer shell construction. To get a good fit, carefully measure the dimensions of your door opening, rather than your existing storm door. And finally, remember to choose a storm door that opens on the same side as your entry door.

Step 1

A. Before buying a storm door, measure the door opening. Take the height and width of the inside edges of the brick molding on the entry door. Select a door that fits these dimensions.

B. Because entry thresholds are slanted, you'll need to cut the frame of the storm door to match the angle of the threshold. To determine the angle of the cut, measure from the outer threshold to the the top of the door opening at the edge of the brick molding (A), and at the front edge of the entry door stop (B), as shown.

C. Subtract ⅛ in. from measurements A and B to allow for adjustments when the door is installed.

D. Measuring from the top of the storm door frame, mark the position of the adjusted points A and B on the corner bead.

Tools
- tape measure
- pencil
- hacksaw
- hammer
- drill
- screwdriver

Materials
- storm door unit
- wood spacer strips
- 4d (1½-in.) casing nails

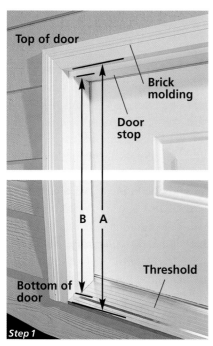

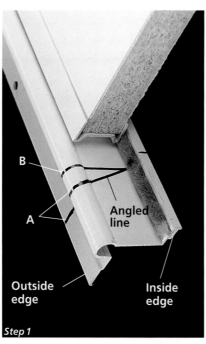

Take the outside (A) and the inside (B) dimensions of the door opening.

Draw a line from point A on the corner bead to point B on the inside edge.

Measure the gap between the line and the hinge side of the door frame.

the corner bead.

E. Draw a line from point A to the outside edge of the frame and from point B to the inside edge, as shown. Draw an angled line from point A on the corner bead to point B on the inside edge.

F. Use a hacksaw to cut down through the bottom of the storm door frame, following the angled line. Hold the hacksaw at the same slant as the angled line for a smooth, straight cut.

Step 2

A. Position the storm door in the opening and pull the frame tightly against the brick molding on the hinge side of the storm door.

B. Draw a reference line onto the brick molding, following the edge of the storm door frame.

C. Push the storm door tightly against the brick molding on the

latch side. Measure the gap between the reference line and the hinge side of the door frame.

D. If the distance is greater than ⅜ in., install spacer strips to ensure the door will fit snugly: Remove the door, and nail thin strips of wood to the inside of the brick molding where the storm door's hinges are located. The thickness of the wood strips should be ⅛ in. less than the width of the gap.

Step 3

A. Attach the sweep to the bottom of the door. Replace the storm door and push it tightly against the brick molding on the hinge side.

B. Drill pilot holes through the hinge side frame of the storm door and into the brick molding.

C. Secure the frame with mounting screws spaced every 12 in.

Step 4

A. Remove any spacer clips that are holding the frame to the storm door. Close the storm door, drill pilot holes and attach the latch side frame to the brick molding. Use a coin to maintain an even gap between the storm door and its frame.

B. Center the top piece of the storm door frame on top of the side frames. Drill pilot holes and screw the top piece to the brick molding.

Step 5

A. Adjust the height of the bottom sweep so it brushes the top of the sill lightly.

B. Attach locks and latch hardware as directed by the manufacturer.

Classic Screen Door

Although wood screen doors are no longer as common as they once were, they still offer a graceful charm that aluminum screen doors simply can't match. This handcrafted door, which was installed in just three days, does more than just keep out bugs and let in fresh air—its graceful accents also complement the look of this vintage home.

Reproduction wood screen doors such as this one are available in ready-to-assemble kits in a wide range of styles, and you're sure to find one that will perfectly complement your home. Each design has different details that you'll need to assemble according to the manufacturer's instructions, but the basic installation method is the same. Here's how to assemble and install this classic screen door:

Step 1

A. Before ordering a screen door kit, carefully measure the top, middle and bottom of the door opening. Also measure the height from the head jamb (the horizontal part of the door frame at the top) to the threshold along each side jamb.

B. If the opening isn't exactly square, order a door to match the larger dimensions and trim it to fit.

Step 2

A. Spread weatherproof glue liberally onto the joints of the precut door frame.

B. Draw each joint closed with two pipe clamps. Place one clamp above the door and one below the door to distribute the pressure evenly and prevent bowing.

C. Glue and clamp the spandrel (middle) rail together.

Step 3

A. Miter-cut the parts of the screen frame to length and screw

Tools
- four 4-ft. pipe clamps
- caulking gun
- spline roller
- hammer
- pry bar
- plane or belt sander
- screwdriver

Materials
- precut screen door kit
- weatherproof glue
- construction adhesive
- ⅛-in.-dia. rubber spline (20 lin. ft.)
- 2d, 4d galvanized finishing nails
- fiberglass or aluminum screening
- 3-in. full-surface hinges (3)
- turnbuttons (10)
- galvanized screws
- cedar-shingle shims
- pneumatic door closer

Draw the joints in the door frame closed with two pipe clamps.

Press the spline into the groove with the concave wheel of a spline roller.

Shim the door until it's exactly centered in the door frame opening.

them together. Paint or stain them.

B. Trim the the inside of the door frame with ¼-in. lattice strips, using 2d finishing nails.

C. Fasten the spandrel rail and the quarter-circle brackets to the inside of the door frame with construction adhesive and 4d finishing nails.

Step 4

A. Cut the screening 8 in. wider and longer than the screen opening; a big overlap makes it easy to handle.

B. Clamp one end to the screen frame, then pull the other end taut.

C. Use the convex wheel of a spline roller to gently press the screening into the grooves in the back of the frame. Flip the tool over and use its concave wheel to push in the rubber spline that secures the screening.

Step 5

A. Pry off the old stops from around the inside of the doorway.

B. Place the screen door in the opening and check its fit. Plane or belt-sand the edges and ends to allow a ³⁄₁₆-in.-wide space around the entire unit.

C. Paint or stain the door.

Step 6

A. Use cedar-shingle shims to hold the door centered in the opening. To avoid cutting mortises, hang the door in the opening with three full-surface hinges.

B. Attach the hinges directly to the door and to the outside casing, using galvanized screws.

C. Use the turnbuttons to secure the screen frame to the door. On the inside, nail new stops to the side and head jambs.

D. Install a lockset and attach a pneumatic door closer. Turn the closer's valve screw to adjust the tension until the door closes and latches securely without slamming.

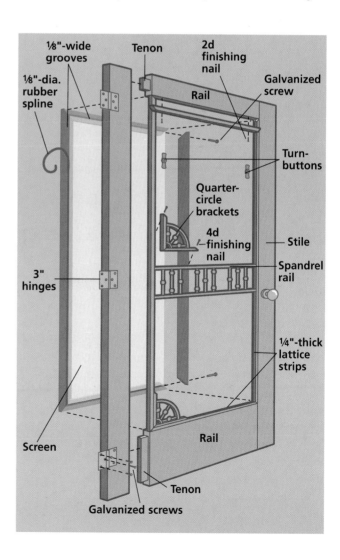

BIFOLD CLOSET DOORS

Raised-panel bifold doors such as those shown at left are a stylish replacement for old-fashioned sliders. These doors are a convenient addition to any closet, since they provide easy access to the entire storage area without requiring too much clearance room.

Replacing or upgrading a set of bifold doors is an easy task. The model we install here operates by means of six posts: a top and bottom pivot post on each jamb-side door and a top guiding post on each lead door. In addition, you need to install a track at the header and a bottom bracket at each jamb.

Tools
- tape measure
- screwdriver
- plane
- circular saw

Materials
- pair of bifold doors with hinges & mounting hardware
- screws

Step 1

A. Measure the width of the closet opening. Subtract ⅞ in. from that measurement to allow clearance between the doors.

B. Divide this total by two to determine the width of each bifold pair.

C. Purchase a pair of bifold doors to fit the measurement. If your doorway isn't a standard size, you have two options. You can either order the doors too wide and plane them to your measurements, or order them too narrow and reduce the size of the closet opening (see step 3A).

Step 2

A. Pop the old doors out of the sliding track by simultaneously lifting and pulling inward. If necessary, unscrew the roller hardware from the upper inside surface of each door.

B. Unscrew the metal door track from the header.

C. Remove the floor guide by backing out the screws and separating the guide into two pieces.

Step 3

A. If necessary, adjust the size of the door to fit the dimensions of the opening.

If the doors are too large, plane the door to fit. If they're too small, reduce the width of the doorway by nailing a 1×4 to each side jamb and attaching ¾-in. cove molding to hide the filler strips.

B. Fasten the overhead door track for the new doors by driving 1½-in.-long screws up into the header. Position the tracks so that the installed doors will be ¾ in. back from the outside of the casing.

C. If the closet opening has a valance, screw a 2×2 mounting strip to the back of the valance. Position it so the door track is flush with the

Step 3

Screw the jamb bracket to the side of the opening. The bracket supports the pivot post on the bottom of the door.

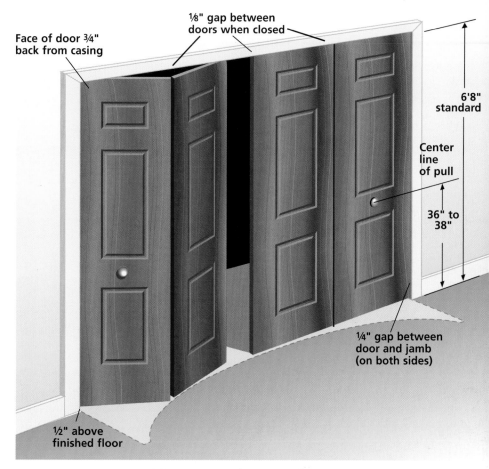

⅛" gap between doors when closed

Face of door ¾" back from casing

6'8" standard

Center line of pull

36" to 38"

¼" gap between door and jamb (on both sides)

½" above finished floor

valance, then drive the screws up through the track and into the 2×2.

D. Fasten an L-shaped jamb bracket to each side jamb. Be sure the center of the bracket aligns precisely with the center of the overhead door track.

Step 4

A. Lay the doors facedown and attach the hinges. Each pair of doors requires three hinges.

B. Check the height of the doors in the opening. They're designed to fit a standard 6 ft. 8 in. opening, but if the floor is carpeted or tiled, you may need to trim them.

C. Screw a pivot post to the top and bottom of the two doors. Position each steel post bracket exactly ⅝ in. from the door edge.

D. Attach a guide to the top of the doors where they meet in the center.

Step 5

A. Fold one pair of doors closed, lift it into position and insert its two top pivots into the track. Slip the bottom pivot post into the jamb bracket.

B. Repeat this process for the other pair of doors.

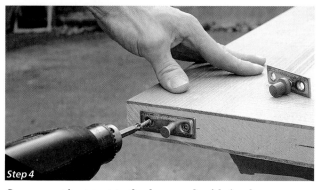

Step 4

Screw one pivot post to the doors at the side jambs.

C. Close both doors and check for equal spacing along the side jambs and down the center.

D. Adjust the door height by turning the bottom pivot clockwise to lower it or counterclockwise to raise it.

E. Align the door vertically by loosening the screw in the top pivot point guide and sliding it left or right.

The bottom pivot can be positioned anywhere along the length of the pivot angle for an additional vertical adjustment.

Adding Shelving & Storage

Discover how
these ingenious new
ideas can add
welcome storage
space to your home.

Adding Shelving & Storage

If you think you've exhausted all your home's storage and shelving possibilities, look again. The projects here can help you spot new storage space that may have been hidden along a stairway, inside a wall or above a kitchen cabinet.

The carpentry skills required for these projects range from simple to advanced. Begin with one that's suited to your skill level, and build your confidence before proceeding to the more complicated projects.

Display Shelving

Small ornamental shelves can provide a spot for collectibles, display objects and household items. Mantel shelves and wall boxes are an attractive alternative to traditional shelves and relatively simple to build. The unique design of bin-and-shelving units is both practical and appealing—and the detailed instructions for this project make it ideal for a beginning carpenter.

Recessed Shelving

Recessed shelves make use of the storage space hidden between wall

studs. You simply build a cabinet, insert it into a hole in the wall and add a face frame. The possibilities for recessed shelving are almost limitless—an ordinary wall can become a bookcase, a kitchen soffit can become a wine rack, a basement stairwell can become a pantry.

These projects are affordable and easy to build in a weekend, even for a do-it-yourselfer with relatively little carpentry experience. Just make sure you don't accidentally cut into electrical wires or ductwork when you open up the wall.

Wall Units

The first two projects here, a wall-to-wall bookcase and an entertainment center, are quite simple because they're constructed with stock kitchen cabinets. This approach puts these projects well within the reach of a do-it-yourselfer with average carpentry skills. You simply screw the cabinets

together and attach them to the wall as a unit. The matching moldings give the units a built-in look. If you take care in matching the cabinets to your wall trim, the results can be as impressive as a custom-built unit.

If you have advanced carpentry skills, consider the last project in this section. It describes how to build an impressive floor-to-ceiling wall unit in a weekend or two, for a fraction of the retail cost.

Shelf Add-Ons

The final step in customizing a wall unit is adding the wiring and lighting. By selecting the right light fixtures and concealing the wires, you can transform an ordinary set of shelves into an elegant showcase for your collectibles. Another shelf add-on, glide-out shelves, makes it easier to access the items at the back of a deep cabinet.

MANTEL SHELF

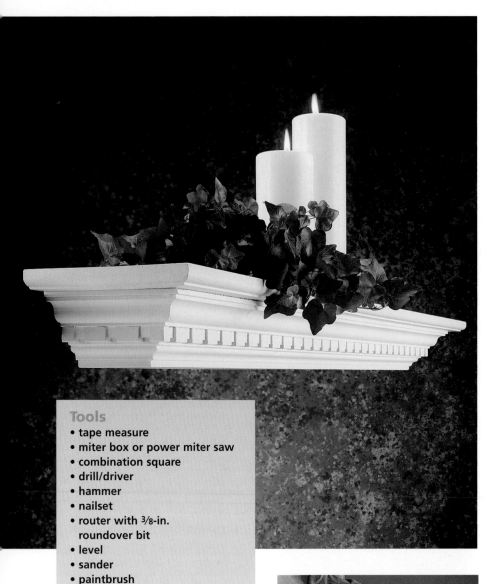

Tools

- tape measure
- miter box or power miter saw
- combination square
- drill/driver
- hammer
- nailset
- router with 3/8-in. roundover bit
- level
- sander
- paintbrush
- miter box

Materials

- 1x8 poplar or oak (6 ft.)
- 2x4 poplar or oak (4 ft.)
- 2x2 poplar or oak (6 ft.)
- 3/4 x 3 3/4-in. crown molding (5 ft.)
- 1/2 x 5/8-in. dentil molding (5 ft.)
- wood glue
- #8 x 2 1/4-in. wood screws
- #6 x 1 1/2-in. trim-head screws
- 3 1/2-in. drywall screws
- 2d & 4d finishing nails
- sandpaper
- wood putty
- antique white paint or stain

Step 1

Position the center supports along the ledger, drill pilot holes and fasten.

Although this mantel appears to be made from a solid piece of milled hardwood, its looks are deceiving. We used stock moldings to hide a simple support framework, and an antique white paint to disguise the inexpensive poplar lumber. For a natural finish, you could build the mantel from oak, then stain it.

Step 1

A. Cut the 2×4 shelf bottom, 2×2 center supports and 2×2 end supports to size. Miter one end of each support at 45 degrees.

B. Draw lines on the top face of the shelf bottom, 13 and 14½ in. from each end.

C. Position the end supports, drill pilot holes and attach with glue and 2¼ in. screws.

D. Cut the 2×2 ledger to length and test-fit it between the end supports so the back edges of the ledger and bottom are flush.

E. Position the center supports against the ledger along the reference lines. Drill countersunk pilot holes for the screws. Attach the center supports with glue and screws.

Step 2

A. Cut the front crown molding and the two returns to size. Miter the ends at 45 degrees.

B. Position the front crown so the top edge is flush with the top edge of the supports and the lower edge rests against the front edge of the bottom.

C. Drill pilot holes; attach the front crown to the supports and the bottom with wood glue and 4d finishing nails.

D. Attach the two return crown moldings in the same way. Nail through the joints with 2d nails from both directions.

E. Set all the nail heads.

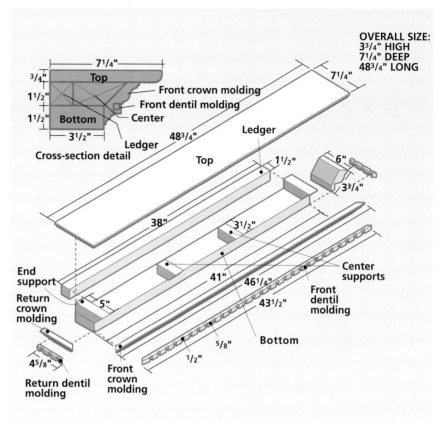

OVERALL SIZE:
3¾" HIGH
7¼" DEEP
48¾" LONG

7¼"

¾"
1½"
Top
1½"
Bottom
3½"

Front crown molding
Front dentil molding
Center
Ledger

Cross-section detail

48¾"
Ledger
Top
1½"
6"
3¾"
38"
3½"

End
support
Return
crown
molding

41"
46¼"
43½"

Center
supports
Front
dentil
molding

5"
5/8"
Bottom
1/2"

4⅝"
Return dentil
molding
Front
crown
molding

Attach the front crown molding and the returns to the bottom and supports.

Step 3

A. Cut the top to size. Smooth with medium-grit sandpaper.

B. Round both the ends and the front edge with a router fitted with a ⅜-in. roundover bit set for a ⅛-in. shoulder.

C. Place the top facedown. Mark the positions of the supports on the underside. Drill pilot holes; attach the top to the supports with glue and 4d nails. The back edges of the top and supports should be flush. Set the nailheads.

Step 4

A. Cut the front and side dentil molding to size, mitering the intersecting ends at a 45-degree angle. Cut through the "tooth" part of each piece so the pattern will match at the corners.

B. Position the front dentil molding and the two returns on the crown molding. Drill pilot holes and attach with glue and 4d nails, keeping the mitered joints tight. Nail the joints from both directions with 2d nails. Set the nailheads.

Attach the dentil molding to the crown molding, keeping the joints tight.

Step 5

A. Position the ledger on the wall, making sure it's level.

B. Drill pilot holes; attach the ledger to the wall with 3½-in. drywall screws driven into wall studs.

C. Fit the shelf over the ledger. Drill pilot holes for 1½-in. trim-head wood screws through the top and into the ledger.

D. Remove the shelf from the wall. Apply wood putty to all the nail holes. Scrape off any excess putty.

E. Sand the shelf until smooth and finish with paint or stain. Allow it to dry thoroughly.

F. Position the shelf over the ledger. Mount the shelf with 1½-in. trim-head screws driven into the pilot holes.

G. Fill screw holes with wood putty and touch up the finish.

BIN & SHELVING UNITS

Tools

- circular saw
- clamp
- drill
- hammer
- ⅛-in. drill bit with ⅜-in.-dia. counterbore
- small handsaw
- sanding block
- level

Materials

- ¾-in. medium-density fiberboard (2 ft. x 4 ft.) or 1x6 lumber (4 ft.)
- ¼-in. tempered hardboard (2 ft. x 4 ft.) or 1x8 lumber (3 ft.)
- #8 x 3-in. brass oval-head screws & finishing washers or #10 x 3-in. brass oval-head screws & finishing washers
- ⅜-in. dowel
- cotton swabs
- 1⅝-in. wood screws
- wood glue
- sandpaper
- toggle bolt anchors
- acrylic or latex paint or wood stain & clear acrylic finish

These unique bin-and-shelving units can support a glass or wooden shelf—and you can add or subtract V-sections to adjust the unit to fit the available wall space in a small bathroom. The shelves can also be mounted diagonally on the wall to create a stair-step effect.

If you plan to paint the shelves, you can use medium-density fiberboard (MDF) for the bins and hardboard for the backboard—the surfaces of these materials will accept paint well. If you're using a hardboard backboard, use #8 oval-head screws.

If you prefer a stained wood finish, use 1×6 lumber for the bins and 1×8 lumber for the backboard. If you're using a solid wood backboard, use #10 oval-head screws.

Step 1

A. Cut six shelving pieces from fiberboard or 1×6 lumber. Cut one piece 5½ × 8¼ in. and label it "A" on a piece of tape. Cut five more pieces 5½ × 7½ in. and label them "B" through "F."

B. Position the pieces in order, as shown in photo, placing piece "A" at the far right and working left.

C. Clamp piece "B" to piece "A" at a right angle. Mark the location of two screws on "A," ⅜ in. from the lower edge and 1 in. from each side.

Mark the location of a third screw centered between the first two.

D. To make the pilot holes for the screws, use a counterbore bit. Drill deep enough to create a ¼-in.-deep counterbore in the top section of the pilot hole.

E. Drill pilot screw holes through "A" and into "B." Secure "A" to "B" with 1⅝-in. wood screws.

F. Clamp "C" to "B" at a right angle and join as above. Repeat for "D" through "F."

Step 1

Position the pieces for assembly, with piece A at the far right.

Step 2

Mark the position of the assembly screws on the backboard.

Step 2

A. Lay the V-sections on the front of the backboard, with the upper points flush with the top edge of the backboard. Trace the edges of the V-sections onto the backboard.

B. Cut off the backboard along the lower outline. Draw lines on the front of the backboard showing the location of the wood screws inside the V-sections.

C. Mark the position of three screws along each side of the V-sections, avoiding the lines for the wood screws.

D. Drill holes through the backboard at the new marks, using a ⅛-in. drill bit.

Step 3

A. Place the V-sections front-edge down. Place the backboard front-face down on top of it, with the edges aligned.

B. Keeping the pieces aligned, drill the pilot hole closest to the center V, creating a ¼-in.-deep counterbore. Drive a wood screw through the hole. Recheck the alignment.

C. Drill counterbored pilot holes and drive in the screws at the ends of the unit.

D. Drill counterbored pilot holes and drive in all remaining screws.

Step 4

A. Cut a ½-in. piece of dowel to make plugs for the counterbored screw holes. Bevel one end of each plug by sanding or filing it slightly.

B. Apply wood glue to the inside surface of the holes, using a cotton swab. Tap the plugs into the holes as far as possible with a hammer; the fit should be quite snug.

C. Wipe away any excess glue with a damp cloth. Let the glue dry thoroughly before proceeding.

Step 5

A. Sand the outer edges of the backboard and the edges of the shelves. Cut off the excess plugs with a small handsaw, taking care not to scratch the wood surface.

B. Sand the plugs flush with the surface, using rough sandpaper on a sanding block. Sand the entire unit until smooth.

C. Paint the unit, or apply a stain and clear acrylic finish.

D. Mark the position of mounting screws on the front of the backboard, centered over each V-section and 1 in. down from the top. Drill pilot holes with a ⅛-in. bit.

Step 6

A. Position the shelving on the wall. Tap a small nail partway into the wall through one screw hole.

B. Place a carpenter's level on top of the shelving. With the nail holding it at one end, slide the other end up and down until the unit is level. Use a nail to mark the placement of the screw on that end.

C. Remove the shelf. Drill pilot holes for toggle bolt anchors into the wall at the marks. If there's a stud at a mark, drive a wood screw directly into the stud instead.

D. Place the shelving in position on the wall. Screw it to wall studs (using washers) or follow the manufacturer's instructions for installing the toggle bolt anchors, running each bolt through a finishing washer and into the holes.

WALL BOXES

Wall boxes offer almost endless display possibilities. They can be any size or depth, painted or stained and can be used alone or in groups. You can add glass shelves for an open curio case or create a display ledge by placing the open side against the wall. Other ideas include adding a picture frame molding or hinged shutters to the outside of the box.

Step 1

A. Decide on the dimensions of the wall box. The outside dimensions will be 1 in. higher and wider than the display opening. The depth will be 1¼ in. deeper than the display area, since the back is recessed.

B. Cut the backboard of the box to the exact dimensions of the display opening.

C. Cut the top and bottom of the box, making them as long as the backboard and as deep as the display area plus 1¼ in.

D. Cut the sides the height of the backboard plus two thicknesses of the material you're using, and the same depth as the top and bottom of the box.

Step 2

A. Place the backboard on 1×2 boards to raise it ¾ in. up from the work surface. Apply a bead of wood glue to its top edge. Position the top upright against the glued edge, with the side ends aligned.

B. Secure the top to the backboard, using brads placed 1 in. from the back and side edges of the board. Space the remaining brads at

Tools
- jigsaw or circular saw
- drill
- counterbore drill bit
- sanding block
- nailset
- hammer
- paintbrush

Materials
- ½-in. hardwood, A-A plywood or medium-density fiberboard
- 1×3s
- 1×2 scraps
- wood glue
- 16 x 1½-in. brads
- ¼-in. tempered glass shelves
- ¼-in. x ¾-in. pine or oak molding
- wood filler
- sandpaper
- paint or stain
- #8 wood screws

Place the backboard on 1×2s to raise it up. Place the top upright against it.

Glue the narrow strip of the mounting rail to the top back of the box.

the top of the box, with the angled edge pointing down, as shown. Anchor the strip with brads driven down through the top.

Step 6

A. Position the wide strip of the mounting rail on the wall, making sure it's level. Point its angled edge up so it will fit under the matching angle on the wall box. Mark the placement on the wall.

B. Use a ⅛-in. drill bit to drill screw holes through the mounting rail and into the wall, at stud locations, if possible. Where there is no wall stud, install plastic toggles into the holes.

C. Secure the rail to the wall with #8 wood screws.

Step 7

A. Mount the wall box onto the mounting rail.

B. Have tempered glass shelves cut by a glazier to fit the display area of the box, less ⅛ in. on the side and back edges. Install the shelves.

4- to 6-in. intervals. Recess the brads with a nailset.

C. Attach the bottom to the backboard in the same way.

Step 3

A. If you're adding a glass shelf, mark its position by aligning the sides and marking lines along the front edges. If you're not adding a shelf, skip to step 3D.

B. Cut molding strips equal to the depth of the display area, less ⅜ in. Sand the ends.

C. Align the molding strips on the marked lines ¼ in. from the front edge. Attach the strips with glue and 1½-in. brads. Recess the brads with a nailset. Fill the holes with wood filler.

D. Attach the sides to the box, using glue and brads driven into the edges of the backboard and the top and bottom pieces.

Step 4

A. Sand the ends of the sides flush with the top of the box, using rough

sandpaper on a sanding block. Sand the top of shelf using medium and fine sandpaper. Repeat for the bottom of the box.

B. Sand the front and back edges. Fill the nail holes and the plywood edges with the wood filler. Sand them smooth.

C. Paint or stain the box.

Step 5

A. On a piece of 1×3 at least 8 in. longer than the box, mark a continuous line along one long side, 1 in. from the edge.

B. Clamp the board at the ends, then use a circular saw or a jigsaw to bevel-cut the board at a 45-degree angle along the long line, angling the blade toward the closer edge.

C. Cross-cut the pieces to a length that equals the width of the back piece.

D. Lightly sand the sharp angled edges of the mounting rail pieces. Glue the narrow strip of the mounting rail to the underside of

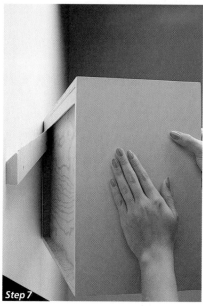

Mount the box, fitting the angled edges of the mounting rail pieces together.

PICTURE FRAME SHELVES

Finding more storage space is easy—if you know where to look. Picture frame recessed shelving, for example, is an easy, attractive and versatile way to create built-in shelving inside the walls of your home. This space-saving project simply involves opening a wall, installing a shallow wooden cabinet in the hole and adding shelving and a hardwood face frame.

Step 1

A. Locate the wall studs in the area you want to put the shelves. Cut a small hole in the wall, and use a flashlight to make sure there aren't any plumbing ducts or electrical cables in the wall. If there are, patch the hole and choose another spot.

B. Mark the cutout area on the wall, using a level as a guide. The sides of the cutout should follow the edges of the wall studs, and its height should allow for the thickness of a 2×4 header and sill plate.

C. Use a jigsaw to cut out along the marked lines.

Step 2

A. Cut the center stud at the top and bottom edge of the opening with a reciprocating saw.

B. Fit the saw with a flexible 12-in. blade and cut any fasteners between the cut portion of the stud and the finish layer on the opposite side of the wall.

C. Use a flat pry bar to remove the cut portion of the stud. Take care not to damage the opposite wall.

Step 3

A. Measure between the flanking studs at the top and bottom of the hole. Cut a header and a sill from 2×4 lumber to those measurements.

B. Attach the header and the sill to the cripple (cut) stud and the flanking studs, using 3-in. screws.

Tools
- flashlight
- pencil
- level
- jigsaw
- reciprocating saw with flexible 12-in. blade
- flat pry bar
- drill/driver, bits
- portable drill stand
- pegboard scraps
- pipe clamps
- hammer
- tape measure
- utility knife
- paintbrush

Materials
- wood glue
- 1½-in. finishing nails
- 3-in. finishing nails
- 1½-in. wood screws
- 3-in. wood screws
- 1-in. wire nails
- pin-style shelf supports
- tapered shims
- 1x4 oak lumber
- ¼-in. oak plywood
- 1x3 oak face frames
- 2x4 header and sill plates
- stain & varnish
- wood putty
- sandpaper

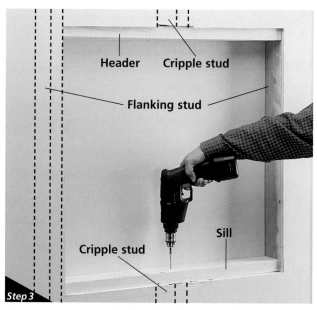

Header Cripple stud

Flanking stud

Cripple stud Sill

Step 3

Secure the header and sill to the cripple and flanking studs.

Step 4

A. Measure the height of the opening between the header and the sill and the width between the studs.

B. Cut the 1×4 shelf side pieces 1¾ in. shorter than the measured height of the opening.

C. Cut the 1×4 top and bottom pieces ¼ in. shorter than the measured width of the opening, to allow for adjustments during installation.

D. Drill two rows of holes on the inside face of each side piece, sized to hold pin-style shelf supports, using a portable drill stand and a scrap piece of pegboard as a template.

If you prefer to install metal shelf standards, you can skip this step.

Step 5

A. To assemble the cabinet, glue and clamp the side pieces over the top and bottom pieces.

B. Drill counterbored pilot holes into the butt joints. Secure them with 1½-in. screws.

C. Measure and cut a ¼-in. ply-wood back panel flush with the out-side edges of the cabinet.

D. Attach the back panel with 1-in. wire nails positioned every 4 to 5 in. along the outer edge.

Step 6

A. Place the cabinet in the opening. Shim it until it's level and plumb and its front edges are flush with the surface of the wall.

B. Drill pilot holes. Secure the cabinet to the flanking studs, header and sill with 1½-in. finishing nails driven every 4 to 5 in. and through each of the shims.

C. Trim the shims even with the cabinet, using a utility knife.

Step 7

A. Measure the inside height and width of the cabinet.

B. Cut 1×3 horizontal pieces equal to the width of the cabinet, and vertical pieces 5 in. longer than its height.

C. Glue and clamp the horizontal pieces between the vertical pieces to form butt joints.

D. Reinforce the joints by drilling pilot holes and driving 3-in. finishing nails through the vertical pieces and into the horizontal pieces.

Step 8

A. Position the face frame around the cabinet. Drill pilot holes and attach it with 1½-in. nails driven into the top, bottom and side panels and the framing members.

B. Set the nails; fill the holes with wood putty.

C. Sand the unit. Finish with stain and varnish.

D. Add shelf pegs. Cut 1×4 shelves ⅛ in. shorter than the measurement inside the cabinet. Sand and finish the shelves; install them in the cabinet.

Step 6

Shim the cabinet until it's level and plumb, and secure it with nails.

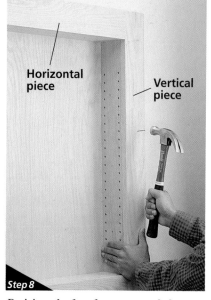

Horizontal piece

Vertical piece

Step 8

Position the face frame around the cabinet and nail it in place.

KITCHEN WINE RACK

A wine rack in the soffit above your kitchen cabinets is an easy, inexpensive project that can provide elegant storage for a dozen wine bottles. If you collect rare wines, you'll want to store them in a cool room in the cellar. But these recessed nooks are a convenient way to keep everyday wines within easy reach.

The wine rack is easy to construct—it's simply a plywood box framed with decorative molding and installed into the soffit. However, before starting this project, it's important to make sure that there are no heating ducts or hot-water pipes running through the area that could overheat the wine.

Tools
- tape measure
- drywall saw
- jigsaw
- hammer or pry bar
- router with
  1/2-in. straight bit
- screwdriver
- nailset
- paintbrush & tools

Materials
- 1/2-in. birch plywood (1/2 sheet)
- 1/4-in. plywood or hardboard
- 4d (1 1/2-in.) finishing nails
- 3/4-in. wire nails
- 1 1/8-in. decorative doorstop molding
- 3/4-in. flat screen molding
- 3/4-in. brads
- wood glue
- wood putty
- 1 3/4-in. wood screws
- paint

Step 1

A. Cut a small hole in the wall with a drywall saw. Proceed only if you don't see any obstructions in the soffit or any heat sources (such as ducts or pipes) nearby. If you do, patch the hole and choose another spot.

B. Mark and cut a 9×26-in. hole in the soffit with a drywall saw. If the bottom of the framing extends into the opening, create more space by cutting it lengthwise with a jigsaw. Pry out the waste with a hammer or pry bar.

Step 2

A. There will most likely be at least one stud in the hole. Pull the nails that secure it in place.

B. Move that stud to the left edge, screwing it to the top and bottom framing.

C. Move or add a stud on the right edge as well.

Step 3

A. Cut two 9×11-in. pieces of ½-in. plywood for the sides of the rack.

B. Cut three 11×25-in. pieces of ½-in. plywood for the top, bottom and horizontal shelf.

C. Cut ten 4×11-in. pieces of ½-in. plywood for the vertical dividers.

D. Cut one 9×26-in. piece of ¼-in. plywood or hardboard for the back.

Step 4

Using a router with a ½-in. straight bit, cut ⅛-in.-deep × ½-in.-wide grooves in the top, bottom and shelf, spaced 4¼ in. on center.

Step 5

A. Nail the top and bottom pieces between the two sides with finishing nails. Secure the back with wire nails.

B. Slide the horizontal shelf into the plywood box. Secure to the box with finishing nails.

C. Spread glue into the grooves and slide the vertical dividers into them. Let the glue dry.

Step 6

A. Miter the doorstop molding to fit around the perimeter of the rack, allowing it to extend over the outer edge by ⅛ in. Attach it with wood glue and brads.

B. Attach the screen molding to the shelf and the vertical dividers with brads.

C. Set and fill all the nail holes with putty.

D. Slide the rack into the wall opening. Drive two screws into the upper frame and one screw into each side. Paint the wine rack to match the surrounding wall.

If necessary, cut along the bottom of the soffit. Pry out the waste, taking care not to damage the surrounding drywall.

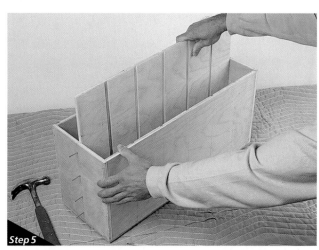

Slide the horizontal shelf into the plywood perimeter and attach it to the sides and back of the box with finishing nails.

Attach the decorative doorstop and screen molding with wire brads. Set the brads and fill all the holes with wood putty.

STAIRWAY PANTRY

The wall of a basement stairwell is the ideal spot for a trio of recessed cabinets. The 14½-in. bays between standard wall studs are just the right size for these spacious custom-made pantry shelves.

Choose an interior wall with enough room behind it for cabinets of a desirable depth, such as a partition wall that encloses a basement staircase. If the staircase doesn't have a partition wall, you can build a 2×4 stud wall to hold the cabinets.

We built these cabinets out of birch-veneer plywood, using ¾-in. plywood for the sides, tops, bottoms and shelves, and ¼-in. plywood for the backs.

Step 1

A. Cut the rough openings in the wall for the cabinets.

B. Using the 16d nails, attach 2×4 sill plates between the studs, keeping them about 3 in. above the stair stringer. The existing top plate and wall studs will form the top and sides of the openings.

Step 2

A. Carefully measure the height, width and depth of each rough opening to get the starting dimensions for the three cabinet frames.

B. To ensure easy installation, size the cabinets ⅛ in. smaller than the dimensions of the rough openings.

C. Cut the sides, tops and bottoms of the plywood frames to size with a table saw or a circular saw.

D. Glue and screw the pieces together with simple butt joints, using 1⅝-in. wood screws.

E. Cut the back panels to the overall dimensions of each frame. Fasten one side edge of the back to the frame with the wood screws. Check for square, then fasten the remaining edges.

Materials
- 2x4 sill plates
- ¾-in. birch-veneer plywood
- ¼-in. birch-veneer plywood
- ¾ x 1½-in. oak trim
- ⅛ x ¾-in. oak edge banding
- wood glue
- shelf standards (4 per cabinet)
- shelf support clips (4 per shelf)
- 2-in. & 1⅝-in. wood screws
- 16d common nails
- 2d & 4d finishing nails
- sandpaper
- paint or varnish

Tools
- tape measure
- table saw or portable circular saw
- screwdriver
- drill
- hammer
- painting or staining tools

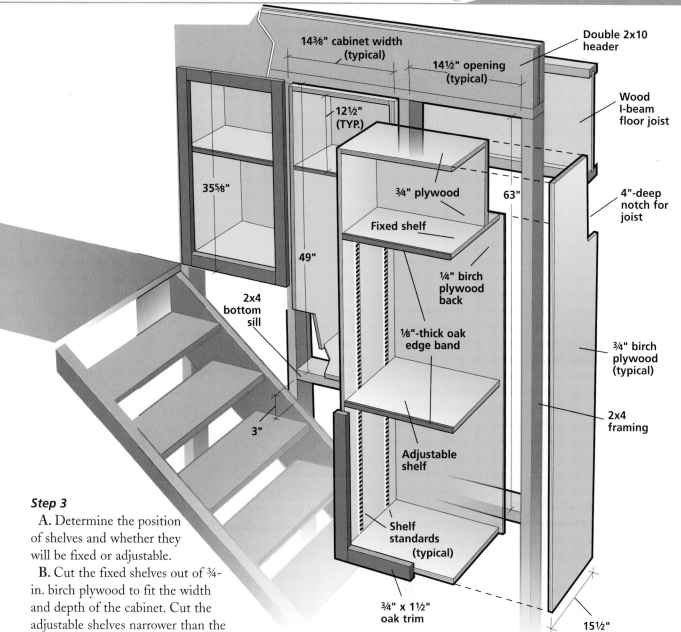

Double 2x10 header

14⅜" cabinet width (typical)

14½" opening (typical)

Wood I-beam floor joist

12½" (TYP.)

35⅝"

¾" plywood

63"

4"-deep notch for joist

Fixed shelf

49"

¼" birch plywood back

2x4 bottom sill

⅛"-thick oak edge band

¾" birch plywood (typical)

3"

Adjustable shelf

2x4 framing

Shelf standards (typical)

¾" x 1½" oak trim

15½"

Step 3

A. Determine the position of shelves and whether they will be fixed or adjustable.

B. Cut the fixed shelves out of ¾-in. birch plywood to fit the width and depth of the cabinet. Cut the adjustable shelves narrower than the fixed shelves to allow for the thickness of the shelf standards, and ⅛ in. shorter to allow for the oak edge banding.

C. Glue and screw the fixed shelves to the cabinet sides and back, using 1⅝-in. screws.

D. Glue the oak edge banding to the front edge of the adjustable shelves.

E. Attach the shelf standards for the adjustable shelves to the side walls of the cabinet, 1½ in. from the front and back of the cabinets.

Step 4

A. Cut ¾ × 1½-in. oak trim to fit around the front edges of the cabinets. Center the trim on the front edges of the cabinets to create a ⅜-in. overhanging lip on both sides of the cabinet panels.

B. Glue and nail the trim to the cabinets and the front edges of the fixed shelves, using 4d nails.

C. Place the cabinets in the openings and shim until level.

D. Secure the cabinets with twelve 2-in. wood screws driven through the sides of the cabinet and into the wall studs.

Step 5

A. Smooth all the surfaces and edges of the pantry with sandpaper.

B. Apply two coats of polyurethane varnish or paint to protect the pantry from wear and dirt accumulation.

WALL-TO-WALL BOOKCASES

It can be surprisingly easy and affordable to create an impressive wall-to-wall bookcase such as this one. The trick is to assemble it from the wall cabinets made by kitchen cabinet companies or the knockdown cabinets that are sold in furniture stores.

Step 1

A. Make a drawing of the existing wall space, including all the dimensions. Take it to a showroom, home center or lumberyard.

B. Show the salesperson your drawing and describe your built-in project. Inspect the cabinets on display. Ask to see planning guides as well as manufacturers' catalogs.

C. Choose a cabinet style and select specific sizes and features from the planning guide.

Step 2

A. Position the base cabinets; use shims to level them.

B. Screw the base cabinets together through the face-frame stiles, using 2½-in. screws placed 4 in. from the top and the bottom.

C. Secure the base assembly to the wall studs with 3-in. screws. Don't overtighten them, or the doors and drawers won't operate properly.

Step 3

A. Using 2½-in. screws, attach the upper cabinets together as you did the base cabinets.

B. Place the upper cabinets onto the base cabinets as a single unit. (If you prefer, you can also install them individually and then fasten them together.)

C. Attach the upper cabinets to the wall, using 3-in. screws.

Step 4

Trim the bookcase with baseboard and crown molding that matches the trim used in the rest of the room as closely as possible.

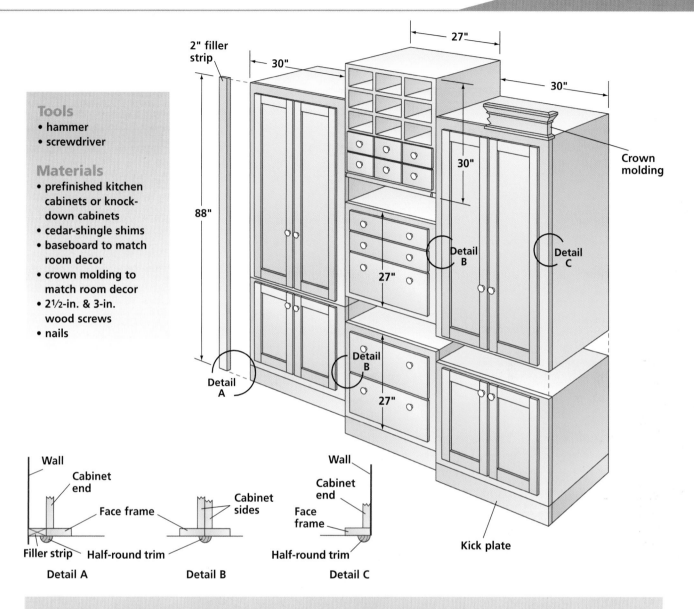

Tools
- hammer
- screwdriver

Materials
- prefinished kitchen cabinets or knock-down cabinets
- cedar-shingle shims
- baseboard to match room decor
- crown molding to match room decor
- 2½-in. & 3-in. wood screws
- nails

2" filler strip

30"

27"

30"

88"

30"

Crown molding

30"

27"

Detail B

Detail C

Detail B

27"

Detail A

Kick plate

Wall

Cabinet end

Face frame

Filler strip

Half-round trim

Detail A

Wall

Cabinet end

Face frame

Cabinet sides

Half-round trim

Detail B

Wall

Cabinet end

Face frame

Half-round trim

Detail C

CHOOSING CABINETS

To determine the quality of the cabinets you're considering for your built-in projects, ask these questions:
- How are the cabinets constructed? What material are the carcasses made from?
- Are the drawer sides made of solid wood or plywood? Check for sturdy metal drawer slides and strong dovetail or rabbet joints.
- Do the doors have self-closing hinges that are easy to adjust?
- Are the doorknobs, drawer pulls and shelf hardware included?
- Is the finish water- and alcohol-resistant? (Important for areas where food or drink will be served.)

- Are matching filler strips, moldings and trim pieces available?
- Will someone from the showroom come to my house to take exact measurements? (If not, you'll be responsible if something doesn't fit.)
- Once an order is placed, how long will it take for the cabinets to arrive?
- Is there a delivery charge to bring the cabinets to the house?
- Is installation available?
- What will the cabinets cost? (While you won't get an exact figure until you place the order, you should be able to get a rough idea of the cost.)

ENTERTAINMENT CENTER

This handsome cherry entertainment center is built entirely from stock kitchen cabinets. The upper half of the center cabinet houses the television and the VCR; its base cabinet has three roll-out shelves for videos and supplies.

Good-looking home entertainment centers like this one are usually expensive to buy and difficult to build from scratch. However, stock kitchen cabinets offer a timesaving shortcut for the do-it-yourselfer. Once we had all the materials, it took just two days to assemble the cabinets.

This unit is composed of five stock cabinets. The center television unit is a 36-in.-wide × 84-in.-tall utility cabinet, turned upside down. Flanking it on either side is a standard 18-in.-wide × 30-in.-tall wall cabinet, topped by a 48-in.-tall bookcase.

Tools
- screwdriver
- drill
- portable circular saw
- hammer
- clamps

Materials
- 36-in.-wide x 84-in.-tall utility cabinet
- 18-in.-wide x 30-in.-tall wall cabinets (2)
- 48-in.-tall bookcases (2)
- matching plywood skins
- matching crown molding
- matching 1x4
- matching cove molding
- ¾-in. plywood or 2x4s (base)
- ¾-in. plywood (TV shelf panel)
- roll-out shelves & mounting hardware
- ¾-in. x 1-in. wood strips
- contact cement
- 2d & 4d finishing nails
- 2½-in. wood screws

When building with stock kitchen cabinets, the biggest challenge is making the finished project look like custom furniture rather than a bunch of stacked-up boxes. The secret is in the accents—the baseboard, molding, shelves, fluted filler strips, prefinished skins and glass-paned doors—that are offered by cabinet manufacturers specifically for this purpose.

Building with stock units does require you to sacrifice some design features. For example, most stock cabinets don't come with slide-back doors. However, our television cabinet has hinges that open to 170 degrees—more than enough for a clear view of the set.

Also, most kitchen cabinets aren't finished on the inside. Although you might not mind staining them yourself, we wanted an exact match throughout the unit, so we bought prefinished plywood "skins" and glued them to the inner surfaces of the cabinets. This is optional, but it makes the unit as attractive with the doors open as it is when they're closed.

Before you buy your cabinets, carefully measure each piece of equipment you plan to put inside them, including any wires, jacks or picture tubes that project from the back, and any knobs that stick out in front. Figure out where you'll need to drill holes in the cabinet backs and shelves to run the electrical wiring. Also be sure to allow enough space around electrical components to avoid overheating.

Here are the steps we followed to assemble this entertainment center; they will remain essentially the same for any stock cabinets you choose.

Step 1

Remove the baseboard molding from the wall where the entertainment center will be placed.

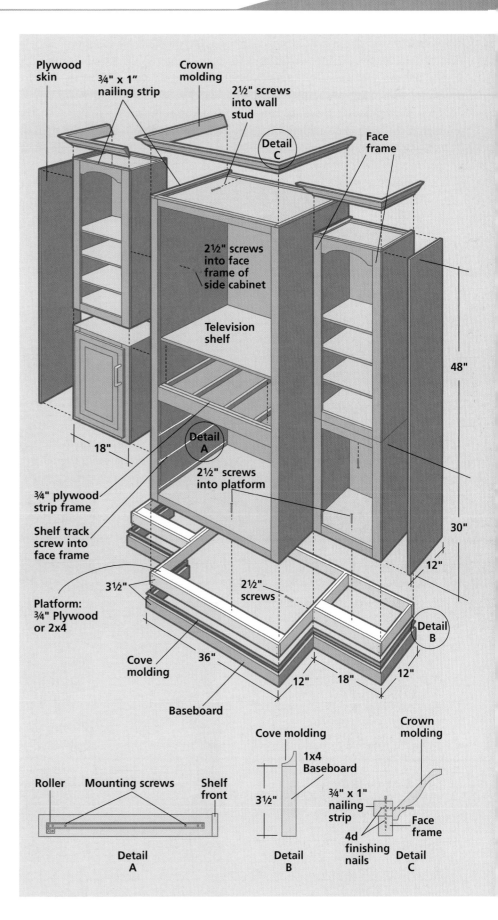

Step 2

Build a 3½-in.-high base platform for the cabinets, as shown in the photo. (The platform raises the cabinets off the floor and will be concealed by baseboard molding.)

Make the platform out of ¾-in. plywood or 2×4s set on edge, to the exact dimensions of the cabinets. If you make it out of plywood, you can add a front backing strip to provide extra support, as shown. Fasten the pieces together with 2½-in. screws.

Step 3

A. Using a portable circular saw, carefully cut off the toekick on the bottom of the large utility cabinet.

B. Flip the cabinet upside down so that the larger compartment is on top. Set the cabinet on the center of the platform.

Step 4

Build up the height of the television shelf so its surface is flush with the face frame. (This will make it easier to slide in the television and access the control buttons.)

A. Cut four or five narrow plywood strips. To determine their width, measure the height of the face frame from the shelf bottom, and subtract the width of the plywood panel (and the plywood skin, if you're using one).

B. Lay the strips across the shelf, equally spaced. Secure with glue and toenailed 2d finishing nails.

C. Cut a ¾-in. plywood panel to fit over the strips. Secure it in place with 4d finishing nails. (Always drill pilot holes before screwing or nailing into the stock cabinets.)

Step 5

A. Clamp one of the bookcase units to one of the wall cabinet units. Drive a pair of 2½-in. screws through the cabinet frame and into the bookcase frame.

B. Lay the assembled unit on its side on a blanket or pad.

C. Cut a plywood skin to span the exposed side of both cabinets to conceal the joint between them. Glue it down with contact cement.

D. Repeat steps 5A to 5D for the other bookcase.

Step 6

A. Place the two assembled bookcase units onto the platform. Attach them to the middle television cabinet, drilling pilot holes first. Drive the screws through the side of the cabinet and into the face frame of the bookcase.

B. Drive a 2½-in. screw through the bottom of each of the base cabinets and into the platform below.

C. Drive a screw through the upper rear panel of each cabinet and into a wall stud.

Step 7

A. Cut the prefinished plywood skins for the interior surfaces of the television compartment.

B. Glue the plywood skins in place with contact cement, starting with the one that covers the inside top of the cabinet.

C. Glue the plywood skin over the raised bottom shelf.

Since this surface may not be visible (depending on the size of your television), you may prefer to stain the shelf instead.

D. Install the plywood skin on the back of the cabinet.

E. Install the plywood skin on the left- and right-side panels.

Build a 3½-in.-high platform base to support the cabinets.

Use a circular saw to cut the toekick off the bottom of the large utility cabinet.

Use wood strips and plywood to raise the TV shelf even with the face frame.

Fasten a wall cabinet to a bookcase with two screws into the face frames.

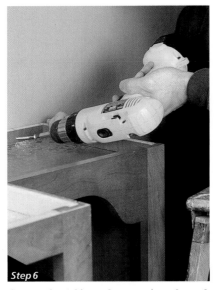

Secure the cabinets by screwing through the upper panel and into wall studs.

Line the interior of the TV cabinet with prefinished plywood skins.

Step 8

A. Screw the metal tracks that support the roll-out shelves into the bottom of the television cabinet.

B. Fasten the front end of each track to the edge of the cabinet face frame.

Step 9

Install the specialty hardware and decorative trim, as follows:

A. Hide the platform below the cabinets with a matching baseboard secured with 4d finishing nails. We used a solid 1×4 topped with a cove molding secured with 2d nails.

B. Nail ¾ × 1-in. wood strips along the tops of the cabinets, flush with the outside edge, to provide fastening support for the crown molding.

Step 10

A. Miter-cut the matching crown molding to size.

B. Drill pilot holes and nail the crown molding to the strips, using 4d finishing nails.

C. Cut the old baseboard to fit the remaining wall space alongside the new unit. Install the baseboard.

D. Install your TV and entertainment equipment.

Attach the metal tracks for the roll-out shelves to the edge of the face frame.

Conceal the platform with a 1×4 topped with a cove molding.

Miter-cut the crown molding, drill pilot holes and nail it into place.

ADDING SHELVING & STORAGE

FLOOR-TO-CEILING SHELVES

A wall of floor-to-ceiling shelves allows you to transform an ordinary room into an inviting den or library. Built-in shelves are also sturdier and make better use of space than a freestanding bookcase. For the best results, select a wood finish and trim that matches the room's existing wall moldings.

A built-in bookcase isn't literally "built into" the wall, but installed against it. Since only the front, and perhaps one side, of the bookcase is exposed, it appears to be recessed into the wall. For this project, we used finish-grade oak plywood and a solid oak face frame that gives the shelves the look of an expensive solid oak shelving unit, at a fraction of the cost.

If you're installing floor-to-ceiling shelves in a corner, as shown here, you'll need to add ½-in. plywood spacers to the support studs that adjoin the wall. The spacers will ensure that you can install face frame stiles of equal width on both sides of the unit.

This is a challenging project that requires good carpentry skills and may take a few weekends to complete—but the final outcome will be well worth the effort.

Step 1

A. Mark the location of two parallel 2×4 top plates on the ceiling, using a framing square as a guide. Mark the front edge of the outer top plate 13 in. from the back wall and the other top plate flush against the wall.

B. Mark the location of the ceiling joists. If necessary, install blocking between them to create a surface on which to anchor the top plates.

C. Measure and cut the top plates from 2×4 lumber.

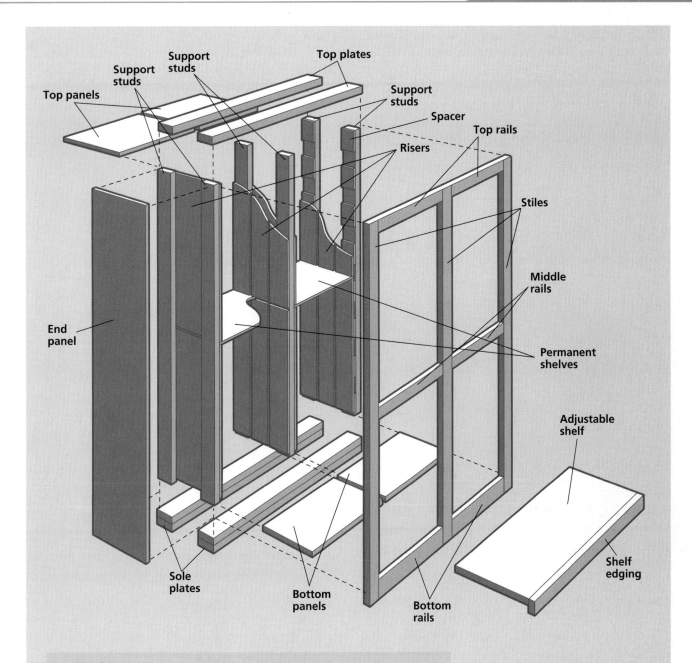

Support studs

Support studs

Top plates

Top panels

Support studs

Spacer

Top rails

Risers

Stiles

Middle rails

End panel

Permanent shelves

Adjustable shelf

Sole plates

Bottom panels

Bottom rails

Shelf edging

Tools

- ruler or tape measure
- framing square
- screwdriver
- hammer
- drill with ¾-in. straight bit
- plumb bob
- level
- router
- sander
- circular saw
- paintbrush

Materials

- 2x4 lumber (top & bottom plates, support studs)
- ½-in. plywood
- ¾-in. plywood
- 1x3 lumber (stiles & top rails)
- 1x4 bottom rails
- metal shelf standards & clips
- wood glue
- shims
- 1¾-in., 2-in. & 3-in. screws
- 4d (1½-in.) finishing nails
- shelf-edge molding
- paint or stain

D. Place each plate in position. Level them, shimming if necessary. Attach the plates to the ceiling with 3-in. screws driven into the joists or blocking.

Step 1

Position the top plates and level them. Attach them with screws driven into the ceiling joists or blocking.

Step 2

A. Cut four bottom plates from 2×4 lumber. Screw them together to form two double-high bottom plates.

B. Align the bottom plates with the top plates, using a plumb bob suspended from the outside corners of the top plates. Shim the bottom plates to level them.

C. Anchor the plates with 3-in. screws toescrewed into the floor.

Step 3

A. Cut the six support studs from 2×4 lumber. Install four of them at the corners of the unit with 3-in. screws toescrewed through the studs and into the plates.

B. Install the center support studs midway between the end support studs. Toescrew them to the bottom plate first with 3-in. screws. Use a level to make sure that the studs are plumb, then attach them to the top plate.

Step 4

A. Where the shelves fit into a corner, use 2-in. screws to attach ½-in. plywood spacers on the inside faces of the support studs, spaced every 4 in. Don't extend the spacers past the front edge of the studs.

B. If the side of the unit will be exposed, cut a ½-in. plywood end panel to the floor-to-ceiling height.

C. Attach the panel to the support studs with the front edges flush, driving 1¾-in. screws through the support studs into the end panel.

D. Measure and cut ½-in. plywood panels to fit between the support studs on the top and bottom of the unit. Attach them to the top and bottom plates with 1½-in. (4d) finishing nails.

Step 3

Install the center support studs midway between the end support studs.

Step 4

Attach an end panel to the support studs on the exposed side of the unit.

Step 5

Measure, cut and install the upper risers above the permanent shelves.

Step 5

A. Measure and cut the lower risers from ½-in. plywood. Cut grooves in them to hold the metal shelf standards.

B. Install the lower risers on each side of the 2×4 support studs so the front edges are flush with the edges of the studs. Secure the risers to the support studs with 1½-in. (4d) finishing nails. On the riser that adjoins the wall, drive the nails through the spacers.

C. Measure and cut the permanent shelves from ¾-in. plywood to fit between the support studs, just above the lower risers.

D. Set the shelves on the risers and attach them with 1½-in. (4d) finishing nails driven down into the risers.

E. Measure and cut the upper risers to fit between the permanent shelves and the top panels. Cut grooves in the risers to hold the metal shelf standards. Nail the risers to the support studs.

Step 6

A. Measure and cut 1×3 stiles to fit from the floor to the ceiling along the front edges of the exposed support studs.

B. Drill pilot holes and attach the stiles to the support studs so they're flush with the risers, using glue and finishing nails driven at 8-in. intervals into the studs and risers.

C. Measure and cut 1×3 top rails to fit between the stiles. Drill pilot holes and attach the rails to the top plate and top panels with glue and finishing nails.

D. Measure and cut 1×4 bottom rails to fit between the stiles. Drill pilot holes and attach the rails to the bottom plates and bottom panels, as above. The top edge of the rails should be flush with the top surface of the plywood panels.

Step 7

A. Fill all the nail holes. Sand and finish all the wood surfaces.

B. Measure, cut and install metal shelf standards in the riser grooves, using the nails or screws that come with the standards.

C. Measure and cut the adjustable shelves ⅛ in. shorter than the distance between the metal shelf standards.

D. Cut the shelf-edge molding; attach it to the shelves with glue and finishing nails.

E. Sand and finish the shelves.

Step 8

A. Insert shelf clips into the metal shelf standards.

B. Install the adjustable shelves.

C. Cover any gaps between the floor-to-ceiling shelving unit and the walls and floor with a molding that's been finished to match the shelving.

Attach the stiles and rails to the front edge of the unit.

Cover gaps at the walls and floor with matching molding.

ADDING SHELVING & STORAGE

LIGHTING A WALL UNIT

Tools	Materials
• router	• plastic wire tracks
• drill with hole saw or Forstner bit	• plastic wire organizers
	• 12V transformer
	• vent screens
	• outlet strips
	• grommet plates

Adding electrical accessories to a wall unit can make it both more attractive and more useful. For example, low-voltage halogen lights can turn an ordinary bookcase into an elegant display case; these fixtures use very little electricity and can be left on permanently. And adding an electrical outlet strip to an entertainment center allows you to connect electronic equipment without using cumbersome extension cords.

When adding lights or other electrical accessories to a wall unit, try to keep the wires hidden from view. Inexpensive wire organizers and wire tracks inside the built-in can help hide the cords and keep them neat.

If the unit contains incandescent lights or electronic equipment, such as a television, computer or stereo, it's a good idea to install vent screens in the shelves or walls to dissipate the heat they generate.

To provide a convenient place to plug in electronic components or light fixtures, you can attach an outlet strip inside the unit. Some models have a remote on-off switch that will control up to four receptacles, a telephone jack or a cable TV outlet. For computer equipment, use a strip that has power-surge protection.

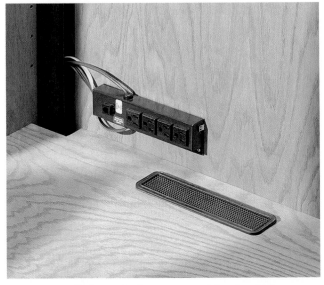

Vent screens dissipate the heat generated by electrical gear.

Installing Halogen Lights

Step 1

Cut holes in the top panel of the wall unit to accommodate the low-voltage light fixtures.

Cut small grooves into the shelves and risers for the wires.

Step 2

Install the low-voltage light fixtures, running the wires through the grooves.

Cover the wires with plastic wire tracks in the grooves. Leave several inches of space around the lights to prevent heat accumulation.

Step 3

Install a 12V transformer to convert the 120V current from an ordinary wall receptacle to low-voltage power for the lights.

Hiding wires

Here are some ideas that can help hide the electrical wires that provide light and power to your wall unit or cabinet:

• Cut a plastic wire organizer to the desired length and tack it inside the cabinet to keep electrical cords and cables neatly tucked away out of sight (photo, right).

• Drill a hole to run cords and cables through the side of the unit or cabinet. To reduce the chance of splintering, use a hole saw or a Forstner bit.

• Install grommet plates over the holes, slipping the groove in the grommet around the wires (photo, below).

• Grommets are available in a variety of materials and finishes. For a coordinated look, select hardwood grommets, which can be stained to match the color of your wall unit.

Wire organizers hide cords and cables.

MINIATURE LIGHT SYSTEMS

Miniature light systems are available in both low and regular voltage, and fall into four main categories: mini-tracks, strips, pucks and fluorescents. Low-voltage systems require a transformer but offer greater energy efficiency and smaller lights.

Mini-tracks. Miniature versions of track lighting, the tracks can be cut to length and run almost anywhere with connectors that can turn corners. Bulbs can be placed anywhere along the track.

Strip lighting. These bulbs are set in a fixed pattern and usually left exposed. However, this is a good option inside cabinets, and less costly than mini-tracks.

Puck lights. Low-voltage halogen puck lights are good for display-case or undercabinet lighting. You can adjust the direction of the light, and some can be recessed within a shelf.

Fluorescent fixtures. These fixtures, often used under cabinets to light a countertop, have narrow tubes and a plastic cover to diffuse the light.

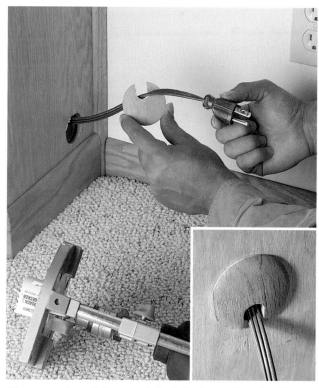

Grommet plates help conceal the holes for cords and cables.

GLIDE-OUT SHELVES

Adding full-extension glide-out shelves to a base cabinet helps make more efficient use of hard-to-reach storage space by providing easier access to items tucked in the back.

Glide-out and roll-out shelf extensions are most common in kitchen cabinets, but they have many other uses, as well. For example, roll-out shelves are also used in the entertainment center (pages 118-121).

Step 1

A. Determine the width of the glide-out shelves by measuring the inside of the cabinet and subtracting 3½ in. This allows space for two standards and brackets (1¼ in. each) and two slides (½ in. each).

B. Cut two 1×4s to that measurement for each shelf. These will be the front and back pieces. Use a jigsaw to cut out the top edge of the front pieces to make a drawer pull.

C. Cut two 21¼ in.-long pieces for the sides of each shelf.

D. Cut the bottom from ½-in. birch plywood.

Step 2

A. Rout a ⅜-in.-deep × ½-in.-wide groove into each 1×4, ½ in. up

Rout grooves and rabbets in the 1×4s.

Tools	Materials
• tape measure	• 8-ft. 1x4 poplar (2)
• level	• ½-in. birch plywood (½ sheet)
• jigsaw	• full-extension drawer slides (2 per shelf)
• circular saw	• shelf standards (2 sets)
• router with ½-in. straight bit	• brackets (4 per shelf)
• hammer	• wood glue
• finishing sander	• 4d (1½-in.) finishing nails
• screwdriver	• 120-grit sandpaper
	• 180-grit sandpaper
	• sanding sealer

from the bottom edge.

B. Cut a ⅜-in.-deep × ¾-in.-wide rabbet across the inside face of each end of the shelf front and back.

C. Spread glue onto the shelf front rabbets and attach the shelf sides, using three 4d finishing nails.

D. Spread a bead of glue along the groove in the shelf front; slide the bottom into place. Glue and nail on the shelf back. Clamp the pieces square and let the glue dry.

E. Smooth all surfaces with a finishing sander and 120-grit sandpaper. Wipe off all dust and coat the shelf with sanding sealer. Let dry for one hour.

F. Lightly hand-sand the shelf with 180-grit sandpaper. Apply a second coat of sealer.

Apply glue to the rabbet joint and nail the front of the shelf to the sides.

Step 3

A. Position the front standards 2½ in. from the inside edge of the face frame. On a frameless cabinet, measure from the front edge of the cabinet.

B. Use a level to make sure the standards are perfectly vertical, then secure them with screws.

C. Install the rear standards 17¹⁄₁₆ in. from the first set, measuring from center to center.

D. Bolt two metal shelf standard brackets to each drawer slide, making sure they're 17¹⁄₁₆ in. on center.

Step 4

A. Mount the drawer slides to the cabinet by snapping the metal clips into the slots in the standards.

B. Detach the sliding rail from each slide by pressing down on the release lever.

C. Screw a sliding rail to each side of the shelves, ½ in. up from the bottom edge.

D. Install each shelf by aligning its sliding rails with the slides inside the cabinet and pushing it all the way in. The rails will automatically lock into place.

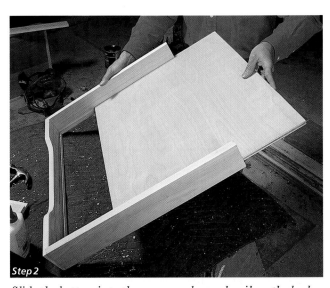

Slide the bottom into the grooves; glue and nail on the back.

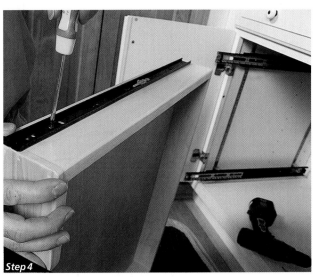

Attach a sliding rail to each side of the shelves.

Planning *your* Landscape

Planning and design are the first steps in creating a landscape you'll enjoy for years to come.

Every landscape project should start with an integrated vision of how all the elements in the yard fit together. You don't want to suddenly discover that the only sunny place for the platform deck you've always wanted is right over the garden bed you painstakingly put in the year before.

A good landscape plan will enhance the beauty of your home and the characteristics of your yard. Even more important, it will take into account what you like to do outdoors and how much time you want to spend maintaining your landscape.

Redwood Deck Photo Courtesy of California Redwood Assoc.

Planning Your Landscape

*These timesaving design tips and techniques
can help turn your yard into an inviting place
to play, dine and relax.*

QUICK REFERENCE

*Designing Your Landscape
pages 133-135*

*Make a Small Space Look Bigger
pages 136-137*

*Create a Beautiful,
Low-Maintenance Yard
pages 137-139*

Helpful Terms

Foundation planting: Trees, shrubs and flower beds that smooth the visual boundary between the house and the yard.

Lawn edging: Edging strips of metal, plastic, brick or wood that prevent weeds and lawn grasses from invading flower beds and soil from washing out over the lawn.

Visual balance: A pleasing distribution of visual weight (the places where the eye tends to linger) in a landscape.

Visual boundary: The dividing line between different parts of a landscape.

Designing Your Landscape

Professionals know that it's easier to create a successful landscape when you follow the principles of good design, which include purpose, simplicity, balance and unity.

Purpose

As you start to design your landscape, divide it into separate areas, each with a specific design goal. For a front entry, the goal might be visual appeal. For a secluded backyard patio, the primary goal might be privacy.

Next, consider the purpose of each space and the elements that are necessary to fulfill that function. For example, a sunbathing deck should be placed where it will receive afternoon sunlight, while a deck for family meals and entertaining might benefit from afternoon shade.

Simplicity

Good landscape designs are simple. A simple design is more attractive, easier to maintain and cheaper to build. Don't try to cram many different plants and materials into a landscape. The result will only be a visual hodgepodge of confusing colors, textures, shapes and sizes.

A simple composition—with smooth lines, large shapes and a few building materials—will have a soothing and calming emotional effect. For example, a landscape that consistently uses brick in garden walls, walkways and patios will be much more pleasing than one that mixes wood decking, concrete walkways, rubblestone retaining walls, a brick patio and a timber raised bed.

The same guidelines apply to plantings. A yard that contains only a few flower species is usually more pleasing than one that's crammed with dozens of different kinds of trees and plants. For the same reason, flower gardens are usually more pleasing when they're composed of a few kinds of plants massed together in unified groups.

Visual Balance

To create a pleasing visual balance, consider where your eye goes first or where it tends to linger as you view a scene. Don't try to create a landscape that looks perfectly balanced or try to arrange all the elements in perfect

In this garden, the strong vertical lines of columnar trees balance the horizontal line of a large expanse of lawn.

symmetry; this just produces a formal, static impression. Instead, use different elements to create an impression in which the visual weight is roughly equal. For example, balance the large mass of a house on one side of the yard with the large mass of a shade tree on the other.

If there's any visual element that threatens to dominate your landscape, consider balancing it with its opposite. For example, balance large areas of subdued, monochromatic color with a few spots of dramatic color. Balance the strong horizontal line of a large lawn or deck with the vertical line of a fence, an arbor or a row of columnar trees.

Unity

A unified landscape is one that fits in visually with its surroundings. A good landscape will complement not only your home, but also the surrounding neighborhood. Unity makes a landscape seem natural, which makes it a more comfortable,

---

KEEPING YOUR LANDSCAPE SIMPLE

Use no more than two or three different building materials. For example, repeat the same natural stone in all the paths, patios and retaining walls.

Limit the number of different plant species. Unless you're a dedicated hobby gardener, limit yourself to one or two tree species, three or four shrub species and six to eight types of flowers.

Use color with restraint. Broad splashes of a few strong colors are more effective than a kaleidoscope of different hues.

DESIGNING YOUR LANDSCAPE *CONTINUED*

reassuring living environment.

Gradual transitions between the different elements in a landscape will greatly improve its sense of unity. That's why a foundation planting of shrubs and flowers is so essential to a home landscape—it creates a gradual transition between the house and the yard that unifies the house with its surroundings. For a pleasing landscape, look for ways to soften other boundaries, such as between the yard and the adjacent properties.

Another way to create a sense of unity is to copy the style, color or building materials used in your home. If your house is made of brick, use brick for paved surfaces and garden walls. If your house has brown roof shingles, build a stone or masonry retaining wall in the same shade of brown. If your house has Victorian detailing, copy some of the details on a wood fence and gate.

UNIFYING YOUR LANDSCAPE

Use local rock and wood products. Since these materials will be common in the area, they will seem natural and familiar. For example, in a mountainous region a granite retaining wall will be more unified with its surroundings than one made of sedimentary sandstone. Local materials are also likely to be cheaper.

Use your home's interior decorating materials. For example, if your kitchen has slate floor tiles, use similar paving tiles on the adjoining outdoor patio.

Use the same trees, plants and building materials that are used in neighboring yards. If your street has a canopy of stately oaks and you fill your yard with birch trees, they will look out of place. Also, the plants that are flourishing in your neighbor's yard will be likely to thrive in your yard, too.

MAKE IT INTERESTING

Include a few elements that focus and draw the attention of the senses, the intellect or the emotions in each area of your landscape.

Use contrasting colors, textures and patterns. For example, make a large lawn more interesting by juxtaposing it with the coarser texture of natural stone walkways and bright flowering plants.

Add landscape accessories—such as ponds, garden statuary, trellises, arbors and decorative benches—to provide visual interest.

Attract birds, butterflies or other wildlife. Include a birdbath and bird feeders, or a flower garden that appeals to butterflies.

Pique the mind by adding an interesting piece of statuary to the landscape.

Add a self-circulating fountain or waterfall to provide both visual appeal and the musical sound of cascading water.

Create other appealing sounds with wind chimes or by attracting songbirds.

Include fragrant flowers in your garden to greet visitors with a soothing scent.

Arouse the viewer's curiosity with a pathway that disappears around a corner.

Create emotional interest with family keepsakes, such as an heirloom mailbox or wagon, or children's palm prints in a concrete walkway.

Don't go overboard and create too much interest. Too many plants, pots, colors and accessories isn't interesting—it's jarring and unattractive. Design your landscape for simplicity and unity, then add just a few elements to provide interest.

This secluded garden nook, almost surrounded by roses, appeals to the senses of sight and smell.

DESIGN TIPS

• Whenever you spot a landscape that you like, take a moment to identify what pleases you about it. Is it the color of the flowers, the line of the walkways or the consistent use of brick or natural stone? Learn why certain yards appeal to you, and others don't.

• Realistically consider your time budget. Do you enjoy yard work and welcome it as a way to relax and get some exercise? Or do you prefer a low-maintenance landscape so you have more time for other activities?

• Follow the scale of your landscape. A very large yard, for example, calls for large trees, wide paths and spacious lawns. But a small house with a small yard will look best with dwarf tree species and potted plants. Here, a large shade tree would overpower the house and look out of proportion.

• Place larger or more coarsely textured elements where they'll normally be viewed at a distance; place small, fine-textured items nearby, where they can be fully appreciated.

• Take a cue from the style and building materials of your home. If it's a rustic cottage, complement it with a cozy English garden. If it's faced with natural flagstone, design patios and walkways made of a matching natural stone.

• If you can't afford to do a complete foundation planting to soften the transition between your house and yard, focus on the corners. A small bed of ornamental shrubs at each corner will do wonders to help a house blend in with the landscape.

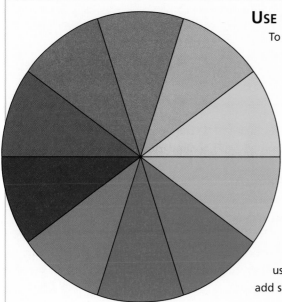

USE COLORS TO CREATE MOOD

To create color harmony in your landscape, consult the color wheel. Combine colors that are next to each other or opposite each other. In general, avoid other strong color combinations.

Colors that are next to each other on the wheel are soothing and reassuring. Use these combinations in quiet, private areas of the landscape. For example, a garden composed of blue and purple flowers will create a restful impression.

Colors that are opposite each other on the wheel tend to exaggerate and enhance one another. For example, blues look brighter when contrasted with yellow. Use these combinations in active, social areas of the landscape, such as a children's play area or a deck.

Other color combinations tend to be jarring to the eye, and it's usually best to avoid them. However, you can use them sparingly to add surprise, drama or interest to a landscape.

STAY IN BALANCE

You can extend the idea of visual balance to any design principle, element or function:

Balance coarse textures with fine textures. Lawn grass is a fine-textured surface that should be balanced with a coarse-textured element, like a stepping-stone path or a broad-leafed tree or shrub.

Balance straight lines with curved lines. Most homes and building sites are square with straight edges. Design curved paths or plant areas with sweeping edges to balance the landscape and save it from monotony.

The straight vertical lines of this fence are balanced by the horizontal branches of a trained apple tree. A tree trained to grow flat against a wall, as pictured here, is called an espalier.

Balance living plants with structural surfaces. Structural surfaces, such as wood, stone and brick, should make up about half of your landscape; the rest should be composed of lawn or other living plants.

Make a Small Space Look Bigger

Whether you have a small patio or deck, a narrow side yard or an odd-shaped pocket of ground, the following six techniques can help you turn that space into an inviting area to play, entertain and relax.

Keep It Simple

Turning a small space into a garden means making the most of the available space—and finding space where you thought there was none. Since small spaces tend to highlight the details of every texture, surface and color, a hodgepodge of plants and materials will make them feel cluttered and small. However, a simple, unified design will make even a tiny space look open and inviting. Here are some easy ways to give small spaces a big look:

Select a unified theme and eliminate everything that doesn't fit—in a small space, anything that doesn't reinforce your theme will weaken it.

Create a long-term plan for the entire space, even if you won't be doing all the work at once.

Make your yard more appealing by replacing a large lawn with flower islands and borders.

Tie the space together by repeating just a few colors and building materials.

Choose just a few plants that work together and repeat them throughout the space.

Replace Lawn with Paving

In a small space, brick, stone or wood paving is a better choice than lawn. It looks good, requires little maintenance and is more functional than a carpet of grass. Choose a small-scaled material that won't overwhelm the space, such as brick pavers—they're nonskid and can be laid in many patterns.

It's hard to grow lawn in a shady area. A wood-chip path bordered with azaleas and rhododendrons may be a better solution.

Wood is another good choice—and you can orient the boards to make the space look bigger. Here are more paving ideas:

Before paving an area, mark the boundaries with a garden hose or heavy rope to see how it will look.

Test to be sure the paving is the right size. For example, an eating area for eight requires at least 144 sq. ft., plus 8 × 6 ft. for a barbecue.

Choose a paving material that matches or harmonizes with the colors and surfaces of your home.

Paving often looks best when plants spill over the edges or grow between the stones.

Put Walls to Work

Walls and fences can support a vine, create a private space, screen off an undesirable view or provide a backdrop for a sculpture or fountain. Since high walls can feel claustrophobic in small spaces, consider building a low wall or fence topped with a row of lattice. Here are some other smart ways to enhance walls:

Open up a wall by creating a window that looks out on an interesting view.

Camouflage an ugly wall or fence by placing a row of colorful plants in front of it.

Install a wall-mounted mirror to add light to a dark space and reflect a planting bed.

Plant vines on a trellis next to the wall, instead of on the wall itself. It can be hard to paint a vine-covered wall or to remove the vines without damaging the finished surface of the wall (see **Vines**, pages 237-238).

Pick Plants That Fit

To avoid constant pruning or replanting, choose plants that won't grow too large for your space. Here are some tips for picking the right plants:

Consult with your local nursery or extension service to find out what types of small trees grow well in your area.

Small trees are ideal for tight spaces. Some, such as this Japanese tree lilac, also offer fragrant blooms.

Consider a small tree. Small and dwarf trees are perfect for confined spaces. A dwarf apple tree, for example, will grow only 6 to 10 ft. high.

Consider large shrubs, such as pineapple guava or xylosma, which can be trained to look like small multitrunked trees.

Choose plants that grow up, not out. Select vines or shrubs (like heavenly bamboo, twisted juniper or yew pine) that will grow vertically.

Use Pots, Barrels and Baskets

A single pot of vibrant tulips can transform a dull corner into an inviting oasis (see **Container Gardens**, pages 259-265). You can group containers, use them as accents, suspend them from rafters or place them on low walls or pedestals. Here are more ideas for containers:

Make sure every container has a drainage hole, so the roots won't become water-logged and suffocate.

Prevent damage from water seepage by putting saucers under small containers and raising large containers on bricks.

Grow container fruits and vegetables. A single plant in a bushel basket can yield pounds of

Simple, yet effective, this arrangement of flower-filled terra-cotta pots breaks up an otherwise stark expanse.

fruit or vegetables.

Don't rely solely on flowers. Shrubs and trees can add fall color and year-round interest to a landscape.

Water and feed container plants regularly; their roots can't travel to seek out food and water.

Stretch Your Boundaries

Use color, pathways and focal points to make a small space feel bigger. Cool colors, like blue and purple, tend to recede; place them at the far end of the space. Warm colors, like red and orange, seem to jump forward; use them sparingly. You can also use walkways to create a feeling of expanded space. Adding a few steps down to a pond or up to a deck will make a short path seem longer. Here are more tricks that can make a small space seem larger.

Design a gently curving path. Curving paths tend to feel more spacious than straight paths.

Plan a path that leads out of view or ends at a gate. This effect creates the illusion of extended space.

Add interesting focal points. A large container plant, fountain or overhead plant can draw the eye and make a space seem bigger.

Bring an outside view into the garden. Frame the view with an arching trellis or selectively prune a tree to make it visible.

Create a sense of greater depth by grouping plants that have varying sizes, shapes and textures.

CREATE A BEAUTIFUL, LOW-MAINTENANCE YARD

You can have a breathtaking yard and still have time to enjoy it. The secret is to work smarter, not harder. The following labor-saving tips can help you save both time and effort.

Lawn Timesavers

The following tips can help reduce the amount of time you'll need to spend caring for your lawn.

Make Mowing Easier

• Consider replacing some of your

Evergreen dwarf periwinkle, punctuated by spring blooms, is an easy-care lawn substitute that spreads quickly.

grass with a lower-maintenance surface, such as a brick patio, a wood deck or a gravel pathway.

• Eliminate sharp curves and corners and connect areas of lawn so you can mow them in one pass.

• Place mailboxes, boulders, lampposts and other impediments out of the way, perhaps in a planting bed.

• Cover slopes with ground covers that don't require mowing, like cotoneaster and juniper (see **Ground Covers**, pages 240-241).

• Design pathways for mowing convenience. With a 21-in. mower you can mow a 36- to 40-in. grass path in two passes.

• Don't set paving stones in grass; you'll be constantly struggling to keep them clear.

• Install brick or concrete mowing strips at the edge of the lawn, level with the soil, so that the mower wheels will ride on top of the strip.

• Plant trees and shrubs on grass-free islands and mulch the soil below their branches. Remove low branches from existing trees so you won't have to dodge them as you mow.

Reduce Raking and Fertilizing

• Leave grass clippings where they fall—they feed the lawn and won't cause thatch or smother lawn grass (unless they're in dense clumps). Leaving clippings on the lawn can reduce the amount of fertilizer you need to add by 20 to 30 percent.

• Use a mulching mower. Mulched clippings decompose in two weeks.

• Fertilize your lawn just two or three times a year with a slow-release fertilizer. One application of slow-release fertilizer will work for six to eight weeks, and it won't overstimulate your lawn or cause a quick surge of top growth.

Garden Timesavers

Use these ideas to create easy-care gardens and flower beds.

Choose Easy-Care Flowers

• Use fewer varieties. A grouping of one type of flower can be more attractive and easier to maintain than a mixture of plants.

• Avoid plants that must be staked, like delphiniums and hollyhocks.

• Choose plants that don't require special care (such as pruning, dead-heading or heavy feeding).

Position Plants for High Impact

• A few plants massed together will require less maintenance than the same number scattered about.

• Plant flowers where they'll be seen—at the front entrance, beside a walkway or near a deck. Another way to highlight flowers is to plant them in a raised bed or against a backdrop of green foliage.

Design for Low Maintenance

• Make your flower beds narrow enough that you can easily reach across them. A bed wider than 2½ ft. can be difficult to work from one side.

• Install edging strips of metal, plastic, brick or wood between the gardens and lawn. Edging will prevent weeds and lawn grasses from invading flower beds and soil from washing out over the lawn.

• Fertilize less by using slow-release fertilizers. Some of the products for flowers are effective for three to four months, while others work for eight months or more.

• Add a thick layer of organic mulch over gardens and flower beds to reduce weeding and watering chores (see **Mulching**, pages 194-195).

Tree and Shrub Timesavers

Careful planning and selection can ensure that your trees and shrubs are both beautiful and low maintenance.

Choose with Care

Ask before you buy. Extension services and nurseries can help you select low-maintenance trees and shrubs.

Select pest- and disease-resistant plants. For example, some crabapple varieties are susceptible to diseases such as apple scab and fireblight; others are disease-resistant.

Choose trees with noninvasive roots that won't break the pavement or intrude onto the lawn, such as common hackberry or serviceberry. Pass on fast-growing and fast-spreading trees, like carrotwood and poplar.

Choose shrubs that require little pruning or thinning. For example, an informal hedge of Japanese barberry will need little or no pruning, while a boxwood, yew or myrtle hedge will need a lot.

Plan Before Planting

Give trees and shrubs enough room for their mature height and width. Where space is limited, check out the compact and dwarf forms of popular trees and shrubs.

Group plants with similar needs in one place, where they can all be watered and fertilized together. For example, put drought-resistant plants together in one area and those that require more moisture in another.

Avoid trees that drop foliage, flowers or fruit—or plant them where you can leave the debris where it falls. Cover the ground under trees with shade-tolerant ground covers, like pachysandra or periwinkle.

The seasonal flowers displayed in this charming entryway provide color where it counts. The plants include annual purple lobelia and an assortment of roses.

FOUR EASY-CARE GROUND RULES

1. Stick to plants that are proven successful in your climate. Before you plant, ask around to find out what plants grow well in your area. Also, be sure the plants you've chosen are well suited for the site you have in mind. Don't plant a sun-loving plant in the shade or a water-loving plant in a dry spot.

2. Prepare the soil before planting. Plants won't thrive unless the soil provides all the nutrients, air and water they need. Have your soil tested and add any amendments it needs before you start planting (see **Breaking New Ground**, pages 200-205).

3. Eliminate weeds before planting. The more weeds you get rid of in the beginning, the fewer you'll have to worry about later. After planting, discourage weed growth by maintaining a thick layer of organic mulch.

4. Automate irrigation. One inexpensive solution is a timer attached to the faucet that turns the water on and off (you still have to move the hose). The ultimate irrigation systems are automated pop-up sprinklers for lawns and drip irrigation systems for plants. They're expensive, but they mean you won't need to water by hand.

Improving your Landscape with Structures

Walks, patios, decks, lighting and other enhancements can greatly increase your enjoyment of your yard.

Although most homeowners are willing to take on some home improvement projects themselves, they're often less confident when it comes to improving their landscape. However, even a big project like a walk, a patio or a deck can be surprisingly easy when you approach it the right way. Planning ahead, getting the right materials and tools for the job and understanding basic building techniques can ensure that you'll get professional-looking results every time.

Redwood deck photo courtesy of California Redwood Assn.

Walls, Walks & Patios

Retaining walls, walks and patios prevent erosion,
minimize yard maintenance and increase
the usable living space in your yard.

QUICK REFERENCE

Helpful Terms

Deadman: A piece of lumber and a cross-piece that extend back into the hillside to anchor a retaining wall.

Dry-laid path: A mortarless path made of pavers or stone set on a bed of sand.

Rebar: Metal reinforcing rods that are embedded in concrete or masonry walls.

Subbase: A layer of compacted, crushed stone that provides a stable foundation for walls, walks and patios.

Tamper: A hand tool used to pack down layers of soil, sand or gravel.

RETAINING WALLS

A retaining wall can hold back a hillside or turn a steep slope into usable space. But retaining walls aren't just limited to slopes—you can use them anywhere to define the edges of garden beds, outdoor living areas or groups of trees and shrubs.

A quick check of your neighbors' retaining walls will probably reveal that many of them are bulging, cracking or leaning. That's because most residential retaining walls aren't built properly. A long-lasting retaining wall must be properly constructed and have a good drainage system, as described below.

Not Too Tall

Even a small retaining wall must be able to contain enormous loads—a 4-ft.-high, 15-ft.-long wall may need to support up to 20 tons of saturated soil. This means that there are some limits to do-it-yourself construction. Don't try to build a wall over 4 ft. tall (3 ft. for mortarless stone) by yourself—hire a professional builder. If your slope is taller than that, consider step-terracing. If you must build a taller wall yourself, have a landscape architect or structural engineer design it for you.

Build It Right

Poor drainage is the main cause of retaining wall failure; excess moisture can lead to oversaturated soil and frost heaving. That's why, with very few exceptions, all retaining walls require a gravel subbase and drainage system.

Excavation. The depth of the excavation will depend on the soil, the building materials and whether the ground freezes in winter. Where the ground freezes, mortared and concrete walls require deeper footings and nonmortared walls must be built on gravel-filled trenches. (For a nonmortared wall where the soil drains well and the ground doesn't freeze, you may be able to get by with simply removing the topsoil.) Dig down far enough to place the first row of the wall below ground level.

Battering. To ensure stability, both the drainage area and the completed wall should lean into the hill 1 in. for every 1 ft. of height. This receding slant is called "battering."

Anchors. Timber walls 4 ft. or higher must be secured to the hillside with deadmen anchors. Deadmen aren't necessary for interlocking-block systems or geo-grid systems (in which weblike tiebacks are buried in the backfill).

Lining. Line the drainage area with enough landscape fabric to contain all the gravel and keep topsoil from washing into it from above. Start by draping the fabric from the top of the hill down across the trench, leaving the top section in place on the slope above the wall until you've completed the wall and the gravel backfill.

Subbase. After the excavation is completed and lined, lay at least 4 in. of compactible gravel onto the landscape fabric, extending at least 6 in. behind the wall. Compact this subbase thoroughly with a heavy hand tamper.

Gravel backfill. Lay down 4-in. perforated drainage pipe over the subbase. At least one end of the pipe should be unobstructed so that runoff can escape. Lay the first two rows of the retaining wall on the gravel base in front of the drainpipe. Backfill behind them with coarse gravel and tamp it down. Add the gravel as you build each row of the wall, tamping as you go. (If you add all the gravel at the end it won't compact thoroughly.)

Finishing. Once the top row of the wall is in place, fold the landscape fabric down over the gravel to form a large C facing downhill. Cover the fabric with 6 in. of topsoil and compact lightly.

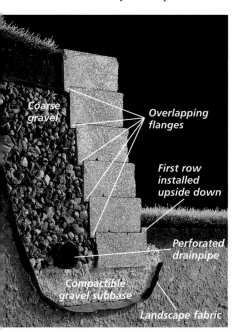

Coarse gravel

Overlapping flanges

First row installed upside down

Perforated drainpipe

Compactible gravel subbase

Landscape fabric

RIGHT: *Deadman anchor.*
LEFT: *Cutaway diagram showing the construction of an interlocking-block retaining wall.*

WALL MATERIALS

TIMBER	**PROS:** A wall up to 4 ft. high can be a do-it-yourself project. You may be able to build an even taller wall if you have an engineer calculate the loads and design the wall, including the support and drainage system.
	CONS: Not as long-lived as masonry. Making square cuts is challenging. Also, the components are heavy and hard to manage alone. Plan on about three days to build a wall that's 4 ft. tall by 15 ft. long.
	NOTES: Use 8-ft.-long, 6x6 pressure-treated wood designated for "ground contact" and have all materials delivered. All timber walls require deadmen at least every 4 ft. at midwall height or higher. Follow instructions for landscape fabric, drainage and backfill. Pin the first tier of timbers to the ground with #4 rebar.
INTERLOCKING CONCRETE BLOCK	**PROS:** Interlocking-block systems (also called segmented retaining walls) are mortar-free and easy to assemble. The walls can taper, turn, wrap and curve and are available in many textures, shapes and colors. These systems can be used for walls up to 20 ft. high. They use various construction techniques, including: • Keyed & battered design. Blocks key into one another and are stacked to lean into the hillside. • Backfill trap. Backfill is shoveled into the webbing, trapping blocks individually. • Geo-grid nets. Geo-grid plastic net tiebacks attach to the block and are buried 5 ft. into the hillside at the specified heights.
	CONS: You can't mix and match systems from different manufacturers. Block systems that use metal pins to tie the blocks together can be difficult to line up exactly.
	NOTES: Tell the supplier where to unload the materials and make sure the forklift will be able to get to that spot. Use the manufacturer's guidelines to determine how many blocks, pins and tiebacks you'll need. Follow instructions for landscape fabric, drainage and backfill. When stacking blocks, sweep off each layer; small pebbles can disrupt the pattern. Top walls with flat blocks (capstones) attached with construction adhesive.
STONE, BRICK OR CINDER BLOCK	**PROS:** Stone walls have a handsome, rustic appeal. You can save money by collecting stones and doing the work yourself. Brick walls provide a tailored, formal look. Cinder block is inexpensive and can be reinforced with steel and concrete.
	CONS: Building a stone wall is harder than it may appear. It can be difficult to fit the stones together properly, and it takes experience to make solid, natural-looking mortar joints. Dry stone walls are easier to build but have less holding power. Bricklaying also requires a certain level of skill. Cinder block walls usually need to be faced with stucco, brick or stone or covered with plantings to make them attractive.
	NOTES: A mortared wall requires a footing and a drainage system that will defeat frost heaving. Follow instructions for landscape fabric, drainage and backfill.
CONCRETE	**PROS:** Strong. Well-designed and properly built concrete walls rarely fail.
	CONS: Bare concrete is unattractive. You can veneer the finished wall with masonry or embed decorative designs in it. If it does fail, patching may not be possible and removal is costly. Walls over a few feet high should be formed and poured by a professional who has experience with vertical pours.
	NOTES: Dig footing or gravel bed below frost line. Follow instructions for landscape fabric, drainage and backfill. Form wall with 3/4-in. plywood and 2x4 bracing. To strengthen, install #4 rebar wired in 12-in. grids. While concrete is wet, vibrate mechanically or strike forms every 6 in. with a rubber mallet.

How to Build a Retaining Wall Using Interlocking Block

Step 1

A. Dig out the slope to create a battered (see page 143) surface for the retaining wall. Allow 1 ft. of space for the gravel backfill between the back of the wall and the hillside.

B. Use stakes to mark the ends of the front edge of the wall and any corners or curves. Connect the stakes with string. Using a line level, adjust the string until it's level.

C. Dig a trench for the first row of blocks and the gravel subbase. The depth of the trench should equal the height of the blocks plus 8 in. Measure down from the string as you work to make sure the trench remains level.

Step 1

D. Line the excavation with sheets of landscape fabric that have been cut 3 ft. longer than the height of the wall. Arrange the sheets so that they overlap by at least 6 in.

Step 2

A. Spread a 6-in. layer of compactible gravel subbase into the trench, and compact it with a hand tamper.

B. Lay the first row of blocks in the trench, aligning the front edges with the string. If you're using flanged blocks, install the first row of blocks upside down and backward in the trench to provide a solid basis for the rest of the wall.

Step 2

C. Check the blocks frequently with a level; adjust their position as necessary by adding or removing gravel beneath them. Sweep off the top of the blocks before beginning the next row.

Step 3

A. Lay the second row of blocks according to the manufacturer's instructions, staggering the vertical joints. As you work, make sure all the blocks remain level.

B. Place 4-in. perforated drainpipe over the gravel subbase behind the blocks. Make

sure that at least one end of the pipe is unobstructed so that runoff water can escape.

C. Add 6 in. of coarse gravel behind the blocks and pack it thoroughly with a hand tamper (but don't crush the drainpipe).

D. Lay additional rows of block until the wall is about 18 in. high.

Step 3

Stagger all the vertical joints and sweep off each row before adding the next one.

E. Fill behind the wall with coarse gravel, and pack it down with the hand tamper.

Step 4

A. Lay the remaining rows of block, except the capstone row, backfilling and tamping as you go.

B. Fold the end of the landscape fabric down over the gravel backfill.

Step 5

A. Apply construction adhesive to the top row of blocks, following the manufacturer's instructions. Lay the capstones in place.

B. Use topsoil to fill in behind the wall (over the landscape fabric) and in front of the base of the wall.

C. Add sod or other plants as desired above and below the wall.

CREATING HALF-BLOCKS

Half-blocks are often needed for corners and to ensure that the vertical joints between the blocks are staggered between rows. To make a half-block, score a full block with a circular saw outfitted with a masonry blade, then break the block along the scored line using a hand sledge and a brick chisel.

PATHS

The brick-paver walkway and decorative fence columns of this entryway create a unified look that complements the brick veneer of the house.

A well-designed path provides safe, easy access to your home while enhancing the charm and value of the property. Fortunately, installing a new pathway is one of the easiest home improvement projects you can do yourself.

Although building a path mostly involves common sense, it does require some skill and a lot of elbow grease. If you're not sure how to proceed, seek professional advice. A landscape architect, contractor or designer can answer questions that are specific to your site or handle the entire project for you.

Walkways can be classified into two types—primary and secondary. Before you start planning, it's a good idea to know which type of path you're designing:

• Primary paths are the main paths that lead from the front or the back of the house to a street, sidewalk or driveway.

• Secondary paths branch off the primary path and often wind through a seating area or garden.

If you're designing a primary path, select a surface material that won't get slippery when wet and that can be set firmly and evenly, such as cut-stone slabs or brick pavers.

Routing

In most homes, the primary path to the front door is set in a straight line, probably because a straight path is the fastest and easiest way to approach a house. Curved designs are more commonly used for secondary paths. Since a secondary path doesn't have as much foot traffic as a primary path, it can be narrower, less obtrusive and more casual in design.

Although there are no hard-and-fast rules for designing either kind of path, professional designers suggest the following guidelines:

• Curve a path around an existing tree or garden feature (such as a boulder or shrub) or follow the dripline of your trees (the circular line around the outside edge of the tree branches).

• Design a meandering path that winds around special features of your yard, such as a unique plant, a garden sculpture or a striking view.

• Use a straight, narrow walkway to make a small yard appear longer (this will be especially effective if the end of the path is hidden from view).

• Create a curving path, or one laid on the diagonal, to draw the eye from side to side and make a garden look wider.

• Soften the look of a straight path by adding a border of plants or flowers on either side.

Width

Primary paths should be at least 48 in. wide, to allow two people to comfortably walk along side by side. Landscape designers also suggest that the width correspond to the dimensions of one of the architectural elements of your house, such as the combined width of the front door and its trim.

Secondary paths, which are more likely to be used by only one person at a time, can be narrower—30 to

This walkway made of large pavers repeats the colors of the house and creates a striking contrast with its luxuriant garden.

36 in. wide.

Be sure all paths are wide enough to accommodate any yard equipment you might use. For example, a lawn mower or garden cart requires a span of 3 or 4 ft., while a tractor may need 5 ft. or more. When in doubt, make the path wider than absolutely necessary, to ensure that it will be comfortable, safe and easy to follow.

Installation Tips

The most difficult part of building a walkway may be choosing among the many different styles and materials that are available (see **Choosing Path Materials**, page 148). There are two approaches to designing paths: continuous-surface paving and stepping-stones. Choosing which type to build is mostly a matter of personal taste. However, bear in mind that a continuous walkway is a more permanent addition to your property. If you like to change your landscaping scheme every few years, you may prefer a stepping-stone path that can be easily altered or removed.

The instructions for installing most pathway materials tend to be very similar. Whether you choose to make your path of brick, concrete pavers or cut stone, keep these essentials in mind:

• Most walkways (except for grass paths and stepping-stones over 4 sq. ft.) require a base of coarse crushed stone to keep the path level and to keep weeds from invading it. Your soil type and climate will determine how deep the base needs to be. Landscape contractors and stone suppliers can provide specific instructions for your area—but in general, you can figure on a 4-in. base if you have a mild winter and well-drained soil. In other areas you may need to dig deeper—check the local building codes for the requirements in your area.

• If you have heavy clay soil, improve your drainage by placing 4-in.-dia. perforated PVC drainpipe down the center of the path, enclosed within the gravel base. The drain holes should face down.

• Prepare your path so water drains off the surface. You have two options: Install it so the fin-ished surface will be ¼ to ½ in. above the adjacent grade, or slope the path away from your foundation or driveway, at a rate of ¼ inch per ft. of path.

• Apply a leveling course of 1 to 2 in. of sand over the base. This will allow you to move the stones or bricks around until they're firmly seated. If you like, you can place a layer of landscape fabric between the gravel base and the sand, to prevent the sand from filtering down through the gravel.

• Use professional-quality edging to hold bricks, concrete pavers and small stones in place. Edgings, which are commonly made of aluminum, steel or plastic, are relatively inexpensive and typically available in 7½-ft.-long sections.

PATHS *CONTINUED*

CHOOSING PATH MATERIALS

Gravel and Crushed Stone

These nonslip materials offer an inexpensive, fast-draining path surface. They come in many colors and sizes, and are easy to install. Gravel is sold in both bag and in bulk form. Bulk stone costs less, but suppliers usually charge a delivery fee. Small gravel (¾-in.-dia. or less) is the most comfortable to walk on. A gravel path will need an edging to keep the stones from traveling.

Brick Pavers

Brick pavers can be laid in countless patterns, including intricate herringbone designs. For curved paths, choose a basic end-on-end pattern to avoid extensive brick cutting. Brick pavers are affordable, low maintenance and easy to handle. However, always use paving bricks, not wall bricks. Paving bricks are harder and more durable, especially in cold or wet climates. For a nonskid surface, choose bricks with a rough surface. Use a rigid edging to securely contain the bricks and prevent them from spreading and shifting underfoot.

Stone

Natural stone is an especially elegant surface. It's also expensive and difficult to lay. You can lay stones in sand or set them in concrete with mortar joints. However, a mortared path should be done by a professional, since it will crack unless properly installed. Stone is sold by masonry suppliers, in both irregular shapes and squares or rectangles sized in 6-in. increments. A local stone is most likely to blend well with the surroundings.

Mixed Materials

Mixed materials, like the brick, ceramic tile and broad stones that are used in the path above, can create a striking and unique look. More traditional paving combinations include stepping-stones and gravel, or brick with pebbles. When planning a mixed path, lay out the sample materials in your yard to see how they'll work with the surroundings.

The mixed materials that compose this bold path create a unique look that adds distinction to the surroundings.

Mulch Paths

Mulch offers an earthy, casual look that's best suited for informal paths in low-traffic areas. Choose a material that fits the surroundings, such as bark, pine needles or wood chips in a wooded area. Since organic mulches will decompose, you'll need to refresh them every year or two.

Grass Pathways

Grass can unify a yard by creating the feeling of a single garden, rather than separate planting areas. A grass path is inexpensive and easy to start with seed or sod, but it requires regular maintenance. It can also be difficult to maintain a grass path in areas that have deep shade, heavy traffic or compacted soil. You can form a grass path in almost any size and shape, but be sure to make it wide enough to mow easily.

Concrete Paths

You can make concrete paths that look like stone by using special kits that have molds and coloring agents. Finish the path with edging plants.

Broad stepping-stones laced with low-growing plants create an informal path that complements this rustic home and its garden beds.

BUILDING A LOOSE-FILL PATHWAY

A loose-fill pathway is a simple, inexpensive alternative to a concrete or paved path. This kind of path uses lightweight loose materials, such as gravel, crushed rock, bark or wood chips to "pave" a prepared surface. Most loose-fill materials are available in a pre-bagged form, which makes them relatively easy to transport and use.

Because the materials are not fixed within the path, you'll need an edging around the perimeter of the path to hold them in place. You can fashion an edging from common building materials, such as wood, cut stone or brick pavers. For the best effect, use a material that's used in the house or other structures in your yard, and select a loose-fill material that complements the texture and color of the edging.

Loose-fill paths can be adapted to a wide range of shapes, designs and settings. The project below uses brick edging set in soil—an approach that's best suited for lightly traveled pathways in well-drained soil.

How to Build a Loose-Fill Pathway with Brick Edging

Step 1

Step 3

Step 5

Step 1
A. Mark the outline of the path with a thick rope or garden hose.

B. Excavate the area to a depth of 2 to 3 in. Rake the site smooth.

Step 2
A. Dig a narrow edging trench, about 2 in. deeper than the path, on either side of the excavated area.

B. Test the depth of the trench by placing a brick paver in it on end—the top of the brick should stand several inches above ground.

C. If needed, adjust the trench to bring the bricks to the correct height.

Step 3
A. To prevent weed invasion, line the trench with landscape fabric, overlapping the sheets by at least 6 in.

B. Push the ends of the sheets into the edging trenches.

Step 4
A. Set the bricks vertically into the edging trenches. Arrange them side by side, with no gaps between them.

B. Using a trowel, replace the soil behind and beneath each brick and pack it down. Adjust the bricks as necessary to keep the rows even.

Step 5
A. Finish the path by spreading the loose-fill material (gravel, crushed rock, bark or wood chips) between the brick edging.

B. Level the surface with a garden rake. The loose material should be slightly above ground level.

C. Tap each brick lightly on the inside face to help set it into the soil.

D. Inspect and adjust the bricks yearly, adding new loose-fill material as needed.

PATHS *CONTINUED*

How to Build a Sand-Set Flagstone Walkway

Step 1

A. Outline the walkway site and excavate it to a depth of 6 in., to allow enough room for the edging and stakes. Add a 2-in. layer of compactible gravel subbase and smooth

Step 2

the surface with a rake.

B. Install an edging of 2×6 pressure-treated lumber at ground level around the perimeter of the path.

C. Drive 12-in. stakes on the outside of the edging, spaced 1 ft. apart. The tops of the stakes should be slightly below ground level. Attach the edging to the stakes with galvanized screws.

Step 2

A. Test-fit the stones over the walkway base to find an arrangement that minimizes the number of cuts you'll need to make. The gaps between the stones should range between ⅜ in. and 2 in. Use

a pencil to mark the stones for cutting, then remove them and place them beside the walkway in the same arrangement.

B. To cut the flagstones, score along the marked lines using a circular saw with a masonry blade set ⅛ in. deep (wear a dust mask or respirator when cutting flagstones). Set a piece of wood underneath the scored line on the stone. Use a masonry chisel and hammer to strike along the scored line until the stone breaks.

To avoid injury, always wear safety goggles and thick work gloves when cutting stone or brick.

Step 3

A. Lay strips of landscape fabric over the walkway base, overlapping the edges by 6 in.

B. Spread a 2-in. layer of sand

Step 3

over the landscape fabric to serve as the base for the flagstones.

C. With a short 2×6, make a screed for smoothing the sand by notching it to fit inside the edging. The depth of the notches should equal the thickness of the stones.

D. Smooth the base by pulling the screed from one end of the walkway to the other. Add sand as needed until the base is smooth and level.

Step 4

Step 4

A. Beginning at one corner of the walkway, lay the flagstones onto the sand base (reproducing the pattern used in the test fitting). If necessary, add or remove sand beneath the stones to level them, then set them by tapping them with a rubber mallet or a length of 2×4.

B. Fill the gaps between the stones with sand, then spray the entire walkway with water to help the sand settle. Add more sand until the gaps are completely filled and tightly packed.

Make a screed for smoothing the sand by notching the ends of a short 2×6 to fit inside the edging. The depth of the notches should equal the thickness of the stones, which is usually about 2 in.

PATIOS

Site planning is the first step in building an attractive, comfortable patio. When choosing the spot, keep the following issues in mind:

Sun. Do you want the patio to be sunny or shady, warm or cool? What time of day will you be using it?

Trees. Trees add shade, but also shed leaves, branches and sap—and heavily shaded patios are more likely to develop moss and fungus.

Privacy. Stand and sit in the patio site and look around. If you don't like the view or it isn't private enough, consider a fence or hedge.

Size. A patio should be at least as large as a standard indoor room—100 sq. ft. or more.

Drainage. Don't pick a low spot where water tends to collect. If the patio is next to the house, you may need to reposition gutter downspouts. To do this, add pipe along the wall, or connect the downspout to an underground pipe.

Underground surprises. Before beginning any project that involves digging, you must locate all buried utility lines and structures. Ask your utility company or building department for help locating any underground service lines, sewer pipes or fuel and septic tanks beneath the site. In addition to the safety factor, you don't want to build over utility lines. Although pavers can be removed to gain access to utilities, they don't always reinstall evenly.

Professional Advice

Even if you do the work yourself, getting professional advice can often make a project more successful. For example, a landscape architect can make the most of your site by creating a design that complements the architectural style of your house. If

This inviting cobblestone patio is approached by a flagstone and gravel pathway. Ground covers and container plantings add warmth and color.

your plan includes working around a tree, an arborist can help keep it from damaging the patio, and vice versa.

Keys to Success

Building a patio is not a complicated job, but there's a lot of heavy work involved and you'll want to do careful work to ensure that the patio will last as long as possible. For a durable, attractive patio, keep in mind the following points:

• The most important part of any patio project is excavating and creating a flat base with the right slope for proper drainage. To drain properly, the area should slope down at least ¼ in. per ft.

• Construction will be easier if you

pick a site that's relatively flat and level. If that's not possible, consider hiring a contractor to do the heavy excavating work.

• The right tools can help you produce the best results in the shortest time. You may already have most of the tools you'll need, but you can also rent tools to simplify some tasks. Check with a local rental store or landscape center for prices and availability.

• Poorly installed edging is the main reason patios begin to fall apart after a few years. There are many different types of edging on the market; find out what's available in your area before you begin your patio project.

PATIOS CONTINUED

How to Build a Brick Paver Patio

Installing brick pavers is one of the easiest ways to create a durable, distinctive, easy-care patio. Brick pavers come in many colors and shapes that can be laid in interesting patterns, and since each unit rises and falls independently, the patio won't crack when the ground freezes and thaws.

Some designs and patterns require that you cut pavers to fit. To cut pavers, use a circular saw outfitted with a diamond-tipped or masonry blade. Always wear eye protection and work gloves when cutting pavers. Also, a patio project warrants renting a gas-powered plate compactor to thoroughly tamp down the subbase and the pavers.

Step 1

A. Outline the patio, using stakes and strings for straight edges, and a garden hose for curved edges. Using a line level, adjust each string until

This brick paver patio uses a running bond pattern surrounded by a fan border.

it's level. Once you've marked the shape of the patio, add 6 in. around the perimeter for the edging. Spray-paint this outline on the grass to define the area you'll be excavating.

B. Excavate the site, digging at least 5 in. deeper than the depth of your pavers and making sure you reach undisturbed soil. Drive in a stake and mark the finished level of the patio on it. Don't backfill low spots with soil; instead, fill them with the gravel you're using for the subbase.

C. Use a long 2×4 or a string line across the area to find any bumps or dips. Correct them by removing or adding subbase.

D. After excavating, run a plate compactor over the entire area, to tamp the surface down evenly. If the soil is damp, sprinkle some of the crushed stone subbase over it.

If your patio extends to the edge of the house, compact right up to the building line. Soil under the eaves is often less compacted than soil farther away from the house.

Step 2

A. Lay a geotextile designed for paver construction over the area. (Don't use polyethylene sheeting or garden landscape fabric.) The textile will keep water from saturating the soil base, which can cause settling.

B. Spread a 3- to 4-in. layer of subbase over the area and compact it evenly. (The best subbase material is 100 percent crushed limestone or granite, grade ¾-minus.)

C. Using the plate compactor, work the edges, then crisscross the patio diagonally in both directions; add more stone and repeat until the subbase is 4 in. thick.

Step 1

Use a long 2×4 to check for high and low spots.

Step 2

Pack the subbase with a plate compactor.

Step 3

Install the edging before laying the pavers.

D. Check the slope of the subbase with a straightedge and a string line to be sure the grade is still level. If you find any bumps or dips, add or scrape away some of the subbase and recompact the area. Finishing the subbase as perfectly as possible will prevent later shifting that can lead to an uneven surface.

Step 3

The next step depends on the type of edging you're using. Some types of edging, such as formed concrete (which is appropriate only in mild climates) are installed after all the pavers are set. However, most other types of edging, including the rigid plastic edging shown here, are installed at this point.

To install rigid plastic edging, place it around the edges of the patio, below the string outline. Anchor it by driving galvanized spikes through predrilled holes and into the subbase. To allow for possible adjustments, drive only enough spikes to keep the edging in place.

Step 4

A. Using a line level, recheck the string guides to make sure they're still level. Check the level of the edging by measuring down from the string at several points. Add or remove subbase to adjust the level.

B. Spread 1 in. of coarse masonry sand over the subbase. To get an even layer, place long 1-in.-dia. dowels on the subbase every 6 ft. Shovel on a layer of sand, water it with a hose and pack it lightly. Then level it by dragging a 2×6 over the dowels. When the sand is completely level, remove the dowels, fill the grooves with sand and tamp them smooth.

Step 5

A. Lay the first paver in a corner, making sure it rests firmly against the edging. Lay the next paver tightly against it. Set the pavers by tapping them into the sand with a mallet. Use the depth of the first paver as a guide for setting the rest (use a straightedge to check). Work

outward in sections, fitting the pavers together very tightly. Avoid stepping on the sand as you work.

B. Once all the pavers are down, sweep a layer of dry sand over them. Pack down the whole area with the compactor, then saturate the patio with water and allow it to dry.

Repeat this step until the joints are completely filled. Don't take shortcuts here—a tightly set and fully packed paver patio won't be susceptible to the shifting that can tear other patios apart.

Once the patio is complete apply a sealer to bring out the color of the pavers and protect them from stains. Before sealing the pavers, clean them with an acid-based cleaner made for pavers (available at landscaping yards). Reapply the sealer every two to five years, depending on your climate and how heavily you use the patio.

Redwood deck photo courtesy of California Redwood Assn.

Decks

The comfort and elegance of an outdoor living room make it one of the most cost-effective home improvement investments you can make.

Helpful Terms

Galvanized hardware: Zinc-coated, rust-resistant fasteners used with wood.

Heartwood: The nonliving central wood of a tree, more durable than the sapwood. The premium choice for decking.

Joists: Horizontal pieces of framing lumber that support the floor of a deck.

Pressure-treated (PT) lumber: Wood treated with an insecticide-preservative to resist moisture and decay.

Ultraviolet (UV) rays: Light rays that discolor wood and accelerate wear. Wood decks require a UV-protectant finish.

BUILD A SUNDECK IN A WEEKEND

Build a deck in a weekend? Sounds impossible—after all, it usually takes two days just to dig the postholes and pour the concrete footings. But the 12 × 16-ft. sundeck shown here doesn't require those time-consuming steps, because it's supported by precast concrete footings (or "piers") that rest right on the ground. They're inexpensive, weigh about 45 lbs. and have a molded top that holds 2-by joists.

The thirty footings that support this deck are arranged in six rows laid parallel to the house, about 25 in. apart. The joists are secured by the molded tops of the footings, which simplifies the framing process. Band joists are placed along the outer edge to partly conceal the precast footings. This "floating foundation" system is allowed by building codes nationwide, including areas where frost heaving is a concern.

Tools	Materials
• tape measure	• 16-ft. 2×6 joists (7)
• pencil	• 12-ft. 2×6 decking (38)
• paintbrush	• 2 lbs. 3-in. galvanized
• stakes	deck screws
• level	• 30 precast concrete
• drill or screw gun	footings
• shovel	• wood sealer/protectant

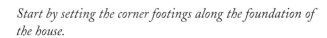

Start by setting the corner footings along the foundation of the house.

How to Build a Simple Sundeck

Step 1

A. Start by placing two corner piers along the house foundation. Space them 14 ft. on center so the 16-ft. floor joist will overhang by 1 ft. on each end. The center of each pier should be about 6 in. from the house.

B. Temporarily place a perfectly straight joist into the slots in the piers, then check it for level. If needed, dig out some dirt from under the high pier to level the joist.

C. Check to make sure that the top of the finished deck will be at least 1 in. below the door threshold. Adjust the height as needed and level. Remove the joist.

D. Once the joist is properly positioned, install three intermediate piers along the house, equally spaced between the two corner piers. Adjust their height as needed by subtracting or adding soil or gravel.

SIMPLE SUNDECK *CONTINUED*

Step 2

A. Set piers in the two outside corners, 10½ ft. on center from the first two corner piers.

B. Temporarily install a straight joist between one of the outside corner piers and one of the corner piers by the house.

C. Shift the outside pier as needed until the joist forms a perfectly square 90-degree angle to the house.

D. Adjust the height of the outside pier until the joist is level. If it's low by a few inches, add dirt or gravel. To raise it more than a few inches, cut a 4×4 post to fit between the pier and the joist.

E. When the joist is level, install four equally spaced piers on that line, extending out from the house.

F. Repeat steps 2A to 2D on the other side of the deck.

Step 3

A. You now have two lines of six piers extending straight out from the house. Place joists across all six rows and level them.

B. Install the three intermediate piers on each row. Adjust their height as needed by subtracting or adding soil or gravel.

C. Lay a side band joist across the ends of the floor joists on one side of the frame. Start it before the intersection with the first joist, about 1 in. from the side of the house.

D. With a pencil, mark the location of each joist on the side band joist. Drill a pair of ³⁄₁₆-in. holes along each line.

E. Attach the side band joist to the joists by driving deck screws through the predrilled holes.

F. Repeat steps 3C to 3E on the other side of the deck.

Step 4

A. Move to the joist farthest from the house. Predrill and screw in short outriggers (12-in.-long 2×6 blocks) at each of the five piers.

B. Mark, predrill and secure the final band joist to the outriggers and the side band joists.

C. Check that the frame is square (by measuring the diagonals) and that each joist is level.

D. Make corrections. Unlike decks with concrete footings, this system allows all the parts to be easily repositioned or adjusted after the understructure framing is completed.

E. Once you're satisfied with the framing, shovel some dirt around the base of any piers that you dug down into the ground.

Step 3

Set the joists into the slots in the concrete piers, then carefully check each one to ensure that it's perfectly level.

Step 4

Screw the band joist parallel to the house in place after installing short 2×6 blocks at each of the concrete piers.

Step 5

A. Seal the ends of the remaining 2×6s with a clear wood preservative or decking stain.

B. Lay out all the 2×6 deck boards on the joists.

If the boards are wet, butt them tightly together; they'll shrink as they dry, forming small gaps between each board.

If the boards are dry, use a 16d nail as a guide to leave a ⅛- to ¼-in. space between the boards.

C. Adjust the decking so that the first and last boards overhang the left and right side band joists by an equal distance.

D. Adjust the decking so that the ends of the boards along the house are perfectly aligned, about 1 in. from the side of the house.

Step 6

A. Beginning with the first decking board on one side, mark the location of each of the six joists on the boards with a pencil line.

B. Drill a pair of pilot holes along these lines.

C. Secure the boards to the joists with deck screws.

D. Snap a line across the outer ends of the boards and trim them straight with a circular saw.

QUICK TIPS

Instead of using a drill for a deck construction job, rent a screw gun. A workshop drill will probably burn out before the deck is done.

Step 7

After the deck is completed, wait several days and apply wood preservative or stain according to the manufacturer's instructions (see **Deck Finishing Tips**, page 161).

Be sure to coat both the deck surface and the band joists along the perimeter.

On the deck shown, the first four steps were done in one day, and the next two construction steps were completed in four hours the next day. Depending on your skills and experience, it may take you more or less time to complete this deck. But either way, this fast, no-nonsense way to build a deck is ideal for the do-it-yourself homeowner.

Step 5

Step 6

Lay the 2×6 decking boards across the joists. Adjust them so that the ends next to the house are perfectly aligned.

Secure the decking to the joists with 3-in. deck screws. Bore pilot holes first to avoid splitting the deck boards.

A GUIDE TO DECKING MATERIALS

While pressure-treated Southern yellow pine is still used for 80 percent of all decks, there are many alternatives available today, including exotic hardwoods and nonwood products that require no finishing and little care.

Pressure-Treated Wood COST: About $1.50 to $2 per square foot.	PROS: PT wood is economical and readily available. If treated with a water repellent every two years, it should last 15 to 30 years.
	CONS: PT Southern yellow pine will check and splinter as it dries. Some PT wood will turn gray if left unfinished (use a semitransparent stain or clear sealer). Protect yourself against PT preservative residue, which is toxic—wear a dust mask during construction, and carefully wash yourself and your clothing when you're done for the day.
Tropical Hardwood COST: About $5 per square foot.	PROS: Ipe is a durable teaklike tropical hardwood that's sold as Ironwood or Pau Lope. It's twice as strong as oak, more durable than redwood or cedar, and resistant to insects and decay. It has a life expectancy of 40 years or more. All grades are virtually knot-free, and its tight grain makes it impervious to water. Treat it just once with a UV-blocking sealer and let it weather.
	CONS: Expensive and heavy. Because it's so hard, you must predrill holes for the fasteners.
Redwood & Cedar COST: About $5 per square foot (higher grades of redwood are much more).	PROS: Redwood and cedar are beautiful, easy to cut, naturally resistant to rot and insects and can be left untreated to weather naturally. Their life expectancy is easily more than 20 years. Select kiln-dried deck heartwood or deck common redwood, or for lower budgets, clear heart, clear, B heart or B grade redwood. For cedar, clear all heartwood is the premium choice.
	CONS: Both are expensive. Avoid redwood or cedar sapwood, which will quickly rot or break down when exposed to moisture.
Plastic-Wood Composites COST: About $3 per square foot.	PROS: Plastic-wood composites are blends of recycled plastic and wood fibers. They're skid-resistant, low maintenance, easy to work, splinter-free and virtually indestructible. Composites can be painted, stained or left to weather (they turn a light gray). Many products come with a 10- to 20-year warranty. Some allow you to run electrical wires inside posts or decking.
	CONS: Some composite lumber has a plastic appearance, and the color may fade over time. The sawdust isn't biodegradable; you must collect it in a drop cloth. Some composite lumber won't span 16- or 24-in. joist spacing. Some building codes don't allow composite lumber.
Vinyl Deck Systems COST: About $7 to $12 per square foot.	PROS: Vinyl deck systems are splinter-free, available in many colors and have good spanning ability. They require no sealers or finishes, and some are resistant to UV rays. You can cut planks to length with a circular saw and cover the ends with vinyl caps. Choose only skid-resistant materials with color-fast, no-fade treatments. Some manufacturers offer lifetime warranties.
	CONS: Relatively expensive. Unless specially treated at the factory, vinyl will fade and become brittle with age, and all vinyl will eventually lose its gloss. The sawdust isn't biodegradable; you must collect it in a drop cloth.

Average costs as of summer 1998.

Build an Easy Hand Railing

Building codes typically require a railing on any deck over 30 in. high—but even if your deck sits low on the ground, you may want to add a railing around two or three sides, especially if it will be used by children or the elderly. Railings can direct the flow of traffic, define a deck's boundaries and provide a backdrop for plants.

A simple butt-joined railing is easy to add to your deck. Measure your deck to determine the length of the railings and the number of balusters you'll need. (To prevent small children from getting their heads trapped, the spaces between the balusters should never be more than 4 in.)

Prefabricated railing kits are another alternative. Many companies offer attractive, fully assembled, ready-to-install railing panels. You simply slide them between deck posts and screw them into place.

Materials

- **2x6s (railings)**
- **42-in. 2x2s (balusters)**
- **2½-in. galvanized deck screws**

Tools

- **drill or screw gun**
- **level**
- **measuring tape**
- **6-in. C-clamp**

How to Build an Easy Hand Railing

Step 1

Predrill the 2×2s.

Step 2

Attach the 2×2s to the band joists.

Step 3

Position the 2×6 railing and attach it to the 2×2s.

Step 1

A. Bevel the lower ends of the 2×2s to ensure that water drips off and doesn't collect there. Align the 2×2s, and draw a center line for the pilot holes. Drill two ³⁄₁₆-in. pilot holes above the beveled end of each board and one ³⁄₁₆-in. pilot hole below the top end of each board.

B. Apply wood sealer to both ends of the 2×2s.

C. Cut a piece of scrap lumber 3½ in. wide to use as a spacer block.

Step 2

A. Clamp a straight piece of scrap lumber to the bottom of the deck band joist to use as a guide strip.

B. Place a corner 2×2 on the guide strip, 3½ in. from the corner of the deck. Use a level to ensure that it's plumb. Attach the beveled end to the band joist with deck screws.

C. Attach the other 2×2s on that side, using the spacer block and the guide strip to position them evenly.

D. Repeat steps 2A to 2C on the other sides of the railing.

Step 3

A. Hold a 2×6 so that it forms a top railing behind the installed 2×2s. Using the level, adjust the 2×6 until it's level.

B. Attach the 2×6 top rail to the 2×2s with the deck screws.

C. Where the top rails meet at a 90° angle, secure them together with two deck screws.

D. Finish the railing by applying a coat of wood preservative or stain.

A GUIDE TO DECK FINISHES

Even if your deck is made of pressure-treated lumber, redwood or cedar, it will be at risk as soon as you complete it. Moisture swells and warps the wood, sunlight dries and shrinks it and ultraviolet rays discolor it. Once you add wear, scratches, grease splatters, ground-in dirt and mildew to this list, you can see why it's important to finish a deck properly.

Selecting a Finish

The ideal deck finish will repel water, protect against mildew and screen out ultraviolet rays. But to make sure you're getting all this, you need to check the label—some products provide waterproofing only, for example. Here's how to take the guesswork out of finishing a new deck or refinishing an old one.

Oil-based finishes provide more and longer-lasting protection, because they penetrate deeper into the wood than water-based products. However, a wood surface must be bone dry before it will accept an oil-based sealer.

Water-based finishes are easier to clean up than oil-based products. They're also more forgiving in damp conditions—you can apply a water-based finish to wood that is still damp. These products also last longer than they used to.

The best deck finishes are sealers and stains; they wear better than paint because they penetrate the wood. Clear sealers have no pigment; stains are available in three pigment levels: solid-color, semitransparent and "tone" (light pigmentation).

Clear deck finishes allow the natural grain of the wood to show through. Since they're transparent, they don't leave lap marks—a common problem with pigmented finishes. However, they aren't the best finishes for blocking UV rays. The UV inhibitors in clear finishes tend to break down quickly and must be reapplied yearly.

Lightly pigmented and semitransparent finishes can add color to a deck while allowing some of the grain to

Color pigments can help protect a deck from UV rays. Generally, the more pigment a finish has, the better it is at blocking UV rays.

show through; they also form an effective UV barrier. (In general, the more pigment a finish has, the better it is at blocking UV rays.) Semitransparent deck finishes last up to three years or more between applications.

Solid-color finishes offer the most effective UV protection, but they generally don't hold up to foot traffic very well. Look for products that are made expressly for deck surfaces, such as solid-color decking stains with Teflon®. During application, pigmented finishes tend to leave lap marks and uneven areas, and they'll show traffic patterns as they wear. Because of this, when you reapply the finish you'll need to feather extra pigment into the worn or uneven areas.

DECK FINISHING TIPS

The best way to finish a new (or newly cleaned) deck is to apply a first coat within a few weeks, and a second coat the next year. After that you can wait two or three years before applying another coat.

If you have new lumber with a waxy buildup (mill glaze), don't finish it right away—wait two or three weeks until the surface weathers. You can tell you have mill glaze if water from a hose beads on the surface, or you can see burnished areas. If water still beads after two or three weeks, sand the deck lightly.

Decks in heavily shaded areas are prone to mildew. Make sure the finish contains a mildewcide. To help keep mildew at bay, apply a deck cleaner annually.

Apply deck finish when the temperature is above 50°F and the weather will be dry for a few days. Wear long pants, long sleeves, eye protection and rubber gloves.

Heavily shaded decks are prone to mildew. Use a finish with a mildewcide and apply a deck cleaner annually.

Before applying a finish or cleaner, protect lawn and plants by wetting them with a hose and covering them with plastic tarp. Rinse again when you're done.

Finish the top, bottom and exposed sides of all boards, and any structural members you can reach. Future maintenance should focus on the surfaces and end grain that are exposed to wear and weather.

You can save time and effort by using power equipment—a garden sprayer or an airless paint sprayer. For deck finishes, you'll need a .011- to .013-in. nozzle tip for your paint sprayer.

For an even finish, do a small section with the sprayer, then back-brush with a paintbrush or roller. Use natural-bristle brushes for oil-based finishes and synthetic bristles for water-based products. After 20 minutes, check for puddles and brush or roll them out.

GIVE YOUR DECK A FACE-LIFT

Painted and stained decks look great at first, but they require a lot of maintenance. As traffic patterns begin to show and successive coats of finish build up, you're left with two choices: sand or chemically strip the existing finish. Both are nasty, tedious chores.

Although sanding hasn't become much easier in recent years, stripping has. A new generation of safe, effective strippers is designed to easily remove a wide range of finishes, including solid and semi-transparent stains, varnishes, water repellents, urethanes and wood preservatives. What's more, most of these deck strippers are biodegradable and safe to use around plants and shrubs. And after you remove the old finish, you can use a product called a "deck brightener" to return the wood to its original color.

We're demonstrating this process on a red cedar deck that has three old layers of gray, semitransparent, oil-based stain. We've selected a thick, water-based gel stripper. This kind of product is easy to control, yet powerful enough to work quickly.

A 1-gallon jug is enough to strip about 150 sq. ft. of decking—and this one even included a packet of deck brightener.

SAFETY FIRST

Stripper Safety

When using any deck stripper, keep these safety tips in mind:

- Always wear goggles and rubber gloves. Even the safest strippers can irritate eyes and skin.
- Brush the stripper on slowly and carefully. Don't cross over onto previously rolled areas.
- Don't walk on areas that are coated with stripper—they're very slippery.
- To keep the process manageable, strip large or multilevel decks in small sections.
- Keep strippers away from bare metal surfaces, such as aluminum thresholds or screen doors; it will spot them.
- Apply strippers in the shade or when the sun is low in the sky. Direct sunlight will evaporate and weaken them.

Step 1

A. First, test the stripper by brushing it onto a 6-in.-square area. Mist the area with water to initiate the chemical action. After about fifteen minutes, scrape the surface lightly with an old chisel. This "scrape test" will show you how fast the stripper is working and how long you'll need to wait before washing it off. On our deck, the stripper had already softened all three coats of the old stain.

B. Use a garden hose to wet all the surrounding vegetation, including the grass. Although the stripper is nontoxic and biodegradable, you'll still want to protect plants, since they're likely to get splashed with a heavy dose.

C. Pour the stripper into a plastic bucket and apply it to the decking with a paint roller fitted onto an extension handle. Then mist the decking with a garden hose to activate the stripper. This is a critical step, because the stripper only works when wet.

D. After about ten minutes, use a long-handled brush to scrub down the surface of the wood. This helps

Step 1

Apply a thick, even coat of stripper to the deck with a standard paint roller attached to a long extension handle.

Step 2

Use a power washer to effortlessly whisk away the stripper and old stain, right down to the bare wood.

Step 3

Scrub the brightener into the decking. The bleaching process will immediately turn the wood several shades lighter.

break down the stain and speeds up the stripping process. After fifteen minutes, scrape a small section of deck with a chisel to see if the stripper has worked its way down to the bare wood.

Step 2

A. To remove the stripper and old stain, use a power washer and a spray wand with a 25- to 40-degree fan tip; the water pressure should be set no higher than 1,500 psi.

It's best to use a washer designed for homeowners. These units produce less pressure than professional models and reduce the chance of damage. To avoid damaging the deck surface, keep the wand moving all the time and don't hold it too close to the surface of the wood. Also, never point the wand at people or pets; it can produce a deep wound.

You can rent a power washer, or you can rinse off the stripper with a garden hose. However, since the hose will generate far less pressure, it will take considerably longer to do the job than a power washer.

B. After washing off the old finish, use a paintbrush to apply stripper over any remaining areas of stain—typically you'll find them between the deck boards, beneath the front edge of steps and in corners where the roller can't reach. Sprinkle those areas with water. After fifteen minutes, blast the stripper off with the power washer.

Step 3

A. The gel stripper worked amazingly well on this deck. One slow pass with the power washer exposed bare, clean wood. But because the stripper also darkened the wood,

we decided to apply the packet of deck brightener that was included with the stripper. The deck brightener is not just for the sake of appearances, however—in addition to lightening the wood, it also neutralizes any stripper that may remain on the deck.

When using a deck brightener, follow the instructions on the package. (In this case, we dissolved the 6-oz. packet of brightener powder into 1½ gallons of water and brushed the solution onto the stripped deck boards.)

B. After applying the brightener, use the brush to scrub it into the surface—and watch as its bleaching action immediately lightens the wood. Wait about ten minutes and rinse it off with the power washer.

C. Once the deck is dry, you can either restain it or protect it with two coats of a clear wood preservative.

Lighting

*Low-voltage lighting is a popular choice for
landscape lighting because of its flexibility, easy installation
and limited energy usage.*

Helpful Terms

Cable: Wires that are grouped together
and protected by a covering or sheath.

Controller: A device that turns lights on
or off, usually triggered by a sensor.

Lighting fixture: The unit that holds the
light bulb in place; many fixtures allow
you to adjust the direction of the light.

Sensor: A device, such as a photocell, that
responds to light or movement.

Transformer: A device that converts
electric energy. A low-voltage transformer
lowers the standard 120 volts to 12 volts.

SAFETY LIGHTING

Keeping your backyard intruder-free and safeguarding guests as they make their way toward your house can be important security concerns. Safety lighting with automatic controllers is one way to secure your property and prevent accidents.

Automatic Lighting

Automatic controllers, which include motion detectors, photocells and timers, turn lights on and off automatically by using triggers. Motion detectors monitor a specific area and switch the lights on when they register movement. Photocells turn on the lights when the surroundings get dark and switch them back off when the light returns. Timers turn lights on and off at preset intervals.

Many lighting fixtures feature built-in controllers,

especially outdoor units that are designed to be mounted on roofs or exterior house walls. But you can also buy separate control units for existing lights.

Where to Put Safety Lights

Areas around your home where safety lighting is especially important include the garage and driveway, all entrances, steps

Floodlights such as these can be adapted for use as safety lighting by adding automatic controllers.

and walkways and any windows that are hidden by shrubs or bushes.

For walkways, a border of low-voltage landscape lighting works best. Choose light fixtures and ground stakes made of tough, weather-resistant plastic.

Lights activitated by motion sensors are the best choice for entryways and stairs. To avoid false alarms set off by blowing leaves or small animals, select a fixture that has pulse-count technology. The pulse breaks the sensor's coverage zone in half and measures how fast an object moves from one zone to the other. Small animals usually move too slowly to trip the light.

You can mount high-intensity motion-sensing floodlights around the backyard or side of your house to discourage intruders. You can also mount one on the garage to help you navigate the driveway at night.

When the sun goes down, built-in photo-cells switch these lights on automatically, making it easy to see the path to the front door.

Lighting the Way

Landscape lighting allows you to enjoy your yard after dark, increases the security of your home and helps you safely navigate your yard at night. Well-designed outdoor lighting can also give your landscape a dramatic new personality in the evening hours. When properly lit, the shapes, colors and textures of landscape elements can be emphasized in new and striking ways.

Picking Parts

The easiest way to add landscape lighting to your yard is with low-voltage lighting. Relatively inexpensive low-voltage lighting systems are sold at many home centers and garden shops. Most systems include a transformer, cable, light fixtures and controls. They come in prepackaged kits, but you can also purchase the components separately and design your own system.

Transformers

The transformer lowers the standard line voltage and supplies power to the light fixtures. If you purchased a prepackaged kit, use the unit supplied, but if you're doing a customized system, consider a larger, more powerful transformer. Add up the wattage required by the fixtures you've chosen and buy a transformer that meets those requirements.

Cables

Low-voltage outdoor cable comes in 16- to 10-gauge wire. The lower the gauge, the thicker the wire and the more current it can carry.

Fixtures

Most light fixtures are made of plastic or metal. There are a variety of styles that produce different effects, such as lanterns, adjustable spotlights, well lights and path lights. Some produce very narrow beams of light, while others work like floodlights, casting wide-angle beams.

Bulbs

You can choose among incandescent, halogen and compact fluorescent bulbs. The incandescent bulbs typically included in starter kits cast a soft, yellowish light. Halogen lamps give off a very bright white light; they usually last longer than incandescents. Fluorescent bulbs also produce more light and use less wattage than incandescent bulbs.

Controls

Low-voltage outdoor lighting can be controlled manually, automatically or with a combination of the two systems. Most kits have automatic controls, such as a photocell that turns the lights on at dusk and off at sunrise.

LEFT: *Use uplighting to highlight a featured area. These well lights are buried in raised garden beds to create a soft glow and outline the patio at night.*

Designing Outdoor Lighting

The best time to plan and install outdoor lighting is when you're planning a new or remodeled landscape. Putting the lights in during the landscaping process saves time, gives you more options for placement and prevents you from having to disturb plantings later.

However, if this isn't possible, you can carefully dig and refill the trenches needed to install your lighting with a minimal amount of disruption.

Like other aspects of landscape design, the most effective landscape lighting designs are simple. To avoid overlighting your yard, position lights in unobtrusive places, such as in garden beds, behind shrubs, in the eaves of a pergola or shining down from tree branches.

Begin planning by taking a nighttime tour of your yard, with a map of the yard in hand. On the map, note any areas that need to be illuminated for safety or security reasons. Then decide which outdoor areas you'd like to use at night, and what you'll be using them for. For example, if you want to barbecue at night, you'll need adequate lighting in the grill area.

Next, note any attractive garden features that you'd like to highlight in the evening hours: Interesting trees or shrubs, sculptures, flower beds or water gardens can all make a striking impression when lit. Also look for architectural features, such as walls, arbors, trellises and gates that would create interesting light effects and patterns.

Use moonlighting to create dramatic effects by filtering light through tree branches. Mount low-voltage lights high in the trees and point them downward.

Lighting Methods

Once you've noted the spots you'd like to highlight, the next step is to determine the best way to light each area. You may want to use some of the lighting methods that professional landscape designers use to establish a specific play of light:

Shadow Lighting

Directs a single beam of light on a specific object with a wall or fence behind it, creating a shadow of the featured object.

Backlighting

Highlights an object from behind, creating a silhouette that stands out from the background. This technique is especially effective with lacy shrubs and single objects.

Moonlighting

Places several spotlights in a tree or large overhead structure, such as a pergola, and directs the light downward to simulate the effect of moonlight. (This techinique is also called "downlighting.")

Use shadowlighting to create a dramatic focal point. This single uplight highlights a plant and casts a shadow on the wall.

Grazing

Focuses a broad beam of light on the high point of a wall or fence and indirectly lights the lower portion of the structure, emphasizing the texture of the surface and any low shadows.

Spotlighting

Emphasizes an interesting architectural or landscape feature with a single beam of direct light.

Uplighting

Highlights trees, shrubs, or architectural features with well lights or floodlights hidden directly below them, creating a dramatic play of light and shadow.

Crosslighting

Places two or more spotlights so that their beams cross at the featured object. This creates a three-dimensional effect.

Side Lighting

Lights a pathway or stairway with a series of small, horizontally mounted spotlights.

INSTALLING A LOW-VOLTAGE LIGHTING SYSTEM

Low-voltage lighting kits are economical and easy to install. They use a transformer that plugs into an outdoor receptacle to reduce the 120 volts of electricity in a standard electrical circuit to just 12 volts. This lower voltage means that even a mild shock is virtually impossible.

The materials needed for most outdoor lighting systems include the lighting fixtures and bulbs, low-voltage connector cable, cable connector caps and a control box containing the power transformer, timer and light sensor.

How to Install Low-Voltage Lighting

Step 1

A. Locate a GFCI receptacle (electrical outlet with a ground-fault circuit-interrupter) on the outside wall of your house or inside your garage. Mount the lighting control box on an outside wall, close to the receptacle. Be sure the sensor won't be covered by plants or other materials.

B. Fasten the cable to the terminals on the control box and tighten the screws with a screwdriver.

C. Check the manufacturer's instructions for the cable you have purchased. Some cable is designed to be covered only by mulch; other cable needs to be buried, usually 4 in. deep. If no other instructions are provided, assume that the cable should be buried, as described below.

Dig a narrow trench 6 to 8 in. deep, directly beneath the control box.

Tools & Materials

- screwdriver
- trenching spade
- hacksaw
- tape measure
- ruler
- low-voltage control box
- low-voltage cable
- outdoor-grade PVC conduit
- pipe straps with screws
- connector caps
- low-voltage light fixtures
- low-voltage light bulbs

Step 2

against the wall, with the bottom resting in the trench. Use the pipe straps to secure the conduit to the wall.

Step 2

Starting at the control box, lay out the cable along the path you outlined in your lighting plan. Choose a path with few obstacles, since you'll need to bury the cable.

Step 3

A. Assemble the lighting fixtures, beginning with the one closest to the power pack. Secure the bulb in the socket, then attach the lens and the hood.

B. Attach the lamp base to the cable with a cable connector cap. Tighten the connector caps according to the manufacturer's directions so it pierces the cable and makes contact with the wires inside.

C. Repeat these steps to assemble and attach the remaining lights in your design.

Step 4

Before you begin digging the trenches, place the lights in their final locations, turn them on and survey your design. Look at the lights from several points of view, but especially from the seating areas around your yard, to ensure that none

D. Measure the distance between the base of the control box and the bottom of the trench. Cut a piece of the PVC conduit to this length.

E. Feed the cable through the conduit, then place the conduit

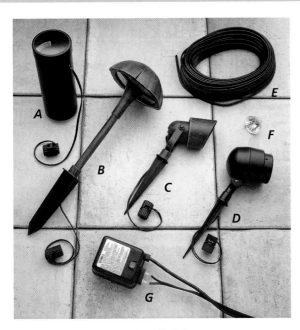

LOW-VOLTAGE SYSTEM COMPONENTS

Typical low-voltage outdoor lighting components include (A) well light, (B) mushroom garden light, (C) adjustable spot, (D) adjustable flood, (E) low-voltage cable, (F) 20-watt halogen bulb, (G) control box containing transformer, timer and a light sensor.

QUICK TIPS

Lighting Your Grounds

To see how low-voltage lights will look before you install them, pass out flashlights to your friends and family members and have them hold the lights where you'll install the lighting fixtures. Ask yourself: Will the fixtures interfere with lawn mowing or walkways? Are any lights aimed at your windows (or a neighbor's window)? Are they easily accessible for service? Do they illuminate any obstacles adequately? Is there enough light?

of the lights is positioned to shine directly into your eyes. Make any necessary adjustments.

Step 5

A. Beginning at the control box, cut a narrow trench about 6 to 8 in. deep along the cable path. At the location of each lighting fixture, make a perpendicular slice across the cable channel with a spade.

B. Using a paint-stirring stick, gently force the cable into the trench so that it's at least 6 in. below ground level. At each lamp location, press the stake into the center of the crossed slices until the lamp is at the proper height.

C. After all the lamps are positioned and the cable is buried, refill the trenches.

Redwood deck photo courtesy of California Redwood Assn.

Other Building Projects

*Fences, gates, arbors and storage sheds add definition
and practicality to your yard. Choose styles and materials
that complement your landscape and lifestyle.*

Helpful Terms

Arbor: A garden structure covered in screen or slats to provide diffused sunlight; often covered with climbing plants.

Auger: A large screwlike tool that can be used to bore postholes into the earth.

Galvanized deck screws: Fasteners that hold better than nails and are easier to remove.

Lattice: Strips of crosshatched material (usually wood) that form a screen pattern.

Molding: A decorative strip, usually of wood, used for ornamentation or finishing.

Posthole: A hole that's dug into the ground to hold a deck or fence post.

FENCES

When you're looking for a way to make your yard more private and well defined, a fence is often the answer. A fence can make your yard safer for kids and pets and create a beautiful backdrop for a garden. Add a gate or two, and you've created a whole new outdoor environment.

All fences are made of the same basic components: vertical fence posts set into postholes in the ground, horizontal rails attached to the fence posts and pickets, fence boards or lattice panels that provide a privacy screen.

Wood Fences

Wood fences come in three styles: picket, lattice and solid board. Since wood components are versatile, you can combine more than one style in one fence—for example, you can top a board fence with a lattice screen.

Since fences must withstand year-round exposure to the elements, use only redwood, cedar or pressure-treated pine for fence construction. These woods offer the best protection against damage from rot and insects. Also, you'll want to use weather-resistant fasteners, such as galvanized or stainless steel nails and screws. You can finish a wood fence with stain or primer and paint, or you can let it weather naturally to a soft, silvery gray. All you'll need to do is apply a clear wood preservative every year to keep it from splitting and cracking.

While many simple fences are easy to design and build, you can also buy prefabricated fencing sections at lumberyards and home centers. Although prefab materials can save you some cutting and assembling time, they're offered in a limited range of styles and are often made of untreated pine, which won't survive for long outdoors.

PVC Fences

Polyvinyl chloride (PVC) is, in some ways, the perfect fencing material. It will never rot, splinter, fade or rust, and it never needs painting. PVC fences are also lightweight and easy to install. However, they're expensive, available in just a few styles and colors, and there are almost no ornamentation options available.

PVC fences have hollow components that require special installation techniques. For example, the posts must be half-filled with concrete and fortified with reinforcing bars.

Ornamental Metal Fences

For those who like a classic look, the wrought-iron fences of yesteryear are being replicated today in durable aluminum and galvanized steel. Tough baked-on polyester finishes provide color and weather protection.

A basic metal fence consists of narrow pickets fastened to horizontal rails. From there, it's up to you to create your own look: fanciful finials, gold-accented scrollwork, twisted, filigreed Florentine circles or creeping rose vines.

Metal fence posts are usually set into a concrete curb or directly in the ground. Metal fence sections can be attached to these posts or between brick pillars or wooden columns.

SWIMMING POOL FENCES

Drowning is the second leading cause of accidental death in children under age three, and a pool can be very tempting to young children. This means that if you have a pool, it's important to fence it off properly. To build a childproof pool fence, follow these guidelines and your local building codes:

• The clearance beneath the pool fence should not exceed 2 in.

• The pickets should be spaced no more than 1¾ in. apart.

• Any horizontal rails should be on the pool side so they can't be used as steps to climb over the fence.

• The mesh of chain-link fences must have openings no larger than 1¼ in. Larger mesh is acceptable if it's woven with wood or plastic slats.

• All gate latches must be securely locked when the pool isn't in use.

• For fences up to 48 in. high, the gate latch should be placed on the pool side, at least 3 in. below the top of the fence.

• If the fence is 60 in. high or more, the gate latch can be mounted on the outside, at least 54 in. above the bottom of the gate.

• The gates should swing open away from the pool, so that if a child leans against the gate, it won't open.

• Gates must be equipped with self-closing hinges and self-catching latches.

FENCES *CONTINUED*

WOOD PICKET FENCE

The classic design of this picket fence is based on the Federal style, which was popular in America during the late 1700s. It features two rows of pickets at different heights, which creates the look of two fences in one design. The shorter, 16-in. pickets mimic the low border fences commonly used around flower beds and gardens. The taller, 32-in. pickets form a traditional boundary fence.

The 5-in.-sq. posts are made of pressure-treated 4×4s sheathed in 1-by trim boards. The 2×2 pickets are sandwiched between three pairs of 1×3 horizontal rails.

Step 1

A. Position the 4×4 posts 7 ft. on center and dig postholes 24 to 30 in. deep, or as required by your local code (see **How to Set Posts,** page 175).

B. Once the posts are in, cut trim boards for all four sides of each post. Rout the decorative flutes and cove detailing, as shown on the diagram. Then nail the boards to the posts.

Step 2

A. Preassemble the pickets and rails into panels. Space the pickets 4 in. on center.

Tools & Materials

- galvanized nails & deck screws
- posthole digger or power auger
- 4x4 pressure-treated posts
- gravel
- concrete
- cedar trim boards, 1x6 & 1x4
- router
- ³⁄₈-in.-dia. core-box bit
- ³⁄₈-in.-rad. cove bit
- 1x3 horizontal cedar rails
- 2x2 pickets, 16-in. & 32-in.
- caps and cove molding

B. Cut short pieces of 2×2s and screw them to the inside of the posts to serve as mounting blocks. Slip the panels down between the posts over the blocks, and secure them with nails or screws driven through the ends of the 1×3 rails and into the blocks.

Step 3

Attach the caps and cove molding to the tops of the posts.

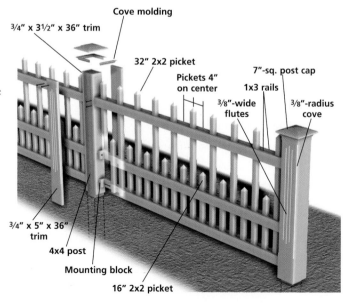

³⁄₄" x 3¹⁄₂" x 36" trim
Cove molding
32" 2x2 picket
Pickets 4" on center
7"-sq. post cap
1x3 rails
³⁄₈"-wide flutes
³⁄₈"-radius cove
³⁄₄" x 5" x 36" trim
4x4 post
Mounting block
16" 2x2 picket

LATTICE PRIVACY FENCE

This 7-ft.-tall privacy fence is perfect for a backyard gardener who's looking for a place to plant climbing flowers and creeping vines. Each panel consists of a 2×8-ft. piece of diagonal lattice set into a 2×4 frame. The frame pieces are grooved to accept the ½-in.-thick lattice. You can position the lattice anywhere along the fence, including close to the ground to support creeping ground-cover plants.

Step 1

A. Position the 4×4 posts 8 ft. on center and dig postholes 24 to 30 in. deep, or as required by your local code (see **How to Set Posts,** page 175). Set them so they extend 80 in. above the ground.

B. Screw horizontal 2×4 rails between the posts. Position the upper rail approximately 4 to 6 in. from the top of the posts, and the lower rail about 6 in. above the ground.

Step 2

A. Cut off the upper corners of the 1×6 fence boards at a 45-degree angle to create the "dog ear" design shown in the diagram.

B. Fasten the 1×6s to the 2×4 rails with 6d nails.

C. Using a table saw with a dado blade, a router or a portable circular saw, cut the ½ × ½-in. grooves for the lattice panels into the 2×4s. (Prefabricated lattice comes in 4×8 ft. sheets in both diagonal and square patterns. Rip the sheets in half lengthwise with a circular saw or sabre saw.)

Step 3

A. Assemble the lattice panels by screwing together the three parts of the 2×4 frame, fastening the 26-in.-long end pieces to the 95-in.-long frame top.

B. Carefully insert the lattice panel, making sure it fits into the grooves.

C. Slip on the bottom of the frame and screw it in place.

Step 4

To secure the assembled lattice panels to the fence, screw through the back of the 1×6 fence boards and into the 2×4 frame. Use at least twelve 2½-in. galvanized deck screws per panel.

Tools & Materials

- 6d (2-in.) galvanized nails
- 2½-in. galvanized deck screws
- posthole digger or power auger
- 4x4 pressure-treated posts
- gravel
- concrete
- 2x4 rails
- 1x6 fence boards
- lattice panels
- table saw with dado blade, or router with ½-in.-dia. straight bit
- circular saw or sabre saw

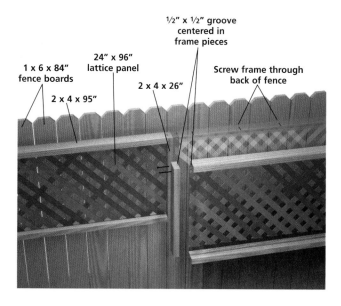

½" x ½" groove centered in frame pieces

24" x 96" lattice panel

1 x 6 x 84" fence boards

2 x 4 x 26"

2 x 4 x 95"

Screw frame through back of fence

GATES

In addition to providing access, a gate can add charm and grace to your landscape—and some of the most elegant and unique gates, like this one, are surprisingly easy to build yourself.

For an even easier project, you can buy a preassembled gate that's made to match a prefabricated fence. However, you'll probably have to special-order it, because most home centers and fence dealers don't carry the matching gates in stock.

VICTORIAN GATE

This gate features fluted posts, dentil molding, turned finials and an elegant picketed gate with a graceful eyebrow top.

To ward off rot and rust, only exterior-grade materials are used to construct this gate. The two posts are pressure-treated 6×6s wrapped with red cedar 1×8s, and topped with dentil molding, shingle molding, a beveled post cap and a finial. The gate is made entirely of red cedar 1×4s. Everything is attached with rust-resistant fasteners and hardware.

Tools & Materials

- **galvanized finishing nails: 3d, 4d, 8d & 10d**
- **6x6 pressure-treated posts (2)**
- **posthole digger or power auger**
- **gravel**
- **wood braces and stakes**
- **60-lb. sacks ready-mix concrete (4)**
- **8 ft. red cedar 1x8s (4)**
- **8 ft. red cedar 1x4s (7)**
- **router**
- **⅝-in.-dia. core-box bit**
- **½-in.-dia. roundover bit**
- **clamps**
- **120-grit sandpaper**
- **miter saw**
- **cedar dentil molding**
- **8 ft. red cedar 1x12 (1)**
- **8 ft. red cedar 1⅛-in. shingle molding (1)**
- **⅜-in.-dia. dowel screws**
- **finials (2)**
- **water-resistant wood glue**
- **table or hand saw**
- **heavy paper**
- **sabre saw**
- **exterior-grade wood putty**
- **paint or stain**
- **shims**
- **gate hinges**
- **latch**

How to Build a Victorian Gate

Step 1

A. Using a posthole digger or power auger, dig two postholes 49½ in. on center (this will allow ½ in. clearance for the latch and ¼ in. clearance for the hinge). Each hole must be at least 12 in. wide and 26 in. deep. Check your local building codes for the required posthole depth in your area.

B. Line the bottom of the holes with 4 in. of gravel.

C. Place the posts in the holes so that they extend 41 in. above the ground and are 49½ in. on center.

D. Align the posts with each other, then check them with a level and adjust until they're both plumb.

E. Hold the posts in position with wood braces and stakes.

F. Mix two bags of concrete for each post. Pour the concrete in the postholes. Adjust the posts as needed until the concrete begins to harden.

G. Allow the concrete to harden overnight, then remove the braces.

Step 2

A. Cut eight 41-in.-long pieces of 1×8 cedar.

B. Rip four of the boards down to 5½ in. wide and nail them to the left and right sides of the posts.

C. Rip the remaining four pieces down to 7 in. wide. After routing (see below), these will be used to cover the fronts and backs of the posts.

D. Before nailing them in place, rout five decorative flutes into each of the boards. Use a router fitted with a ⅝-in.-diameter core-box bit. Set the tool to cut ⅜ in. deep and attach an edge guide (fence) to its base.

E. Clamp the cedar trim board to a workbench. Then clamp a narrow wood strip across each end of the board to mark the starting and stop-ping point for routing the flutes. Position these strips so the flutes begin and end 3½ in. from the ends of the board. Then adjust the router edge guide until it's 3½ in. from the center of the core-box bit.

F. Rout the middle flute, moving the router from left to right. Then slide the edge-guide fence 1 in. in toward the bit and rout the second flute. Move around to the other side of the board and rout the third flute. Slide in the fence another inch and rout the final two flutes, one from each side.

G. Repeat this sequence for the remaining three trim boards.

H. Sand each board lightly. Nail the fluted boards to the fronts and backs of the posts with 8d nails. Nail the edges of the trim boards together with 4d nails.

Step 3

A. Mark the dentil pieces to length. Cut to form miter joints and fasten them to the posts with 4d nails.

B. Cut a 1×8 filler block so that it

Step 2

Rout the flutes into the cedar trim boards using a router fitted with a core-box bit and edge guide.

forms a cap that's flush with all four outside edges of the dentil molding. Nail it to the top of the post.

C. Hold the 1⅛-in. shingle mold-ing in position over the 1×8 cap and the dentil molding and mark it to length. Miter-cut the pieces and

---

HOW TO SET POSTS

All fence projects begin with digging postholes. The posts are typically spaced 6 to 8 ft. apart, depending on the design of the fence. Check your local building code for the required setback from buildings and property lines. Also check the required posthole depth, which will depend on the frost line in your area. The diameter of a posthole should usually be 12 in. or more.

1. Dig the holes with a shovel, posthole digger or rented power auger. If you have many holes to dig, use a power auger.

2. Line the holes with 4 in. of gravel, to ensure proper drainage.

3. Set the posts in the holes and tamp down the dirt all around.

4. Posts that support a gate or that stand at the end of a fence require concrete footings: Dig the hole below the frost line and add 4 in. of gravel. Set the post in the hole, brace it and fill the hole with concrete. Allow to dry overnight.

GATES *CONTINUED*

attach them with 4d nails.

D. Make the beveled post caps by gluing and clamping together three 24-in. pieces of 1×12 cedar (use a water-resistant wood glue).

E. After the glue has dried, saw the laminated blank into two 11-in.-sq. blocks. Bevel-cut the tops on a table saw with the blade tilted to 15 degrees (or use a hand saw). Position the bevel so that the outside 2¼-in.-high edges of the cap are reduced to 1½ in. The flat top surface of the cap should be roughly 6½ in. square.

F. Rout the bottom edges of the beveled caps with the roundover bit. Attach the caps to the tops of the posts with 10d nails.

G. To attach the finials, bore a ¼-in.-dia. × 1-in.-deep hole into the flat center square of each cap and drive a dowel screw into the center of each finial base.

H. Circle the top of each cap with a continuous bead of water-resistant wood glue. Mount the finials onto the caps.

Step 4

A. Cut ten 41½-in.-tall 1×4 pickets and two 41¾-in. 1×4 horizontal braces. On each picket mark two lines, 4 in. and 22¼ in. from the bottom edge. Lay the lower edge of the braces on the marked lines at a right angle

to the pickets. Use a ¾-in.-thick block to maintain consistent spacing between the pickets. Attach with 3d nails.

B. Measure, mark and cut a 1×4 diagonal brace so that it extends across all the pickets and fits inside the horizontal braces. Attach to the pickets with 3d nails.

C. To form the eyebrow curve at the top of the gate, begin by drawing half of the curve onto heavy paper or thin cardboard. Cut out the drawing and lay it onto half of the gate. Trace the pattern onto the pickets. Reverse the pattern and trace the other half. Cut the curve with a sabre saw fitted with a fine-tooth blade.

D. Set the nails and fill holes with wood putty. Paint or stain the gate and posts.

Step 5

A. Stand the gate between the posts and use shims to center it in the opening. Place blocks beneath the gate to keep it at least 2 in. off the ground.

B. With the shims and blocks holding the gate securely in postion, screw the hinges to the post and gate. Check that the gate swings freely, then install the latch.

C. To keep the gate from swinging the wrong way, nail a small cedar stop block to the inside of the post, just below the latch.

Step 3

Trim the posts with dentil molding. Cut the pieces to form miter joints and fasten them with 1½-in.-long finishing nails.

Step 4

Cut out the graceful curve along the top of the gate with a sabre saw fitted with a fine-tooth blade.

*S*HEDS

Sooner or later, most of us face a storage dilemma—where can we stash the ladders, bicycles, lawnmowers and snowthrowers that are cluttering up the garage? Where can we keep the yard tools so they'll be handy when we need them?

The easy answer is a storage shed. The hard part is finding the right one for your needs. What size do you need? What style will look good with your house?

Metal sheds are the least expensive option, and they meet the minimum requirement of pure practicality. But if you want a shed that enhances your landscape, a wood shed is the best option. Wood exteriors offer all three essentials of a good shed: functionality, attractiveness and durability.

Choosing a Shed

There are three basic ways to get a wood shed: Order a set of plans and build it from scratch; buy a ready-to-assemble kit and build it yourself; or hire a contractor to assemble a kit for you.

Building a shed from a plan is the least expensive but most time-consuming option. It also requires that you have moderate to advanced carpentry skills.

For most homeowners, a ready-to-assemble or panelized shed is the best bet. Panelized sheds are available in a variety of woods, styles, sizes and prices. Be sure to choose a kit that uses pressure-treated lumber, cedar or redwood. These woods are the best for resisting decay and insect infestation. Also, all the metal parts should be

SHEDS *CONTINUED*

made of either galvanized metal or stainless steel.

Most panelized sheds come in standard sizes: widths of 6, 8, 10 or 12 ft. and lengths up to 24 feet. Prefabricated panels in standard units make it easy to increase the size of the shed. All the parts are precut, so there's nothing to saw. Even the doors are prehung.

Panelized sheds in prefabricated kits can be delivered to your door and put together quickly and relatively inexpensively. Once finished, a preassembled shed will look like a custom-built one, but will cost far less.

Before Building

Check with your local building department to see if you'll need a building permit for your shed.

Local building codes will also dictate the type of foundation you'll need. In most areas, sheds up to 10 × 10 ft. can be built on concrete blocks set on the ground. Larger sheds must be supported by poured-concrete footings dug below the frost line.

Raising a Preassembled Shed

Step 1

Step 4

Step 6

If you have basic carpentry skills and a good helper, you should be able to erect a modest shed kit in a day or two. (The 10 × 12-ft. cedar shed shown above was built by two workers in about 7 hours.) To assemble a shed kit, follow the manufacturer's instructions. Here are the basic steps involved:

Step 1

Lay concrete foundation blocks over the ground (to promote air circulation under the shed). Use a long, straight 2×4 and a 4-ft. level to check that the blocks are level;

place shims on the blocks until level.

Step 2

Nail a ¾-in. plywood floor onto 2×6 pressure-treated joists. Lay the floor onto the foundation blocks.

Step 3

Preassemble the roof trusses on the floor deck. Nail ½-in. plywood gussets across the joints to strengthen the 2×4 trusses.

Step 4

Raise the prebuilt walls, with the cedar siding attached, and nail them

into place. Fasten two diagonal metal braces to the 2×4 frame to hold each wall square.

Step 5

Place the roof trusses on top of the walls, spaced 24 in. on center. Secure each truss with 3-in.-long screws driven up through the top plate of the wall.

Step 6

Nail plywood roof sheathing to the trusses. Leave space at the peak for a continuous ridge vent, then nail roof shingles onto the sheathing.

CUSTOMIZING A SHED

Most sheds are offered in a basic configuration with a list of optional upgrades and additions. The choices typically include a range of hardware, windows and doors—but can also include a porch, or even a sauna. This means that a customized shed can do double duty as a studio, hobby workshop, potting shed or poolside cabana. Here are some customizing ideas to consider:

• A storage attic loft

• A workbench

• Built-in shelving

• A cupola with a weather vane

• Shutters and window boxes

• A ramp (this is especially helpful if you have a mower, tractor or bike)

• An extra-wide doorway (this is needed for many tractors and riding mowers)

• A skylight to brighten the interior

• Gable or ridge vents to let hot air escape

However, if you end up deciding to make a lot of changes to a standard plan, consider hiring a contractor to help you plan and build a shed that will suit your requirements.

ARBORS

Arbors are becoming increasingly popular with backyard builders, for many reasons. They can support climbing vines and hanging plants or provide filtered shade for a deck, walkway or yard. They're also an excellent way to add vertical interest to a landscape.

Some arbors are designed so that the structure itself provides the shade; others rely on foliage. For deeper shade, you can cover the top of the arbor with a outdoor fabric mesh or climbing vines over a lattice canopy. For a private outdoor room, enclose the sides of the arbor with a lattice screen and plant climbing vines at its base.

While there are many variations, most arbors are constructed with posts and slats. This version of a post-and-slat arbor is a 5 × 5-ft. freestanding structure with an extended overhead. It's made of cedar lumber, which is available at home centers and lumberyards. The posts are secured in the ground with concrete footings. Check your local building code for information on the required footing depth for the support posts.

Tools & Materials

- galvanized deck screws & nails
- stakes
- string
- measuring tape
- posthole digger or power auger
- 10-ft. 4x4 posts (4)
- scrap lumber
- gravel
- 60-lb. sacks ready-mix concrete (4)
- circular saw
- level, line level

- 7-ft. 2x6 tie beams (2)
- 7-ft. 2x4 rafters (4)
- 7-ft. 2x2 cross strips (7)
- wood sealer
- drill
- 3-in. lag screws
- reciprocating saw
- rafter ties
- screw eyes
- wire
- handscrew clamp

How to Build an Arbor

Step 1

A. Lay out the location of the posts, 5 ft. apart, using stakes and string. Check to make sure the layout is square by measuring the diagonals. Adjust the layout as needed until the measurements are equal.

B. Dig the postholes at the corners of the arbor with a posthole digger or power auger (see **How to Set Posts,** page 175).

Step 2

Brace the posts into place with two pieces of scrap lumber. Use a level to make sure the posts are plumb.

Step 5

Use rafter ties (metal tie-down brackets) to attach the rafters to the tie beams.

Step 6

Space the cross strips one foot apart and attach them to the rafters with galvanized deck screws.

Step 2

A. Position the posts in the holes. To brace them in a plumb position, wedge two crossed pieces of scrap lumber against them. Use a level to make sure the posts are plumb; adjust as needed.

B. Drive a stake into the ground next to the base of each of the 2×4s. Secure the 2×4s to the stakes with deck screws.

C. Mix one bag of dry concrete for each post. Pour the concrete into the holes around the posts, and immediately check to make sure the posts are plumb. Adjust as needed until the concrete begins to harden, then let it dry overnight.

Step 3

A. Using a circular saw, measure, mark and cut a 45-degree angle to notch the bottom corners of each overhead piece. Remove a 3 × 3-in. notch from each beam, a 2 × 2-in. notch from each rafter and a 1 × 1-in. notch from each cross strip. Seal the cut edges with wood sealer and let them dry.

B. Position a tie beam 7 ft. above the ground against the outside edge of one pair of posts. The ends of the beam should overhang the posts by about 1 ft.

C. Level the tie beam and clamp it into place. Drill two ⅜-in. pilot holes through the tie beam and into each post. Attach the tie beam to the posts with 3-in. lag screws.

Step 4

A. Extend a level line from the top of the installed tie beam to the opposite pair of posts, marking the location of the second tie beam.

B. Attach the second tie beam, following the same procedure as in steps 3B and 3C.

C. Using a reciprocating saw, cut off the tops of the posts so they're flush with the tops of the tie beams. Brush wood sealer onto the cut ends of the posts.

Step 5

Position the rafters on top of the tie beams and attach them with rafter ties and nails. Beginning 6 in.

from the ends of the tie beams, space the rafters 2 ft. apart, with the ends extending past the tie beams by about 1 ft.

Step 6

A. Drill pilot holes in both ends of the 2×2 cross strips to prevent the ends from splitting.

B. Attach the 2×2s to the tops of the rafters, using 3-in. galvanized screws. Space the strips 1 ft. apart, starting 6 in. from the ends of the rafters. Position the cross strips so they'll overhang the rafters by 6 in.

C. Once the arbor is complete, mound some soil over the concrete footings.

Step 7

Plant a climbing vine, such as clematis or a climbing rose, at the base of each post. Attach screw eyes to the outsides of the posts, then string wire between the eyes. As the vines grow, gently guide them to climb up the wires.

For more information about climbing vines, see **Vines**, page 237.

Landscaping
with
Plants

Beautiful landscapes are the result of careful plant selection, proper planting technique and regular maintenance.

The biggest challenge of landscaping is choosing and maintaining the flowers, trees and shrubs that will create the effect you're looking for. With literally thousands of choices available, the task can seem nearly impossible. Fortunately, you don't need to become an expert gardener. All it takes is a little research to find the best plant for your situation, and a review of basic gardening skills so you can provide the care your plants need to thrive.

Garden Basics

*Luxuriant gardens of flowers, vegetables
or herbs can complement a lawn and add a
beautiful finishing touch to your yard.*

Helpful Terms

Compost: A rich soil amendment made of decomposed organic matter.

Cultivator: A three-pronged fork used to remove weeds and aerate soil.

Mulch: A blanket of material placed over the soil to insulate plant roots and discourage weeds.

Raised bed: A garden bed built up over the existing soil, often bounded by a frame made of wood timbers.

Watering wand: A metal extension that mounts on the end of a hose.

CHOOSING GARDEN PLANTS

With literally thousands of different plants available, it can be daunting to choose those best suited for your garden. The first step is knowing which plants are well suited to the climate, soil and sun conditions at your site. Also, consider how much work you want to put into garden maintenance. Some plants are almost maintenance-free, while others require careful nurturing.

When choosing plants for your garden, strive for simplicity. Grouped plantings of just a few species usually are more attractive than individual plants of many different species. But don't forget to use a range of different categories of plants—lawn, flowers, shrubs and trees. A yard that features a few well-balanced groups of shrubs, flowers and trees is easy to appreciate at a glance.

A good way to begin your selection is to review the basic plant categories and decide which you want to use and how you want to arrange them. Here are the major categories of plants to consider:

Lawn

A lawn can provide a pleasant textural contrast to planting beds and unify the various elements of a landscape. Grass looks best when bordered with informal groups of trees or perennial flowers arranged in a meadowlike plan. Also consider using ornamental grasses, which can add contrasting colors, shapes and textures to planting beds and containers.

Broadleaf Trees

Trees are usually the largest, most dominant landscape elements. Their mature size should be in proportion to the setting; a large tree will overpower a small house or front yard.

Deciduous broadleaf trees provide autumn color, but you'll also have to clean up their leaves in fall. Before planting, consider how a tree will affect the light and shade patterns in

your yard. Also, consider that a well-placed tree can shield the house from the winter wind or summer sun, thus reducing your heating or air-conditioning bills. Although some trees require fifteen to twenty-five years to mature, you can also buy well-established trees and have them professionally planted.

Needle Evergreen Trees

Needle evergreens, or conifers, add strong geometric shapes to a landscape, and in cold climates

Evergreen trees provide year-round color and strong geometric shapes.

they provide welcome winter color. However, because of dry soil, shade and root competition, it can be difficult

Broadleaf trees add large blocks of visual weight to a landscape.

CHOOSING GARDEN PLANTS *CONTINUED*

to grow grass or flowers directly under them. Common evergreens include spruces, pines and firs. The height of a mature needle evergreen tree can range from 6 ft. to more than 150 ft.

Shrubs

Shrubs are medium-size plants that are ideal for bridging the height difference between tall landscape elements, such as trees and buildings, and low-lying gardens or lawns. Shrubs can also provide seasonal color and fruit and they generally require little care.

Shrubs generally look best when arranged in a natural plan, but they can also be planted in rows to create a privacy hedge. Deciduous shrubs lose their leaves in the fall, while evergreen shrubs provide year-round color.

Annuals

Although it includes all kinds of plants, the term "annuals" generally refers to flowers that complete their life cycle in one growing season. There are hundreds of varieties of annuals, and this category includes many of the most popular garden flowers, including marigolds, zinnias and impatiens.

Annuals tend to grow faster and bloom longer than perennials; most of them will provide bright color all summer long. These versatile plants are well suited for flower beds, formal gardens, hanging baskets and planting containers. Some of them, like moss roses, will return spontaneously from last year's seed.

Annuals mature quickly, and many are easy to grow from seed. In cold climates, they may be seeded indoors and transplanted outdoors when the weather warms. In warm climates, they can be seeded directly into the garden.

Perennials

Although it includes all kinds of plants, the term "perennials" generally refers to flowers that survive cold winters by dying back to the ground and growing back from the same roots in the spring.

Perennials are initially more expensive than annuals. However, their longer life, lower maintenance and easier propagation make them far more economical in the long run. And since perennial beds must be thinned every few years, you can often get starter plants free from other gardeners.

In planning a perennial bed, it's important to consider when each flower will bloom. Unlike an annual

Perennials, like the daisies, phlox and sedum shown here, are a good choice for a low-maintenance garden.

Dramatic specimen plants, like this fiery red rhododendron bush, should be used sparingly.

garden, in which most flowers bloom at the same time, the look of a perennial garden will change every few weeks as the various flowers go in and out of bloom. For example, peonies will bloom in early summer, phlox in late summer and asters in the fall.

Bulbs

The term "bulbs" refers to plants that grow from thickened underground roots that store the nutrients needed for the plant's growth (most bulbs are perennial). Corms, tubers, tuberous roots and rhizomes are all included in this category.

Although bulbs such as crocus, iris, daffodils and tulips are best known for their early spring blooms, you can design a bulb garden that will flower continuously from spring to fall. Hardy bulbs, like tulips and daffodils, can be left in the ground through the winter. Tender bulbs, like caladium, must be dug up and stored before the soil freezes.

Roses

Roses are a popular category of woody flowering shrubs, noted for their exquisite flowers and scents. This ancient species includes many varieties, such as shrub roses, climbing roses, miniature roses, tree roses, old-fashioned roses and hybrid tea roses.

Although roses have traditionally been regarded as difficult to grow, today there are many hardy, disease-resistant varieties that require far less maintenance. However, all roses require full sun and sufficient water and fertilizer.

Vines

Vines are climbing plants that can be trained to grow up trellises and

For the most attractive landscape effects, arrange plants in massed groupings.

arbors for an attractive privacy screen or used to soften the look of fences and walls. Although they can take several growing seasons to become established, vines often require little maintenance. Popular vines include clematis, Boston ivy, wisteria and grape.

Ground Covers

Ground covers are low-growing plants that are ideal for areas that won't support a lawn, such as a steep hillside or the heavily shaded area beneath a tree. Common ground covers include Japanese spurge, ferns, hostas and periwinkle. Some take time to become fully established, but they generally require little maintenance.

Vegetables, Fruits and Herbs

This group includes a wide range of plants that have edible leaves, fruit or roots. Although they're usually planted for their food value, many have attractive foliage or fruit and can hold their own in an ornamental flower garden. Some herbs, like mint and lavender, are noted for their pleasing scent.

A container herb garden can be used to enliven even the smallest garden, balcony or windowsill.

Succulent Plants

Cacti and succulents have fleshy tissues that store moisture, making them ideal for arid climates. Noted for their exotic shapes and colors, succulents range in size from low ground covers to the huge saguaro cactus, which can grow to 60 ft. In cold climates, hardy succulents are useful in rock gardens.

Specimen Plants

Specimen plants include any decorative or unusual tree, shrub or flower that draws the eye, such as some succulents, flowering trees or shrubs and climbing roses. For the best effect, limit the number of specimen plants in your yard and place them in a prominent position.

Aquatic Plants

Aquatic plants thrive in and around garden ponds. Some, such as water lilies, prefer deep water. Other species, such as water iris and water poppy, thrive in shallow water or boggy soil.

Choosing Garden Tools

Even an experienced gardener can be bewildered by the extensive selection of gardening equipment available today. However, here's a list of the few tools that are really essential for home gardening.

Trowels

Trowels are useful for weeding and transplanting. A very narrow blade is best for removing deep-rooted weeds; a broader blade is better for general garden chores. To move soil and dig planting holes, choose a trowel with a broad, flat blade. A good trowel is constructed from one piece of steel with a cone-shaped socket. The wooden handle is inserted in the socket and held in place by a riveted pin that extends through both sides.

Spades

The flat blade and square nose of a spade is good for turning soil, removing turf, edging garden beds, digging trenches and transplanting flowers. The medium garden spade is the best all-purpose choice—its blade is about 8 in. wide and 12 in. long, with a

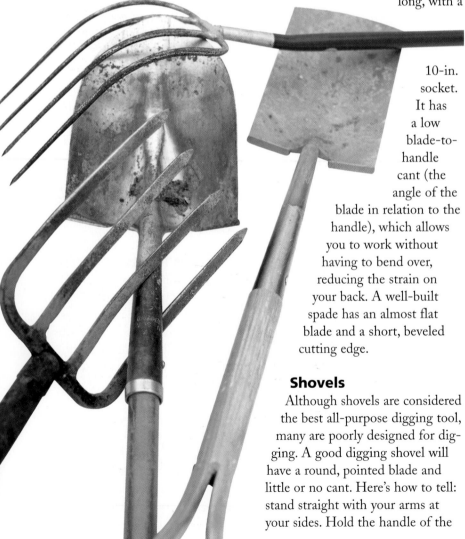

10-in. socket. It has a low blade-to-handle cant (the angle of the blade in relation to the handle), which allows you to work without having to bend over, reducing the strain on your back. A well-built spade has an almost flat blade and a short, beveled cutting edge.

Shovels

Although shovels are considered the best all-purpose digging tool, many are poorly designed for digging. A good digging shovel will have a round, pointed blade and little or no cant. Here's how to tell: stand straight with your arms at your sides. Hold the handle of the shovel in one hand and extend the shovel fully in front of you. In this position, the blade of the shovel should lie almost flat on the floor.

Rakes

Fan-shaped lawn rakes with bamboo or sprung steel tines are useful for clearing dead leaves and debris from garden beds, while rigid steel garden rakes help prepare a tilled seedbed for planting. There are two kinds of rigid steel rakes: flathead and bowhead. Flathead rakes are usually smaller and more lightweight, but since bowhead rakes have a double connection between the head and the handle, they have more spring action. Many gardeners feel they're more comfortable to use, despite the extra weight.

Hoes

The all-purpose garden hoe has long been the standard tool for weeding and slicing soil. It has a slightly angled blade, 5 to 7 in. wide, and an outside beveled cutting edge. However, today there are hoes specially designed for weeding that can almost eliminate the bending and stooping associated with this task. They go by different names, but include oscillating, scuffle and single-prong cultivator types.

Cultivators

If you're weeding and cultivating near plants, a three-pronged cultivator is a good investment. It lets you aerate soil in tight areas without harming plants. Since you can perform just about any hoeing task with a cultivator, you may not need both tools.

The spade's flat blade and square corners make it useful for neatly edging garden beds.

Garden Forks

There are several kinds of garden forks. One favorite, the digging or spading fork, has four heavy tines that pierce soil easily. It's useful for breaking up clods, harvesting onions and lifting and dividing bulbs and perennials. Look for one with a comfortable D-handle, forged-steel head and diamond-back or square tines (which are less likely to bend than flat tines). A compost fork has four scooped, oval tines that penetrate and hold light, loose material. It's handy for turning compost and spreading straw mulch.

Pruners

Pruners are the most basic cutting tool. They range from lightweight shears for trimming and harvesting to heavy tools that can cut ¾-in. branches. Top-quality pruners have replaceable parts and a rubber bumper to absorb the cutting impact. There two basic blade types: curved-bypass blades and anvil blades. If you're left-handed, get a pair that's specially designed for lefties.

Hoses

When it comes to garden hoses, it's worth spending a few bucks more for better quality, because a cheap hose will tend to leak and kink. Hoses are usually made of rubber or vinyl, and the best ones are reinforced with nylon or rayon (however, more plies doesn't necessarily mean a higher quality hose). The strongest hose couplings are made of brass—the thicker, the better. Hexagonal swivels are easier to grip than round ones. Good hoses also have a collar just below the coupling to prevent the hose from kinking at the faucet.

TOOL-BUYING TIPS

It pays to buy quality tools. A cheap tool is likely to break in the middle of a big job or to perform so poorly that it wastes your time and effort. A well-constructed tool, on the other hand, may serve you well for a lifetime. Here are some tips for selecting a quality gardening tool.

Weight. Weight is generally a sign of a higher-quality tool made of thicker metal. Stainless steel is the best quality; carbon manganese is another good choice.

Manageability. If you can't easily lift or control the best-quality tool, get a smaller one. A tool that requires too much effort to use will simply end up collecting cobwebs in your toolshed.

Comfort. Give the tool a good workout before buying. Go through the motions you'll make when using it, testing for weight, strength, balance and comfort.

Red flags. Signs of poor quality include loose screws or bolts, irregularities on cutting edges or a rough, unfinished handle that could give you splinters and blisters.

Durability. A head and socket forged from a single piece of steel ("solid shank" or "solid socket" construction) is the sturdiest.

Handles. Tubular-steel handles are the strongest, but they're heavy. Fiberglass is almost as strong, plus it's waterproof and won't splinter or rot. Wooden handles should be straight-grain ash or hickory.

The garden tools you'll need will depend on the size of your garden. Here's one example of a basic set.

SPRINKLER BASICS

When it comes to watering chores, most homeowners still rely on a garden hose and a few good sprinklers. These tools allow you to customize the spray pattern to fit your yard—and unlike in-ground systems—they're portable and inexpensive. So which tools are best for irrigating a large lawn, misting a freshly sown seedbed, or doing dozens of other watering chores? Here's everything you need to know to make an informed choice.

Wands

As the name implies, wands are metal extensions that mount directly on the end of a hose. Besides giving you added reach, they also work with the spray head to control the volume and force of the water flow. They dispense a concentrated amount of water efficiently, allowing you to direct water to the base of plants, without wetting the leaves or displacing the soil. Wands also allow you to spray delicate plants directly without battering them.

Most wands have three parts: a shutoff valve, a lance and a spray head. On some wands, the lances and heads are joined with standard hose fittings so that individual parts can be switched and replaced as needed. On others, these parts are permanently attached.

Look for wands with a thumb-controlled on/off or trigger valve in the handle–this lets you put the water exactly where you want it and nowhere else. As for lances, you'll find them in lengths from 18 in. to 4 ft. Choose a size that you're comfortable carrying and reaching with. Telescoping wands are also available, but they're less durable than those made with a single piece of tubing.

The spray head you'll find on most pro-style versions is the cylindrical, shower-head type. You can also buy water wands equipped with an adjustable-pattern nozzle.

Water wands extend your reach and direct water exactly where you want it.

Nozzles

Nozzles connect directly to the end of your hose. Because many are tailored for specific watering chores, they're the ultimate in precision and versatility. There are three major types of nozzles:

Fogger Nozzles

Also called misting nozzles, these watering tools create a dense fog that soaks the soil without disturbing it. They're perfect for situations where you don't want to dislodge seeds or damage delicate seedlings. You can screw them onto a wand or directly onto a hose. Three flow rates are available: ½ gal., 1 gal. and 2 gal. per minute. They cost about $5 each.

Pistol-Grip Sprayers

These classic nozzles have undergone some notable design upgrades in recent years. For example, many now have a layer of plastic insulation over the metal body, to prevent

your hands from getting chilled. All-plastic versions are also available, although they aren't as durable.

Multipattern Pistol Sprayers

These all-in-one attachments have several nozzles that provide a variety of sprays, ranging from a mist to a steady stream. Although they aren't as precise as single-pattern nozzles engineered for a specific task, they are more versatile. Since most yard nozzles are used for miscellaneous chores such as washing the car or hosing down the driveway, multipattern sprayers are a useful addition to your watering arsenal.

Sprinklers

Sprinklers are ideal for watering lawns and other large areas because they have a wider spray pattern than nozzles, and you don't have to hold

Fogger nozzles produce a dense mist that's ideal for watering freshly planted seeds.

them. At its simplest, a sprinkler is just a nozzle that sits on the ground —like the classic, two-hole sprinkler with stationary water jets. But today there are more sophisticated sprinklers with moving jets that offer more flexibility and better water distribution. The major types of sprinklers are:

HOW MUCH WATER IS TOO MUCH?

No two yards have the same watering needs. Climate, slope, soil and plant type all determine when, how often and how long you should water. However, there are some basic guidelines for watering wisely. (For more lawn watering tips, see **10 Steps to a Beautiful Lawn,** pages 215-218.)

Reduce evaporation. On a warm day, more than 30 percent of the water from your sprinkler will be lost to evaporation before it hits the ground. Minimize evaporation by watering when the air is calm and the ground and air are cool—typically in the early morning. This time of day is also best for plants; they'll dry quickly as the day warms and be less prone to fungal infections.

Avoid runoff. Apply water at a rate that will penetrate the soil and not run over the ground surface. You can do this by setting your sprinkler to apply the water more slowly, or by moving the sprinkler just before the water starts to run off.

Water deeply. Deep watering promotes strong downward-growing roots. Light watering causes roots to stay near the soil surface, where the water is. Since soil dries from the top down, shallow roots need to be watered more often, and they're also more vulnerable to pests, weeds and diseases.

Don't overwater. With established plants, let the top 2 to 3 in. of soil dry out between waterings. Soil that's constantly saturated doesn't provide enough oxygen for healthy root development and nutrient absorption. A constantly wet environment also encourages the growth of harmful organisms.

Prevent overspray. To avoid watering paved areas along with your plants, adjust your sprinkler to produce a spray pattern that matches the area you're watering. Also, use a sprinkler that sprays high enough to clear foliage, or buy a tripod tower to elevate it.

SPRINKLER BASICS *CONTINUED*

Stationary Sprinklers

These two-hole, "owl eyes" units are durable, easy to use and inexpensive. But because they quickly distribute a lot of water over a fairly small area, you have to watch for runoff on slopes and areas where water penetrates the soil slowly.

Turret Sprinklers

These are stationary sprinklers with a saltshaker-patterned screen over the water outlet. They're a bit more precise than the two-hole models because the screens produce a specific spray pattern and better water distribution. But as with other stationary sprinklers, turret sprinklers are limited to spot-watering small, regular-sized areas.

Revolving Sprinklers

The revolving arms on these units use water pressure to spin their outlet jets and distribute water evenly over a round or square area. The older, nonadjustable models put out a lot of water at once, presenting a runoff problem. Newer models feature adjustable nozzles that you can set to a fine mist—to water a newly seeded lawn, for example.

Traveling Sprinklers

These products are mounted on gear-driven wheels, so they can spray water as they roll slowly along a hose. They're ideal for watering long or large lawns. Their revolving arms can be adjusted to throw water over a wider or narrower path (from 15 to 45 ft. wide).

Oscillating Sprinklers

Oscillators have a spray arm that flips back and forth instead of revolving. In addition to water pressure, they use gears to control how quickly the spray oscillates. This means they can lay down a gentle fan pattern, and runoff shouldn't be

a problem. Newer models also allow you to close down the outer holes at each end of the sprinkler body for a more accurate spray pattern.

While some adjustable models work fine, others will get stuck in one direction when the pressure is too low. Oscillating sprinklers can water an area up to 3,000 sq. ft. But because of their high spray arc, they lose a lot of water to evaporation and wind. Use them when the air is calm and cool.

Rotary and Impulse Sprinklers

These sprinklers emit water through a rotating nozzle that's part of the sprinkler body. They can spray in a full or partial circle up to 70 to 80 ft. in diameter—perfect for large, open areas. The speed and distance of the spray depends on the water pressure, but a gear mechanism slows water distribution enough for effective watering even on slow-draining clay soils.

The major difference between rotary and impulse sprinklers is how they deliver the water: Rotary units emit a continuous spray; impulse units deliver a series of short bursts (their distinctive *chik-chik-chik* has become one of the defining sounds of summer). Although most of these products produce a circular spray, some can be adapted to fit oddly shaped areas.

Some rotary and impulse sprinklers, like this one, let you adjust the spray pattern to cover an asymmetrical area.

SPRINKLER ACCESSORIES

In addition to choosing between sprinklers, wands and nozzles, you also can select from many accessories designed to make using your watering tools easier and more efficient.

Quick-Release Fittings

Snap fittings let you disconnect nozzles and sprinklers without having to run to the spigot to turn off the water. For the best fit, use one brand of snap fittings for all your attachments. Lightly wrench-tighten them—hand-tightened fittings tend to leak or work loose. Also, keep a spare pack of O-rings on hand (the little rubber gaskets that seal joints to prevent leaks).

Tripod Towers

Tripod towers raise sprinklers high above plants, so the spray pattern won't be blocked by foliage. They are especially handy for watering vegetable gardens and large areas.

Most towers come with the sprinklers already attached, but you can also buy the tripod separately, for about $30.

Hose Reinforcements

Hose reinforcements prevent a hose from kinking at the faucet, by maintaining a gentle bend. Two types are available: a metal gooseneck adapter and a short length of hose wrapped in heavy steel spring. They both have couplings that attach between the faucet and hose end.

HOW LONG DO YOU NEED TO WATER?

Amount of water (in. per wk.)	Spray sprinklers (min. per wk.)	Rotary sprinklers (min. per wk.)
0.50	25	115
0.75	38	171
1.00	51	228
1.25	63	286
1.50	76	343

Assumptions: Seventy-five percent sprinkler efficiency. Spray sprinklers producing 1.58 in. per hour. Rotary sprinklers producing 0.35 in. per hour.

MULCHING: THE SECRET TO HASSLE-FREE GARDENING

One of the best things you can do for your garden is cover the soil with a layer of organic mulch that will inhibit weeds, conserve moisture, moderate the temperature and improve the soil. Mulch also makes your yard look neater and more unified and greatly reduces the time you need to spend watering, weeding and fertilizing.

The best time to mulch an established garden is in spring, after the soil is warm enough for active root growth. If you need to mulch in summer (for example, to protect new trees or shrubs), water the soil thoroughly first, at least 6 in. deep.

If your ground freezes in winter, cover your perennials after the ground freezes completely with a 4- to 6-in. layer of loose mulch, such as straw or pine needles. Remove the mulch gradually as the soil begins to thaw in spring.

How to Apply Mulch

Since mulch doesn't kill existing weeds, you'll need to thoroughly weed the garden bed before you start laying down the mulch. The secret of good mulching is making it thick enough. Spread fine mulches (like shredded leaves) 3 in. thick, and coarse mulches (like wood chips) 4 in. thick, but keep the mulch away from plant stems.

Woody mulches—like wood chips, straw and bark—will last for a few years before they need to be renewed. They are also low in nitrogen and will draw it out of the soil as they decay. To counteract this, fortify the soil with a nitrogen fertilizer: in spring, apply 2 lbs. of 10 percent nitrogen fertilizer per 100 sq. ft. Scatter the fertilizer evenly on the mulch, then slowly water it in. Repeat in early summer if plants show any signs of nitrogen starvation, such as weak, stunted or yellowish new growth.

Another tip is to lay landscape fabric under the mulch. Landscape fabric is a tight mesh that lets water and fertilizer reach desirable plants, but blocks the sunlight needed by weeds. It's most useful in permanent plantings and under trees or shrubs. Lay the mesh down before or after planting, cutting holes for the plants. After planting, cover with mulch for a more attractive appearance.

Choosing a Mulch

Mulch should be affordable, easy to use and free of disease and weed seeds. Mulches can be bought, or collected around the yard or from businesses that work with trees or wood products. Here's how the various kinds of mulches stack up:

Lawn Clippings

Although lawn clippings are free and readily available, they're high in nitrogen and fresh clippings will mat and ferment—which can kill plants. To use clippings as a mulch, you need to dry them and then mix in shredded leaves or some other low-nitrogen material. Don't use clippings from a lawn that's been treated with herbicides or that contains weeds or weedy grasses, like Bermuda grass or crabgrass.

Wood Chips

Wood chips make a good mulch that's long-lasting and easy to use. You can rent a chipper-shredder and make them yourself or get them from a professional tree-pruning service. The durability of wood chips

You can use mulch and lawn edging to create a neat, unified look for your garden beds.

Common mulching materials include: (A) chipped bark, (B) shredded leaves, (C) wood chips, (D) landscape fabric, (E) grass clippings, (F) shredded wood, (G) cocoa bean hulls, (H) compost, (I) stone and (J) straw.

makes them ideal for garden paths —they'll stay in place even when pelted with heavy rain.

Pine Needles

You can collect pine needles or buy them at garden centers. They're attractive, free of weeds, long-lasting and perfect for use around shrubs and trees. Don't worry that they might acidify the soil; pine needle mulch creates only negligible changes in soil pH.

Straw

Straw is inexpensive and readily available, especially in rural areas. It's a good mulch for vegetable gardens and winter cover. However, since it decomposes quickly it must be regularly reapplied. Use only straw that's free of weed seeds, and don't use it in fire-prone areas.

Compost

Compost is decomposed organic matter. It's a great soil builder that you can either buy or make yourself. However, compost isn't the best mulch—weed seeds love it, and it can blow away. Instead, work compost into the soil, and mulch over it.

Thorough mulching will discourage weeds, and those that do appear will be weak and spindly, making them easy to pull up.

Leaves

Leaves are a free mulch that decomposes rapidly and improves the soil. However, whole leaves can smother plants, so shred leaves and let them decay for a few weeks before you spread them on the garden.

Chipped or Shredded Bark

Chipped bark is an attractive mulch that decays slowly and won't blow away. Bark is often the best mulch for large areas; it's especially

good at suppressing weeds around trees and shrubs.

Cocoa Bean Hulls

Cocoa bean hulls are attractive and when crushed, they release the scent of chocolate. However, they're very lightweight and liable to be blown away. They also disintegrate easily when stepped on or mowed over.

Stone

Since stone doesn't decay, it isn't an organic mulch, but it does have its uses. It's a good low-maintenance ground cover under trees and shrubs, since it doesn't need to be renewed as often as organic mulch. Put landscape fabric under the stones, otherwise they can be difficult to remove.

MAKING COMPOST

TURN YARD WASTE INTO FOOD FOR YOUR SOIL

Composting is an inexpensive way to turn yard waste into a rich soil amendment. Living plants draw nutrients from the soil as they grow; by spreading compost you can return those nutrients back to the soil so they'll be available to feed your garden plants. Compost also improves soil fertility, drainage and aeration and it's especially beneficial for problem soil—it helps sandy soil hold water and drains and aerates dense clay soil. Learning how to compost is becoming even more important now that so many communities are regulating or banning the curbside disposal of yard waste.

What Is Composting?

Making compost is a simple process of layering organic materials and letting them decay until they shrink and turn into a dark, crumbly substance that looks like rich potting soil.

The organic materials in a compost pile are broken down by the natural microorganisms that feed on them. Although all organic materials decompose eventually, composting speeds that process by creating an ideal environment in which the microorganisms can proliferate and work quickly. Microorganisms can be introduced to the pile by adding soil, old compost or a compost starter.

For efficient decomposition, a compost pile must have the proper balance of these four elements:

Compost is made by layering carbon- and nitrogen-rich organic materials so they can be efficiently decomposed by soil microorganisms.

Greens

Materials high in nitrogen, such as animal manure, grass clippings, discarded vegetables and fresh weeds.

Browns

Materials high in carbon, such as dry leaves, straw, shredded newspaper, sawdust and wood prunings.

Moisture

Efficient decomposition requires moisture; a compost pile should remain as moist as a wrung-out sponge. Water the pile as needed, but if the weather turns rainy for a long time, cover it with plastic to make sure it doesn't get too wet.

Oxygen

Aeration helps build heat, which speeds decomposition; turn piles regularly to ensure a good supply of oxygen.

Composting Methods

Making compost can be as simple as raking your yard debris into a pile and letting it decay. However, this

Turning the pile moves fresh materials to the middle and brings decomposed material to the surface.

CHOOSING A COMPOST BIN

Compost bins hold organic waste neatly and help keep pests out. They can't guarantee better, faster compost, but they can improve the odds by making the pile easier to tend.

You can make your own bin or buy one. If you're buying, you can choose among the four categories of compost bins on the market: compost corrals, continuous-feed bins, stacking bins and compost tumblers.

One important issue is whether a bin is rodent-proof. Most rodent-proof bins have tight-fitting tops and bottoms that keep these unwelcome visitors out. You can also make a bottomless bin rodent-proof by placing it on concrete or on 20-gauge, ¼- or ½-in. galvanized wire mesh.

Compost Corrals PRICE: $40 for a plastic-coated wire-mesh unit; $125 for a more durable cedar-slat type.	Made from wood, plastic mesh or plastic-coated wire mesh, these units simply contain the compost. Some models have a lid or a front gate for easy access to the pile; others must be lifted off the pile before turning. These bins work best for yard waste.
	PROS: Unobtrusive, inexpensive, easy to use, good for cold or hot composting.
	CONS: Most aren't rodent-proof. Finished compost may fall through the mesh or slats.
Continuous-Feed Bins PRICE: Between $48 and $100.	Usually made of plastic, these units have a lid through which you feed material. In three to eight months, a small amount of finished compost will appear at a door in the bottom of the unit; more compost will appear as you add to the pile.
	PROS: Easy to assemble; no turning required. Most are rodent-resistant.
	CONS: Output is slow and sparse. Weed seeds and diseases won't be destroyed.
Stacking Bins PRICE: From $70 to $80.	Designed for hot piles, these units have stackable tiers that you can remove and refill one by one, which makes turning easier. A well-tended pile with the proper ingredients should heat up to at least 120°F, and produce finished compost in about two to six weeks.
	PROS: Fast, easy to use, perfect for larger piles. Rodent-proof when set on concrete or wire mesh.
	CONS: Work-intensive; should be filled all at once. Require twice the space of continuous-feed bins to unstack and refill.
Compost Tumblers PRICE: Vary greatly in quality and cost, ranging from $100 to $400.	These enclosed containers rotate on frames or rollers; this setup tosses the compost so you don't need to turn it with a pitchfork. Because contents can reach at least 120°F, finished compost can be ready in as little as two weeks.
	PROS: Lowest-maintenance. Composting this way is quick, convenient and rodent-proof.
	CONS: Crank-type units are expensive; those with moving parts can be hard to assemble. Large units may be hard to turn.

Making compost *CONTINUED*

approach takes months to produce finished compost. On the other hand, with a little more effort, you can have finished compost in as little as two weeks. These two examples reflect the two methods of composting: cold pile and hot pile. Both work; the best one depends on how much yard waste you have, how fast you want compost and how much effort you want to invest.

Cold Pile

This method is best if you're short on time or energy, or have less organic waste, such as leaves and clippings.

Cold piles are less work, because you don't have to turn them and you only need 3 cu. ft. of waste to start one. But since they don't usually get hot enough to destroy weed seeds and disease organisms, you have to be careful to keep these materials out of the mix. Cold piles also decompose very slowly; they can take up to a year to make compost.

An inexpensive compost bin can be made of wire fencing held together with clips or wire loops. When you want to turn the pile, simply unfasten the clips and remove the fence.

Hot Pile

This method requires more work, but it can yield compost in as little as two weeks. And since the pile reaches 110°F to 140°F, it will kill most weed seeds and plant diseases.

Hot piles must be built all at once in a 4- to 5-ft. cube and turned regularly. As the materials decompose, the pile should shrink to no less than 3 cu. ft.—the minimum needed to maintain heat.

Building a Compost Pile

Whether you're building a cold or a hot pile, you'll need to layer the materials to ensure efficient decomposition and prevent odors. If you're

TROUBLESHOOTING A COMPOST PILE		
Problem	**Cause**	**Solution**
Pile not heating up, little or no decomposition	Not enough nitrogen	Turn pile, add green material
	Not enough moisture	Turn pile and moisten layers
	Pile is too small	Add material to pile
Matted, undecomposed layers	Layers are too thick	Break up pile with pitchfork, make layers thinner
Large, undecomposed pieces	Materials are too large	Screen out and shred them for next pile
Ammonia smell	Too much nitrogen	Add brown material
Rotten-egg smell	Pile is too wet, lacks oxygen	Turn pile, add brown material, protect from rain
	Pile is compacted	Turn pile
Fruit flies and house flies	Too much kitchen waste, not enough oxygen	Add brown material, mix pile, exclude kitchen waste or cover it with browns

building the pile on the ground, loosen the soil and put small prunings down first to ensure good air circulation. Then proceed as if building a pile in an enclosed bin, as follows:

Sift compost to get a perfect amendment for potting or planting soil.

Step 1

Collect equal parts (by volume) of green and brown matter. The waste will decompose most quickly if it's chopped or shredded into pieces no larger than ¾ to 1 in. Use a chipper/shredder to break up woody material, leaves and weeds. If you don't have a chipper/shredder, try breaking the waste with a sharp spade or running it over with a rotary mower.

Step 2

Put down a 2- to 8-in. layer of brown matter, and water it thoroughly with a hose. Then sprinkle over it a shovelful of manure, soil or compost to feed the microorganisms that will make the compost. Follow this with a 2- to 8-in. layer of green matter. Then repeat the process, watering each brown layer as you build.

QUICK TIPS

Critters in Your Compost

Although putting kitchen waste in your compost pile is a handy way to get rid of garbage, it can also attract mice, rats, skunks and other pests. Some municipalities ban food waste from compost piles for that reason. To keep away pests, rodent-proof your compost bin (see page 197).

Most of the insects you'll find in a compost pile—such as ants, beetles, centipedes, earthworms, millipedes, spiders and sow bugs—are either harmless or beneficial. To keep away bothersome insects, like horseflies and houseflies, don't put fresh kitchen scraps in your pile, or cover them carefully with brown material.

Step 3

If you include any kitchen waste, cover it with brown matter so it won't smell or attract pests. Finish the pile with a brown layer, and cap it with a few inches of soil.

You can add yard waste to a cold pile whenever you like. But a hot pile must be built all at once. It will heat up and then begin to cool—track the temperature with a compost thermometer and start turning it when the temperature begins to drop. To get compost in two to four weeks, turn the pile every day or two. To get compost in one to three months, turn the pile once every week or two.

The Ins and Outs of Good Compost

Put In...

High-carbon brown material: Dry corn stalks, dry leaves, dry weeds (hot piles only), hay, shredded newspaper, sawdust, wood prunings, straw, small amounts of shredded leathery leaves (such as eucalyptus, laurel, magnolia and walnut).

High-nitrogen green material: Animal manure, crop plants, fresh grass clippings, green weeds (hot piles only), fresh leafy prunings, fresh kitchen scraps (such as rinsed egg shells, coffee grounds and tea bags).

Keep Out...

Bones, cat and dog waste, cooked kitchen scraps, dairy products, diseased and insect-infested plants (unless your compost pile heats up to 140°F), fatty foods, herbicide-treated grass clippings, grains, mature weeds with seeds, meat, pine needles, pernicious weeds (morning glory, purslane, quack grass), wood ash (if you have alkaline soil).

*B*REAKING NEW GROUND

PREPARE A GARDEN BED IN THE FALL

Perhaps while mowing the lawn for the umpteenth time this summer, you began fantasizing about trading in some of your turf for beds of shrubs, flowers or vegetables.

Exchanging lawn for garden space is a good idea. Garden beds add color, shape and texture to a land-scape, define its boundaries and soften the transition between the buildings and the yard. Plus, they reduce your lawn maintenance time.

However, you don't want to wait until spring to start putting your plan into action. The end of the growing season is the best time to prepare the soil for a garden bed. The amendments and organic materials that you work into the soil in fall will decompose over the winter and be ready to feed next spring's plantings. Plus, you can proceed at your own pace in comfortable weather, and relax through the winter, knowing you're all set for spring.

Plan the Garden

Before you start digging, you need to decide what kind of garden you're going to plant. The major kinds of gardens are flower gardens, vege-table gardens and herb gardens.

Although you can combine any of these categories in one bed, each one has special site considerations. For example, while vegetable gar-dens are often placed in a sunny part of the backyard, flower gardens are usually placed where they'll be visible from the house or the sidewalk, and there are many flowers that do well in the shade.

If you're thinking of putting in a flower garden, consider whether you want annuals, perennials or a combination of the two (see **Flowers**, pages 206-213). If you want a flower bed that will look good in all seasons, you can plant a combination of bulbs, annuals, perennials and flowering shrubs that have staggered blooming times.

Select the Plants

Garden beds can be located in either sunny or shady areas, and the site conditions will determine which plants will flourish in that spot. Be sure to check the needs and preferences of all the plants you're considering—place sun-loving plants where they'll get the light they need and use shade-tolerant plants where there's less sun.

Design the Bed

The next step is to plan the size and shape of your new garden. A pleasing shape is more important for an ornamental flower garden than for a vegetable garden, where ease of use will be the primary consideration.

Although you can make a garden bed any shape, designers often recommend curving lines. Curves are more visually appealing than straight lines and add more interest to a landscape. They're especially attractive next to square or rectangular structures, such as fences, walls and buildings.

While working out the shape, outline the bed on the ground with a heavy rope or garden hose, and make a rough planting plan.

Next, transfer the plan to graph paper with ⅛- or ¼-in. squares, with each square representing a foot. Sketch the outline of the bed

and fill in the plants. Allow enough room for shrubs and perennials to grow to their mature size.

Prepare the Soil

The next step is to remove all the vegetation inside the area you've outlined. Removing grass and weeds before you plant reduces garden maintenance and gives the new plants space to grow without competition for water and nutrients.

If the area has a lot of weeds, you can use a nonselective herbicide first to kill everything inside the outline.

Here are three ways to turn new ground:

Dig by Hand

This method isn't glamorous, but it works. Using a round-point shovel, dig up the sod in pieces, shake it out over the garden bed and toss the remaining grass and roots into the compost pile.

Strip Sod

This method works best when your grass is dense and uniform. Starting at the edge of the bed, slide a sharp-edge spade beneath the sod. Then lever the spade up, tearing the sod from the ground as you push. Don't dig too deep; you want to remove only the grass and about an inch of roots. You'll find that the sod peels back neatly once you get the hang of it.

If you keep the sod intact, you

You can work ground limestone into a garden bed to raise the soil pH, making it less acidic.

can roll it out, grass side down, and place it over the bed through the winter. In spring, you'll work the partly decomposed sod into the soil.

Rototill

Speed and convenience make a rototiller a good choice for larger beds. You can rent one by the half or full day, and the rental fees are low. They're available in both full-size models and miniature versions. A mini-rototiller will fit in the back seat of a car and can easily be handled by one person. Full-size rototillers require a pickup truck; although they're heavy and awkward, they can also be handled alone, as long as you have a ramp.

Before you rototill, check the soil moisture by turning over a shovelful of soil. It should be slightly moist, but not wet. Soil that's too wet will tend to compact and clump.

Breaking new ground *CONTINUED*

Begin tilling at a shallow depth, where the tiller will be easier to control. To work the soil thoroughly, overlap the just-tilled swath by half the tiller's width with each pass. As the dirt begins to loosen, set the tines to dig deeper with each pass, until you've turned 8 to 12 in. of soil. Ideally, follow up by tilling the bed again about ten days later, to turn under any resprouted grass or weeds. If this isn't possible, rake the bed instead.

Get a Soil Test

Once the soil is exposed, have a soil test done to check for fertility and pH level (for more information on soil testing, see **10 Steps to a Beautiful Lawn**, pages 215-218).

Knowing your soil's pH and how to correct it is crucial for a healthy garden. Soil pH is measured on a scale of 1 to 14. Below 7 is acidic, and above 7 is alkaline. The ideal range for most plants is between 6 and 7. Soil pH affects plant growth in many ways. For example, it determines the availability of nutrients and affects the root's ability to absorb nutrients and water.

Correct the pH Level

Adding sulfur or iron sulfate generally reduces pH, making it more acidic. Adding ground limestone raises a soil's pH, making it less acidic. The soil test report should tell you how much sulfur or limestone to mix in to correct the pH of the soil, along with other soil amendments you need to add to the soil to support a healthy garden.

Enrich the Soil

Most soils will also benefit from the addition of organic matter, which improves soil structure and supports beneficial organisms. Examples of organic matter you might add include peat moss, leaf mold, manure or compost.

In clay soils, organic matter promotes drainage and air circulation. In light, sandy soils, it acts like a sponge, holding in the moisture and nutrients that would

These three photos show the process of transforming a dull backyard by adding a flower-filled border. A hose was used to outline the border before the sod was removed.

otherwise wash away. And as the organic matter is broken down by soil organisms, its nutrients are released into the soil.

Add Soil Amendments

Spread an even layer of the recommended soil amendments over the entire bed, along with any organic matter you wish to add.

If you're correcting the structure of a clay or sandy soil, you'll want to add enough new material to equal one-third to one-half of the final soil mix. For example, if you plan to mix the amendments to a depth of 10 in., you'll need to apply a 3- to 5-in. layer of organic matter. To estimate the volume of the soil amendments or organic matter you'll need to buy, refer to the **Soil Coverage Chart** on page 229.

Using a garden fork, shovel or rototiller, turn the amendments into the top 6 to 10 in. of soil—6 in. for flower beds and 10 in. for vegetable beds. It's okay if the soil is lumpy at this point; it will resist erosion better. If you live in a cold climate, the freeze/thaw cycle will help break up the clumps by spring.

Don't apply a fertilizer now; its nutrients will leach out before spring. However, you can plant a cover crop that you'll chop up and mix into the soil later. This protects the soil from erosion and adds more organic nutrients, but it's optional.

Spring Planting

In spring, there's little left to do. If you planted a cover crop, mow it (or cut it off) and turn it under. Use a steel rake to work the topsoil into a fine texture. If you're seeding the bed, follow the directions on the seed packets. If you're putting in container plants, follow these steps:

Step 1

Arrange the plants in their pots on the prepared site and make any final adjustments to your plan.

Step 2

Working with one plant at a time, dig a hole that's twice as deep and twice as wide as the plant's pot. Break up some of the soil that you've dug out and use it to backfill about half of the hole. (This gives the plant's roots the advantage of expanding in loosened soil.)

Step 3

Remove the plant from its pot and loosen the root ball. Spread the plant in the hole at the same level it was growing in its container. Smooth the soil and tamp it all around. Water the hole thoroughly.

Step 4

Once all the plants are in place, cover the bed with 3 to 4 in. of organic mulch (see **Mulching**, page 194) to inhibit weed growth. Keep mulch away from the base of the plants. Water the bed thoroughly.

INSTALLING BRICK EDGING

Brick edging can add a nice finishing touch to a garden bed, especially if the same kind of brick is also featured elsewhere in the landscape. The easiest way to install brick edging is with a sand-set. Here's how to do it:

Step 1

Using a flat spade, dig a flat-bottomed trench around the perimeter of the bed. Make the trench about ½ in. deeper than the height of the edging material.

Step 2

Place a ½-in. layer of sand in the trench and smooth it over with the blade of the spade. Place a strip of landscape fabric over the sand to prevent weeds from growing up between the edging pavers.

Step 3

Lay the bricks side by side in the trench. Place a 2×4 over each brick and tap with a rubber mallet.

Step 4

Spread sand over the bricks and use a broom to work the sand into the cracks.

Step 5

To set the sand, lightly mist the bricks with water.

Step 3

BREAKING NEW GROUND *CONTINUED*

CREATING A RAISED GARDEN BED

If your yard has poor soil that would be difficult to amend, a raised bed is the best way to create a garden. When you build a raised bed properly, fill it with high-quality topsoil and water it frequently, growing healthy plants becomes practically foolproof. And since these gardens are elevated and low-maintenance, they're ideal for children and the elderly.

Raised beds can also serve as a landscape design feature. For example, they offer an excellent opportunity to repeat a structural material that's used in other landscape structures. You can make a raised bed out of almost any material, including brick, stone, interlocking block or wood timbers.

This raised bed is made with 6×6 cedar timbers. Wood timbers are inexpensive, easy to work and blend well with most landscapes. The bed is 5 × 3 ft. and 18 in. deep. The timbers are stacked flush on top of each other in three layers that are secured with galvanized bar nails. Drainage holes are drilled into the frame to keep the plants healthy.

Once the frame is complete, the bed and the frame are lined with landscape fabric to prevent weed invasion and keep the drainage holes from clogging. However, if you'll be planting shrubs or vegetables in the raised bed, place landscape fabric on the sides of the bed only, because these plants have deeper roots.

Before starting the bed, make sure the plants you intend to grow are suited for the site. Vegetables and sun-loving flowers need "full sun"—which means 6 to 8 hours of direct sunlight per day. If you don't have a spot with full sun, build your raised bed in a shady area and plant it with woodland and shade-loving plants.

Tools & Materials

- stakes
- string
- shovel
- level
- drill
- hammer
- saw horse
- reciprocating saw

- 8-ft. 6x6 timbers (6)
- galvanized roofing nails
- 5-in. barn nails (12)
- landscape fabric
- topsoil
- plants
- mulch

A raised bed has both decorative and practical uses. It adds a distinctive design element and allows you to create a garden bed even if you have poor soil.

How to Build a Raised Bed

Step 1

A. Outline a 5 × 3-ft. area with stakes and string to mark the location of the bed. Use a shovel to remove all the grass and weeds inside the area.

Step 1

Remove all the grass and weeds within the staked area.

B. Dig a flat trench, 2 in. deep by 6 in. wide, inside the perimeter of the area just inside the stakes.

Step 2

A. Measure, mark and cut each of the timbers into one 54-in. piece and one 30-in. piece. Use a saw-horse to hold the timbers steady

Step 3

Drive galvanized barn nails into the stacked timbers.

while you cut.

B. Coat the cut ends of each timber with a wood sealer/protectant. Let the sealer dry completely.

C. Lay the first row of the timbers in the trench. Using a level positioned across two timbers, add or remove soil as necessary to level them.

Step 3

A. Lay the second layer of timbers, staggering the pattern to cover the joints in the first layer.

B. Drill 3/16-in. pilot holes through the top timbers into the bottom

layer near the ends of the timbers; drive the galvanized barn nails in with a hammer.

C. Lay the third row of timbers in the same pattern as the first row, staggering the joints.

D. Drill pilot holes through the third layer into the second, offsetting them to avoid hitting the underlying nails. Drive nails through the pilot holes.

Step 4

A. Drill ½-in. drainage holes every 2 ft. into the bottom layer of timbers.

B. Line the inside of the bed with strips of landscape fabric, overlapping each strip by 6 in.

C. Hammer galvanized roofing nails through the fabric to attach it to the timbers.

Step 4

Line the bed with overlapping strips of landscape fabric.

Step 5

A. Fill the bed to within 4 in. of the top with topsoil. Tamp the soil down lightly with a shovel.

B. Add the plants, loosening the rootballs before planting. Apply a 3-in. layer of mulch. Water thoroughly.

MAINTAINING A RAISED BED

Raised beds freeze faster and deeper than in-ground planting beds. Since the outside edge of the bed experiences wider temperature variations than the inner core, consider planting annuals and hardy perennials along the sides and tender perennials and bulbs near the center, where the soil temperature is more stable.

Raised beds also dry out faster than in-ground beds and require more frequent watering. Water the bed whenever the top 2 to 4 in. of soil is dry (depending on the depth of the bed), and before the soil begins to shrink away from the sides of the bed.

Flowers

Flower beds can fill your yard with vivid hues and wonderful scents. Here's how to use perennials, annuals and bulbs to create a full season of color.

Helpful Terms

Annual: Plants that grow, bloom and die in one year; commonly used to refer to a large group of ornamental flowers.

Bulb: A thickened root that stores food for a new plant; commonly used to refer to a group of flowers grown from bulbs.

Perennial: Plants that live more than two years; commonly used to refer to a group of ornamental flowers.

Self-seeding: The process by which some annuals return from the previous year's seed.

GROWING FLOWERS

Flowers can be the crowning touch that delights the eye and adds a splash of color to your yard. The three major kinds of garden flowers are annuals, perennials and bulbs. Perennials and bulbs require the least work, but they tend to have shorter bloom seasons. Annuals must be replanted every year, but they offer the advantage of bold, long-lasting color. Here are some tips for starting a colorful garden that you'll enjoy all summer long:

Ten Self-Seeding Annuals

Bachelor's button (*Centaurea*)
Cosmos (*Cosmos*)
Flowering tobacco (*Nicotiana*)
Larkspur (*Delphinium*)
Love-in-a-Mist (*Nigella*)
Marigold (*Tagetes*)
Moss rose (*Portulaca*)
Salvia (*Salvia*)
Snapdragon (*Antirrhinum*)
Sweet Alyssum (*Lobularia*)

• Choose a site with good drainage and slightly acidic soil, with a pH of 6.0 to 7.0.
• Start small. Use no more than three to five different types of flowers in each bed and group together odd numbers of flowers, using at least three of each flower.

• For a low-maintenance garden, choose self-seeding annuals (see box), and perennials that are well suited to your climate.
• Plan the bed. Sketch in the location of each plant, giving perennials enough space to grow. Use the sketch to figure out how many plants you need to buy.
• Plan for visibility. In a border, put short plants in front and tall plants in back. In an island, put short plants on the outside and tall plants in the middle.

Although you can get the widest selection of seed and starter plants from mail-order catalogs, the best source is often a local nursery, since they usually specialize in plants that will flourish in the surrounding climate. Before buying, compare the selection, price and quality of several suppliers.

• Combine annuals, perennials and bulbs. A properly planted perennial bed will look sparse for the first year or two; fill it in with annuals. Interplant early-blooming bulbs with perennials that will cover the bulb stalks after their blooms fade.
• Remove faded flowers by deadheading: pinching or cutting off the old flower heads. This will keep plants blooming longer and improve their appearance.

A multicolored flower bed is an excellent way to soften the boundaries of a yard and balance the linear appearance of a long fence.

PERENNIALS

Many homeowners shy away from growing flowers because they feel they lack the time or knowledge that flower gardens demand. That's where perennials come in. After planting, they reappear every year, providing a lifetime of pleasure with a minimum of care.

Perennials look great arranged in casual or formal beds. You can make the beds almost any shape that you can easily work and mow around—borders, rectangles and kidney shapes are popular choices.

Serious gardeners favor perennials over annuals. For one thing, since most perennials have a bloom period of just a few weeks, a perennial bed offers ever-changing, elegant beauty that can be more interesting to design than a bed of annuals.

Although roses are some of the most popular garden blooms, they're technically perennial woody shrubs, rather than flowers. Today there are many long-blooming, hardy varieties that aren't difficult to grow, although they do require a sunny location. Hardiness varies.

Coral bells (Heuchera) form low mounds of distinctive roundish leaves topped by tall, wiry stems that bear clusters of bell-shaped flowers in spring and summer. Hardy to -30°.

Coreopsis has a long bloom period and striking yellow flowers. It's also very easy to grow, requiring little water or fertilizer, just sunshine and well-drained soil. Hardy to -30°.

Columbines (Aquilegia) are delicate, airy plants that come in a rainbow of colors and bloom from spring into summer. They prefer cool, moist soil and light shade. Hardy to -40°.

RECOMMENDED PERENNIALS

PLANT	HARDY TO*	HEIGHT	COMMENTS
Five Good Perennials for Sunny Areas with Moist Soil			
Monkshood *(Aconitum)*	-50°	3 to 5 ft.	Blooms late summer, fall; tolerates shade
Daylily *(Hemerocallis)*	-40°	1 to 4 ft.	Blooms early to late summer; tolerates partial shade
Siberian iris *(Iris siberica)*	-40°	2 to 4 ft.	Blooms in early summer; attractive grasslike foliage
Bellflower *(Campanula)*	-40°	6 in. to 3 ft.	Long bloom season; many species available
Garden phlox *(Phlox)*	-30°	3 to 4 ft.	Blooms summer, early fall; easy to grow; long-lived
Five Good Perennials for Dry, Sunny Areas			
Pinks, carnations *(Dianthus)*	-50°	6 in. to 2 ft.	White, pink or red blooms, early summer to fall
Black-eyed Susan *(Rudbeckia)*	-40°	2 to 4 ft.	Gold blooms in summer; good cutting flowers
Purple coneflower *(Echinacea)*	-40°	1 to 3 ft.	Purple blooms in summer; good cutting flowers
Stonecrop *(Sedum)*	-40°	6 in. to 3 ft.	Blooms spring or fall; attractive foliage; long-lived
Coreopsis *(Coreopsis)*	-30°	1 to 3 ft.	Blooms spring to late summer; tolerates extreme heat
Five Good Perennials for Shady Areas with Dry Soil			
Periwinkle *(Vinca)*	-50°	6 to 12 in.	Blooms spring to early summer; good ground cover
Fairy Bells *(Disporum flavum)*	-30°	2 to 3 ft.	Blooms in spring; long yellow flowers
Fern (various species)	-40°	2 to 5 ft.	Tolerates deep shade; spreads quickly
Cranesbill *(Geranium)*	-50°	6 to 18 in.	Blooms late spring, summer; good for woodland gardens
Spotted Nettle *(Lamium)*	-40°	6 in. to 1 ft.	Blooms late spring to summer; good ground cover
Five Good Perennials for Shady Areas with Moist Soil			
Astilbe *(Astilbe)*	-30°	2 to 4 ft.	Blooms early to midsummer; good near water gardens
Bleeding Heart *(Dicentra)*	-40°	2 to 3 ft.	Blooms late spring to early summer; good cut flower
Hosta *(Hosta)*	-40°	6 in. to 3 ft.	Grown for foliage rather than flowers; very long-lived
Cardinal Flower *(Lobelia)*	-50°	3 to 4 ft.	Blooms early to late summer; good in marshy areas
Cranesbill *(Geranium)*	-50°	6 to 18 in.	Blooms late spring, early summer; good in woodlands

Mail-order catalogs sometimes exaggerate hardiness ratings. Check with a local nursery to make sure a plant is truly hardy in your area.

DIVIDING PERENNIALS

Periodic dividing helps keep perennials healthy and prevents them from overgrowing their space. Use a spade or garden fork to dig around the entire plant and lift it out of the soil. Brush the soil off the roots.

For plants that form tight clumps, like this daylily, cut the clump into sections with a sharp knife or pry it apart with two garden forks.

For plants that form diffuse clumps of leafy stems, like coral bells, pull the clumps apart by hand.

Replant strong, young segments with healthy roots—or give them away to a neighbor or a beginning gardener.

Annuals

Unlike most perennials, which bloom for just a few weeks, annuals tend to bloom for the entire growing season, and many are easy to grow from seed. Not only is this an inexpensive way to grow plants, it also makes it possible to experiment with unique varieties. Although most nurseries carry only the best-selling annuals in stock, if you buy seeds by mail you'll have hundreds of options.

Since they're not expected to live through the winter, annuals aren't rated for winter hardiness. Some flowers, such as geraniums, are annuals in northern climates and perennials in more southerly areas, where there's no killing frost. Also, many annuals will self-seed readily, and since they don't require replanting, these flowers can be as easy to grow as perennials.

TOP: *Zinnias are easy-to-grow, long-blooming annuals with big, bold flowers that attract butterflies. When you cut the blooms for arrangements, new ones will develop quickly.*

ABOVE: *Bright orange nasturtiums peek out from behind this white picket fence, softening its geometric lines and giving visitors a warm, friendly impression.*

LEFT: *Impatiens is one of the most popular annuals for bright color all summer long. Since it loves shady spots, try planting a mass of impatiens in a barrel under a tree.*

RECOMMENDED ANNUALS

PLANT	HEIGHT	COLOR	COMMENTS
Ten Good Annuals for Sunny Areas with Moist Soil			
Marigold (*Tagetes*)	1 to 4 ft.	Yellow, orange, red	Easy to grow from seeds
Petunia (*Petunia*)	1 to 2 ft.	Many colors	Thrives in almost any soil
Snapdragon (*Antirrhinum*)	1 to 2 ft.	Many colors	Also tolerates partial shade
Love-in-a-mist (*Nigella*)	12 to 18 in.	Blue-purple	Blooms late into autumn
Cupflower (*Nierembergia*)	6 to 15 in.	Purple	Perennial in the South
China Aster (*Callistephus chinensis*)	9 to 24 in.	Many colors	Prefers warm weather
Larkspur (*Consolida*)	1 to 4 ft.	Mauve, blue, white	Excellent as cut flowers
Geranium (*Pelargonium*)	9 in. to 3 ft.	Red, white, purple	Perennial in zone 10
Canterbury bells (*Campanula*)	2 to 4 ft.	Pink, blue, purple	Long-lasting blooms
Dahlia (*Dahlia*)	1 to 6 ft.	Many colors	Perennial in zone 10
Ten Good Annuals for Sunny Areas with Dry Soil			
Nasturtium (*Tropaeolum*)	1 to 8 ft.	Bright yellow or orange	Good climber on trellises
Cosmos (*Cosmos*)	2 to 7 ft.	Pink, yellow, orange or white	Fernlike foliage
Moss rose (*Portulaca*)	2 to 6 in.	Many colors	Good in rock gardens
Alyssum (*Lobularia*)	4 to 8 in.	White, pink or lavender	Fragrant blossoms
Cleome (*Cleome*)	3 to 5 ft.	Pink	Good background plant
Flowering tobacco (*Nicotiana*)	1 to 3 ft.	Pink, white	Fragrant; tolerates moist soil
Bachelor's button (*Centaurea*)	1 to 2 ft.	Purple, white or pink	Good for cut flowers
Oriental Poppy (*Papaver*)	1 to 4 ft.	Orange-red, white, red or pink	Good in mixed borders
Scarlet salvia (*Salvia*)	1 to 3 ft.	Lavender or red	Tolerates alkaline soil
Larkspur (*Consolida*)	2 to 4 ft.	Blue, rose or white	Good for cut flowers
Five Good Annuals for Shady Areas with Dry Soil			
Forget-me-not (*Myosotis*)	5 to 8 in.	Blue, pink or white	Good for rock gardens
Larkspur (*Consolida*)	2 to 4 ft.	Blue, rose or white	Won't tolerate deep shade
Honesty (*Lunaria*)	2 to 3 ft.	Purple	Tolerates alkaline soil
Foxglove (*Digitalis purpurea*)	2 to 5 ft.	Purple, white, yellow or pink	Biennial grown as an annual
Bachelor's button (*Centaurea*)	1 to 2 ft.	Pink, blue, purple or white	Won't tolerate deep shade
Five Good Annuals for Shady Areas with Moist Soil			
Impatiens (*Impatiens*)	6 in. to 2 ft.	All colors except green, blue	Prolific bloomer
New Guinea impatiens (*Impatiens*)	1 to 2½ ft.	Many colors	Tolerates partial sun
Browallia (*Browallia*)	1 to 2 ft.	Purple or white	Good in container gardens
Wax begonia (*Begonia*)	6 in. to 1 ft.	Red, pink or white	Tolerates acidic soil
Pansy (*Viola*)	6 in. to 1 ft.	Many colors	Won't tolerate deep shade

LEFT: *Moss roses grow rapidly and stay close to the ground, making them ideal for a colorful edging or ground cover.*

Bulbs

Bulbs are a group of colorful flowers that grow from a thickened root rather than a seed. The term includes true bulbs (tulips, daffodils), tubers (begonias), corms (gladiolus) and rhizomes (iris). Although most are perennial, many bulbs have specific climate requirements and must be grown as annuals in some parts of the country.

Like other perennials, bulbs are rated for hardiness. If you plant bulbs that aren't hardy in your area, you'll either need to dig them up and store them each fall, or plant new bulbs every year.

Although bulbs are widely available in pots, it's cheaper to buy them in bulk and plant them yourself. You can find a wide range of rare and unusual bulbs in mail-order catalogs. When choosing a bulb, find out when it will flower. By planting different varieties, you can get a continuous display of flowers over the growing season.

TOP: *Dahlias, which are grown from a tuberous root, come in so many shapes and colors that a dahlia planting like this one can mimic the look of a mixed garden bed.*

ABOVE: *Many bulbs, such as these red tulips and grape hyacinths, can be planted in a random pattern, which is called "naturalizing." This is an excellent way to add natural-looking color to a low-maintenance part of the yard.*

How to Plant Bulbs

Although bulb planting depth varies, generally you'll dig down three times the bulb's diameter (placing the bottom of a 2-in.-wide bulb 6 in. below the surface). Here are two bulb-planting techniques:

1. Dig Individual Holes

To plant a few bulbs, dig holes with a trowel or bulb planter. Make them wide enough so the base of the bulb can sit firmly on the soil.

2. Dig a Planting Trench

To plant 10 or more bulbs in one bed, dig a trench. Excavate the soil to the proper depth. Set the bulbs in place and cover them with soil.

RECOMMENDED BULBS

PLANT	HARDY TO	HEIGHT	COMMENTS
Five Good Bulbs for Spring Blooms			
Tulip *(Tulipa)*	-40°	8 to 24 in.	Many varieties available; good planted in masses
Daffodil *(Narcissus)*	-30°	up to 18 in.	Many varieties available; naturalizes in lawns
Hyacinth *(Hyacinthus)*	-20°	10 in.	Very fragrant; bright, unusual flowers
Crocus *(Crocus)*	-40°	2 to 8 in.	Earliest of all bulbs; can be naturalized in lawns
Bulb iris *(Iris)*	-20°	4 to 20 in.	Delicate, colorful blooms; attractive, grasslike foliage
Five Good Bulbs for Early- to Midsummer Blooms			
Asiatic lily hybrids *(Lilium)*	-40°	2 to 5 ft.	Long bloom period; long-lasting bulbs
Giant allium *(Allium)*	-30°	3 to 5 ft.	Huge lavender flower balls; good filler for background
Tuberous begonia *(Begonia)*	+30°	8 to 9 in.	Spectacular blooms, many colors; does well in shade
American lily hybrids *(Lilium)*	-30°	4 to 8 ft.	Red, pink, orange and yellow blooms
Gladiolus *(Gladiolus)*	+20°	2 to 4 ft.	Blooms 8 to 10 weeks after planting
Five Good Bulbs for Late Summer and Fall Blooms			
Oriental lily *(Lilium)*	-40°	3 to 7 ft.	Spectacular blooms, very fragrant
Gladiolus hybrids *(Gladiolus)*	+20°	2 to 4 ft.	In cooler climates must be dug up and stored over winter
Caladium *(Caladium)*	+30°	8 in. to 2 ft.	Tolerates shade; dig and store for winter in cool climates
Tiger lily *(Lilium lancifolium)*	-40°	4 to 6 ft.	Orange flowers spotted with purple; very easy to grow
Freesia *(Freesia)*	+20°	1½ to 2 ft	Many colors; blooms 10 weeks after planting

Bearded irises, known for their elegant shape and fuzzy "beard," are grown from rhizomes, which are commonly grouped with bulbs.

BULB TIPS

Here are some tips that will help keep your bulbs blooming year after year:

- Plant bulbs in the fall when the soil temperature is below 60 degrees.

- Apply bulb fertilizer when sprouts first appear, to help foliage and flowers grow. Fertilize again when leaves start to die back, to help nurture the bulb.

- Don't snip off flowers when they're at their peak if you want them to rebloom next year. Instead, cut them off as soon as they pass their prime.

- Don't bunch, tie or cut the leaves after the flowers bloom. The leaves produce food to be stored in the bulb, which replenishes the plant for next year.

- Hide yellowing leaves by planting annuals or perennials around the bulbs. Impatiens, marigolds, hostas and coral bells are good choices.

- In cold areas, hardy bulbs (like many tulips, daffodils and lilies) can be left in the ground over the winter. Tender bulbs (like gladiolus and dahlia) must be dug up, stored indoors and replanted in the spring.

Lawns

*The secret of growing and maintaining
a carpet of lush green turf is to make sure you're
mowing, watering and fertilizing correctly.*

Helpful Terms

Aeration: Removal of plugs of matted turf to provide more breathing room for a lawn.

Extension service: The office of a state college that advises state residents.

Soil amendment: Manure, fertilizer and nutrients that are added to soil to enrich it.

Thatch: A fibrous mat of dead grass that lies on the surface of the soil.

Topseeding: Seeding over an existing grass lawn, usually to improve or thicken a lawn.

Topsoil: The layer of fertile soil at the surface of the ground that supports a lawn.

LAWN MAINTENANCE

10 STEPS TO A BEAUTIFUL LAWN

Although the average American homeowner spends two hours a week caring for a lawn, some common lawncare practices are actually worse for your lawn than ignoring it completely. To grow and keep a healthy lawn, you simply need to follow these ten principles of good lawn care.

1. Mow Higher

A lawn consists of millions of grass plants, and every mowing removes part of each plant's leaf. Mowing too short limits leaf development, reducing the plant's ability to produce and store enough nutrients. The lawn becomes thin, weak and can no longer crowd out weeds.

While some of the grasses found on putting greens are meant to be mowed short, higher is better for most home lawns. Every ⅛-in. increase in mowing height increases the leaf surface by 30 percent, promoting deeper roots and hardier growth.

Northern Grasses

Mow lawns no shorter than 3 in. in the spring and early fall, when they're most actively growing. Mow

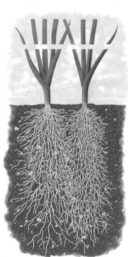

higher (about 4 in.) in the summer, to shade and cool the soil. Mow shorter (2 in. or less) only in late fall and early spring, when the grass is growing more slowly. Gradually raise the mowing height as the grass becomes more active. Don't mow short before the winter dormant period—weeds are still active even if grass isn't.

Protect your lawn by never cutting off more than one-third of its height at one time.

Southern Grasses

Mow lawns highest in the summer and early fall, when they're most actively growing. Cut St. Augustine and Bahia grasses 3 to 4½ in. high, and Bermuda, centipede and zoysia grasses 2 to 3 in. high.

2. Don't Cut Off Too Much at Once

It's important to mow lawns when they need it. If you wait too long, you'll cut off too much of the grass blade at once. The grass plant will put all its energy into replacing the lost leaf area, which stops root growth, food storage and other vital functions.

Follow this rule: Time your mowing so that you don't remove more than a third of the grass blade at once. For example, when you're mowing 3 in. high, don't let the lawn grow higher than 4½ in. You can tell by looking at the lawn clippings—they should be short.

3. Don't Bag Clippings

Instead of bagging grass clippings, let them fall into the soil where they'll break down and feed your lawn, reducing its need for fertilizer. In addition to fewer lawn chores and a greener, deeper-rooted lawn, you'll be helping the environment—grass clippings take up needless space in landfills.

You can leave grass clippings up to 2 in. long on the lawn, but the best solution is to use a mulching mower. Finely mulched clippings will stay out of sight at the base of your lawn and decompose within two weeks.

HOW TO SHARPEN A MULCHING BLADE

1. Put on gloves to protect your hands. Disconnect the mower's spark plug or power cord, then unbolt the blade with a long-handled wrench.

2. Sharpen the outer and inner surfaces with a grinding wheel (above), moving left to right and from the edge inward. Follow the original contour and keep the wheel moving.

3. Slip the center hole of the blade over a screwdriver to check its balance. If one side droops, grind more metal from that side and check the balance again. This keeps both sides equal and prevents vibration.

LAWN MAINTENANCE *CONTINUED*

Both under- and overwatering will weaken a lawn rather than help it grow.

4. Keep Mower Blades Sharp

A dull mower blade won't make a clean cut—instead of slicing through a grass leaf, it will shred it, leaving an unsightly gray tip that invites insects and disease. A mower blade that's heavily nicked will leave uncut grass and make the lawn look hacked up and uneven.

Start every mowing season with a sharp blade. Manufacturers recommend professional sharpening for today's multipitch mulching blades, because shops have the jigs needed to hold the blades at the optimal sharpening angle. However, you can do the job yourself, if you're careful. Small nicks can be smoothed out with a file, but large nicks or cracks call for a new blade. To prevent future damage, clear your yard of rocks, sticks and other debris that might damage a blade.

5. Water Wisely

Since grass roots follow moisture, light watering encourages shallow roots and kills deep ones, resulting in a fragile lawn that's more vulnerable to weeds, pests and disease.

To encourage your lawn to root deeply, don't water too early in the spring. Let the roots reach deeper as the soil dries. Then watch the grass carefully—it will take on a wilted, bluish hue when it really needs water. (Another clue: you'll see footprints after walking across the lawn.)

At that point, fully saturate the soil by watering for an hour or two. Check the moisture level by pushing a spade or screwdriver 6 in. into the soil and moving it forward; the soil should be moist down to the bottom of the roots. After that, water heavily once a week, and twice if it's really hot, dry or windy. Water early in the day so the grass

can dry completely by nightfall (wet grass at night encourages disease).

Lawns need about 1 in. of water a week. Check the amount of water you've applied by putting an empty tuna can on the ground. When it fills up, turn the sprinkler off.

Overwatering fills the air spaces in the soil with water, so oxygen can't get in and carbon dioxide can't get out. The grass roots can't breathe and they begin to rot. Excess moisture also promotes fungus, and trapped carbon dioxide stimulates the germination of weed seeds.

6. Test Your Soil

You can't grow a healthy lawn without balanced, nutrient-rich soil. To assess the condition of your soil, you'll need a soil test, which will describe the makeup of your soil, including its capacity to support a lawn. It will also give you advice on how to improve your soil, based on its levels of potassium, magnesium, and nitrogen.

The cost of soil testing depends on who does it. Most extension services do soil tests for state residents for about $10, while nurseries and private laboratories charge far more— $25 to $100. You can also do it yourself with a soil-testing kit from a nursery or garden catalog ($10 to $18), but these kits only test for a few nutrients. For a more comprehensive professional test kit, you'll have to spend a lot more.

The simplest and most inexpensive kind of soil test simply checks the pH level (acidity or alkalinity) of the soil. On the pH scale, 7 is neutral, lower is acidic and higher is alkaline. Lawn grasses grow best in slightly acidic soil—about 6.7 pH.

7. Improve Your Soil

Good topsoils are biologically active—full of earthworms, microbes and other beneficial microorganisms that keep the soil loose, break down minerals and digest dead and decaying organic matter. These living organisms are what turn plain dirt into the fertile, porous topsoil needed for a lush lawn. However, they can easily be killed off by overfertilizing, too many lawn chemicals or too much salt on walks and drives. The result will be lifeless, compacted soil that can't support a healthy lawn.

To increase the level of beneficial microbes in your soil, use soil activators and avoid spreading chemical insecticides or fungicides all over your lawn. Either spot-treat only the affected areas or use an organic alternative.

If your soil is compacted, consider mechanical aeration. A core aerating machine punches holes into the soil about 2 in. deep and 6 in. apart, pulling out plugs of earth and providing room for air, water and fertilizer, so roots can flourish. You can hire a professional or rent a machine and do the job yourself. Aerate only when grass is actively growing, so the roots can heal and fill the holes before weeds can get established.

8. Don't Overfertilize

Most lawn fertilizers are synthetic, high in nitrogen and fast-acting—but this kind of product can actually weaken grass by overstimulating its growth. Your lawn might look green and lush, but it will be vulnerable to fungus and insect attack, because the forced growth leads to grass with high water content and thin cell walls.

Ideally, you want a fertilizer that feeds your lawn slowly. For this, you'll need either an "organic" fertilizer from a natural source (such as manure, grain, fish or kelp) or a synthetic slow-release fertilizer with a high percentage of controlled-release nitrogen (such as sulfur-coated urea, ureaform or IBDU). If you're not sure what kind of fertilizer you're using, check the ingredient list. Organic fertilizers also help feed microbes and earthworms.

The best time to fertilize your lawn is when it's actively growing.

Fertilizers should only be used to add nutrients that might be lacking in the soil. If your soil is well balanced, fertilize no more than three times a year and don't apply more than 1 lb. of nitrogen per 1,000 sq. ft at a time.

9. Feed Lawns at the Right Time

Any kind of fertilizer can kill your lawn if it's applied at the wrong time. For example, never fertilize a Northern lawn in summer, especially if it's brown—any grass growth you get will be frail and weeds will use the fertilizer to flourish and take over the lawn.

Northern Grasses

Fertilize only once or twice a year. The most important feeding is in fall; this "winterizer" helps nurture the grass through winter and thicken it in spring. You can also feed in spring, at least a month before the hot weather begins. Never feed these grasses in summer.

LAWN MAINTENANCE *CONTINUED*

Southern Grasses

Fertilize only two or three times a year. The best times are in spring (just after the grass turns green), summer and perhaps again early fall. This last application should be at least six to eight weeks before the first killing frost is expected.

10. Get Rid of Thatch

Thatch is a thick mat of grass stems, roots and runners that forms above the soil. Contrary to popular belief, it isn't caused by clippings—the real culprit is poor lawn care. To check for thatch, poke your finger into the turf. If you can easily reach the soil, you don't have thatch. But if you run into a barrier of matted grass more than ½ in. thick, you have a problem. Thatch is like a sponge that soaks up water and fertilizers before they can reach the roots of lawn grasses. A thatchy lawn is more vulnerable to disease, drought and insect invasion.

Dethatching machines and power rakes can remove the top layer of thatch, and core aeration can provide more breathing room for a lawn. For best results, dethatch

Thatch is a fibrous mat of dead grass above the surface of the soil that soaks up water and fertilizer before they can penetrate to the roots of the grasses.

Northern lawns in early spring or fall and Southern lawns in late spring.

However, if you want to get rid of thatch permanently, you have to decompose it. Earthworms and microbes digest thatch where it meets the soil. Encourage them by making sure that the surface soil pH isn't too acidic. Biological dethatching products can add more of the soil microorganisms that decompose dead plant tissue, but they won't dissolve thatch on contact. The best way to get rid of thatch permanently is to combine these approaches with the other nine steps of good lawn maintenance.

LAWN SERVICE TIPS

Thinking of hiring a lawn care service this summer? Look for one that mows high, mulches clippings and only mows when needed. The service should gear their visits to the weather and other conditions. To discourage unecessary mowing, consider a flat monthly rate. Watch out for:

Liming without a soil test. Too much lime is as bad for your lawn as not enough.

Unnecessary pesticides. Make sure they're using pesticides only as needed. And don't do a grub prevention program unless grubs have been a problem.

Overfertilizing. Excessive fertilizing will make it necessary to mow and water more often. Make sure they're using organic or slow-release fertilizers.

LICKING LAWN BUGS

Although insects are a common summer scourge, most homeowners don't prepare for them, while others overreact. If you're tempted to treat your lawn with a broad-spectrum insecticide, be sure it's safe for earthworms and other beneficial insects. Without them, the infestation is likely to become worse.

Healthy parts of the lawn won't need much help fighting off insects, but weaker sections will be more susceptible. The most common culprits are grubs and chinch bugs.

Grubs. Grubs are larval-stage beetles that chew on grass roots; they can proliferate and eventually destroy whole areas of your lawn. Deal with them in spring, by adding beneficial nematodes to the turf to control them. Nematodes are tiny microorganisms that you can buy in a powdered form. Mix the powder with water and apply it directly to the soil with a hose-end sprayer. There are also insecticides that work by impeding the grubs' molting process.

Chinch bugs. Chinch bugs not only draw moisture from the grass blades, they also leave behind their toxic saliva. You can eradicate this goo by applying a premixed insecticidal soap combined with a tablespoon of isopropyl alcohol. Spray this solution on the lawn every few days for a couple of weeks.

Fall Lawn Cleanup Made Easy

Why should you go to all the trouble of removing dead leaves and debris from your lawn in the fall? Because dead leaves literally suffocate the grass, leaving dead spots that will show up in the spring. Also, fall debris provides a cozy place for insects and disease spores to survive the winter cold. The right tools can considerably speed your fall chores and leave you more time to enjoy the crisp fall weather.

A narrow fan rake with flexible tines is the best tool for cleaning leaves and grass clippings from flower beds and beneath shrubs. However, if you have a lot of leaves, you may also want to invest in a hand-held power blower.

Power Blower Tips

When using a power blower, wear eye protection and keep the wind at your back. Here's how to use a power blower efficiently:

Step 1. With the blower on full power, walk around the house and blow all the debris near the bushes onto the sidewalks and driveway.

Step 2. Blow the curbs, sidewalks and driveway clean.

Step 3. With the blower on half power or less, make several small piles of debris 10 to 15 ft. apart on the lawn.

Step 4. Blow all the debris to a central location. Gather the leaves into a bag-lined trash can or use the blower to gather them onto a tarp and drag them into the woods.

Dealing with Debris

The ideal way to process leaves and plant matter is in a compost pile—but that's a very slow way to dispose of a large pile of fall debris. A quicker way to turn dead leaves and broken twigs into valuable mulch or

Fall cleanup is an essential part of good lawn care. The right equipment can speed the process considerably and also turn your dead leaves into valuable mulch.

compost is to use a garden chipper/shredder. The main drawback of a chipper/shredder is the cost; although they start around $150, a good one will run you over $400. If your lot is less than an acre, consider renting a chipper/shredder instead of buying one.

Another option is a leaf shredder. These units cost far less than

chipper/shredders, but they aren't powerful enough to chip twigs or branches. They use a spinning nylon cutting line (heavier than the line on a string trimmer) to quickly shred dry or wet leaves into valuable leaf mulch that you can immediately use on your garden beds. For easier cleanup, they can even be mounted on a garbage can.

THE WAR ON WEEDS

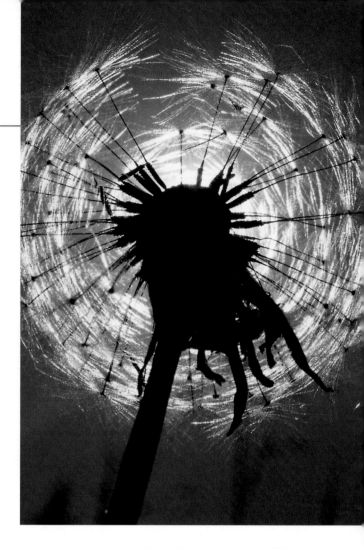

When you consider the tenacity of weeds, it's a wonder that we win any of our battles with them. After all, one dandelion plant can produce up to 15,000 seeds, each of which can survive six years—and produce 15,000 more seeds whenever it does sprout and mature.

The usual response to weed problems is to apply a herbicide. But weed killers can be dangerous to people, pets and turf. The best defense against weeds is a thick, vigorous lawn. Dense grass crowds out weeds and blocks the sunlight they need to germinate. If your lawn has only a minor weed problem, new lawn care habits might be all you need to get rid of them. However, if weeds make up more than 40 percent of your lawn, your best approach is to dig up or kill off the whole area and put in a new lawn (see **Renovating an Existing Lawn,** pages 226-227 and **Putting in a New Lawn,** pages 228-235).

Know Your Enemy

There's no single herbicide, weeding method or lawn care tactic that will work against every weed. To eliminate the weeds in your lawn, you need to know what you have. Some weeds, like dandelions, are easy to identify, but others can be confusing. To sort them out, refer to the chart on pages 222 and 223. If you're still stumped, call your local extension service for help.

There are basically three kinds of lawn weeds: broadleaf plants, grasses and grasslike sedges. Most are annuals or perennials. Annuals complete their life cycle in one season and reproduce by seed. Perennials live several years and spread underground as well as by seed, which makes them harder to control.

- -

CROWD THEM OUT

Most lawn weeds are opportunists that will take root anywhere they can find sunshine and room to grow. Since they can't compete with healthy grass, the best way to prevent weed problems is to follow a good lawn care program (see **10 Steps to a Beautiful Lawn,** pages 215-218). Here are the key lawn care pointers for controlling a weed problem:

- **Fertilize just enough.** Too little fertilizer can lead to a sparse lawn that loses ground to weeds. Too much helps nurture certain weeds. Use a slow-release fertilizer and follow the instructions on the package.

- **Fertilize at the right time.** Most Northern lawns need only one or two applications of fertilizer annually—in fall and perhaps again in spring. Southern grasses might require three feedings—in spring, early summer and early fall.

- **Water deeply and infrequently.** Frequent light watering weakens grass and encourages weed seeds to germinate. Insufficient watering helps weeds that like dry soil.

- **Mow higher.** Mowing too low weakens turf and lets light hit the soil surface, encouraging weed seeds to sprout and grow. Mow at the highest recommended level for your season and grass type, usually between 3 and 4 in. high.

- **Learn to read weeds.** Weeds can help you diagnose and treat soil problems. For example, ground ivy grows best in damp and shady areas where grass won't thrive. You can improve the soil drainage in those areas by aerating the lawn and removing shade-producing tree branches.

SEARCH AND DESTROY

A healthy lawn can keep weeds from sprouting, but what about those you already have? For permanent control, you need to address the problems that caused them in the first place. Here's how to proceed:

Weeding

On small lawns where the number of weeds isn't overwhelming, hand weeding is the best defense, especially against annual broadleaf weeds. Prevent them from spreading by pulling them before they go to seed. Pull perennial weeds before they develop a deep taproot—remove the entire root as shown at right; any root pieces left underground will sprout. If new sprouts show up, keep pulling them up until the roots starve.

Herbicides

Use herbicides only when nothing else has worked or your lawn is completely overrun. Choose a product that's labeled as effective against the kind of weeds you have. Follow the directions—improper use can kill or injure turf or other desirable plants. Also, some herbicides work only at certain temperatures, and others only at certain times of year. When applying a weed killer, always follow the directions on the label. Herbicides fall into three major categories:

Preemergence herbicides kill germinating seeds before they break through the soil. Most preemergence herbicides are synthetic. A natural, nontoxic preemergence herbicide made from corn gluten is safer, but you might have to apply it for several seasons before it will be fully effective. One drawback to these and most other preemergence herbicides is that they kill germinating lawn seed. Check the product label carefully.

Postemergence herbicides kill existing weeds. They come in two forms: contact and systemic. Contact herbicides kill only the part of the plant they touch. Most act quickly and work best against annual weeds. Systemic herbicides enter the plant and kill it all. They're more effective against perennial weeds than contact herbicides, but you might need to repeat the treatment.

When using any postemergence herbicide, don't apply it over your entire lawn; spot-treat isolated weeds or weedy patches.

Systemic herbicides can be selective or nonselective. Selective herbicides kill only certain weeds, while nonselective herbicides will kill any growing plant. For example, selective broadleaf herbicides will kill broadleaf weeds only; they aren't effective against weedy grasses. Nonselective products that will kill both broadleaf weeds and weedy grasses will also kill turf and other desirable plants—so use them on your lawn only when you want to kill an entire area and replant it.

Weed-and-feed products combine fertilizer and herbicides to do two jobs at once. But make sure that the best time for weed control coincides with the best time for fertilizing. Most of these products also pose an herbicide overdose risk if they are used for follow-up fertilizing. Products made from corn gluten with organic fertilizer are the safest weed-and-feed.

How to Pull Up a Weed

A dandelion digger is the homeowner's essential weeding tool. Its forked end probes deep into the soil, allowing you to easily get at the long taproots of perennial weeds.

To remove a weed, push the tool into moist soil, angled downward toward the center of the plant. Wiggle the handle of the digger to loosen the soil around the weed. Then gently pry it up, without piercing or breaking off the taproot. If the plant is large, you may have to loosen the soil on a few sides before you pull it up. Smooth the soil, mix in some compost, and patch the area with lawn seed.

To save effort, weed after a heavy rain or watering. When the ground is soaked through, even deep taproots will come out easily.

Tactical Guide to Eight Common Weeds

Name & Type	Features	Favors	Control	Herbicide
Dandelion Broadleaf Perennial	Bright yellow flowers and a long, fleshy taproot.	Thin turf.	Dig up young plants before they go to seed; cut back any regrowth.	Spot-treat with a selective broadleaf weed killer.
Crabgrass Annual	Coarse, blue- or purple-green leaf blades (smooth or hairy). Flower heads with many fingerlike spikes rising from branching, spreading stems.	Underfed lawns, lawns mowed shorter than 2 in., and lawns watered frequently and lightly.	Maintain thick, deeply irrigated turf. Dig up plants before they go to seed.	Apply pre-emergence crabgrass herbicide in spring, before the soil temperature reaches 60°F.
Ground Ivy (Creeping Charlie) Broadleaf Perennial	Square stems and bright green, rounded leaves with scalloped edges. Plants reproduce by seed and creeping stems that root as they touch ground.	Damp soil and shade.	Water less, improve drainage. Pull up the stems and roots of young plants.	Spot-treat with a broadleaf postemergence herbicide.
Yellow Woodsorrel (Oxalis) Broadleaf Perennial (annual in some regions)	Cloverlike leaves and yellow flowers, each with five petals. Plants spread by roots and seed.	Thin turf that is watered frequently and lightly.	Water lawn deeply and infrequently; fertilize properly. Dig out small plants. (This weed is difficult to control.)	Spot-treat isolated plants with a post-emergence herbicide. Prevent new sprouts with a preemergence herbicide effective on oxalis.

Name & Type	Features	Favors	Control	Herbicide
White Clover Broadleaf Perennial	Three-lobed leaves with a crescent-shaped white band.	Sparse, under-nourished turf with excessive moisture. Spreads by creeping stems.	Water well and apply nitrogen fertilizer. Avoid excessive applications of phosphorus.	Spot-treat with a selective broadleaf weed killer. Two treatments are often needed.
Spotted Spurge Broadleaf Annual	Grows close to the ground in a fast-spreading mat. Small green leaves with a brown-red spot on top. Cut stems exude a milky liquid. Reseeds heavily.	Weak, low-mowed lawns.	Maintain a high-mowed, well-fertilized and vigorous lawn. Pull isolated plants before they seed.	Spot-treat with a post-emergence herbicide and use a pre-emergence herbicide to prevent new growth.
Yellow Nutsedge or Yellow Nutgrass Grasslike Perennial Sedge	Triangular stems and ¼-in.-wide leaves. Reproduces by seed and tubers at the root tips. Tubers often persist, making it difficult to control.	Lawns watered frequently and lightly.	Water deeply and infrequently. Mow high in early- to midsummer. Control is easiest when plants are small.	Spot-treat with a post-emergence herbicide effective on nutsedge.
Quackgrass Perennial Grass	Flat, light green to blue-green leaves. Spreads by seeds and aggressive underground stems (rhizomes).	Dry soil.	Water deeply. Thoroughly dig out roots and pointed rhizomes—remaining pieces will regenerate new plants.	Spot-treat with a nonselective weed killer.

KEEPING YOUR LAWN DISEASE-FREE

Most lawn diseases are caused by fungi that live in the grass blades, thatch and topsoil. They don't usually attack healthy grass, and when they do, the cure is often just a matter of improving your lawn maintenance habits.

Fairy Ring

Preventing Lawn Disease

The first step in preventing lawn disease is to plant disease-resistant grasses suited for your climate and site. Healthy grass will resist most fungi, even in difficult weather. (Some fungi like warm, damp weather, while others flourish in drought conditions.)

Since each disease usually prefers one kind of grass, it's best to plant a mixture of disease-resistant grasses (see **Choosing the Right Grass for Your Yard**, page 234). Remember that when it comes to grass seed, you get what you pay for. The new disease-resistant varieties tend to cost more.

Once you have the right kind of grass, the next step is to maintain it properly. Here are the most important lawn care tips for preventing or controlling a disease problem:

- Mow at the right height.
- Keep mower blades sharp.
- Fertilize at the right time and not too much.
- Water deeply and infrequently in the early part of the day.
- Remove thatch.

For more information and a full lawn care program, refer to **10 Steps to a Beautiful Lawn**, pages 215-218.

Ruling Out Other Causes

To treat a lawn disease properly, you must know what it is—but a brown patch that looks like a disease may really be caused by grubs, drought, dog urine or a gas spill. Before you assume your lawn is diseased, try to rule out all other causes. See the chart below for some symptoms that are commonly mistaken for lawn fungus.

Identifying the Culprit

Once you've been able to rule out other causes, call a professional. Lawn diseases are hard to diagnose; samples will probably need to be analyzed in a lab. (To find a lawn consultant, call your extension office or a landscape-maintenance service.)

Many fungi have specific climate and grass preferences, so lawn diseases vary by region. However, these five are some of the most common:

DIAGNOSING YOUR LAWN PROBLEM	
SYMPTOM	**CAUSE**
Distinct, irregularly shaped brown patches of grass that lift easily, like sections of sod.	White grubs feeding on the roots of the grass.
Lawn is yellowish and lacking in vitality (slow-growing).	Probably needs fertilizer. If the lawn is getting adequate nitrogen, may indicate improper soil pH or an iron deficiency.
Clearly defined brown patches of dead grass.	Probably spilled fertilizer, herbicide or gasoline. If bright green grass surrounds a dead patch, the cause is probably dog urine.
Grass turns from bright green to dull gray-green and starts to die (especially during a summer heat or drought).	Insufficient water, possibly exacerbated by poor sprinkler coverage or hard, compacted soil.

Leaf Rust

Necrotic Ring Spot

Large rings of dead grass. Likes cool, wet weather and Kentucky bluegrass.

Summer Patch

Large rings of dead grass. Likes hot, dry weather after lots of rain and fine fescue or Kentucky bluegrass.

Leaf Rust

Dustlike rust spores on grass blades. Likes warm, moist weather and ryegrass, zoysia or Kentucky bluegrass.

Brown Patch

Small brown areas that may grow and turn into large rings. Likes hot, humid weather and ryegrass or tall fescue.

Fairy Ring

Dark green rings, often with mushrooms. All climates and grasses; cause is undecomposed organic matter (like thatch) under the lawn.

Treating the Problem

After diagnosing the problem, a lawn care professional will recommend how to treat it. Usually the treatment is simply to improve your lawn mantenance habits: water less often, mow higher and aerate the lawn. Some diseases are seasonal and will die off when the weather changes. But if you have an older lawn, consider overseeding it with one of the new, disease-resistant hybrid grasses (see

Choosing the Right Grass for Your Yard, page 234).

Resist the urge to skip the lawn evaluation and simply apply a general-purpose fungicide. Fungicides can be a short-term solution, but they must be applied with care.

Summer Patch

And although they can reduce the spread of a disease, they won't change the conditions that caused it in the first place. If you do use one, follow the label instructions; misuse of fungicides can weaken a lawn by killing beneficial fungi and soil microorganisms.

Doggy Lawns

Because it's so high in nitrogen, a concentrated dose of dog urine has a deadly effect on grass plants—and the resulting dead spots are often mistaken for a lawn disease. A doggy lawn will develop yellow dead patches—and by the time the symptoms appear, it's too late to save the grass. Here's how to deal with the problem:

Once you discover the problem, keep dogs off the lawn to prevent it from recurring. If you catch a dog in the act, you may be able to keep the grass alive by immediately soaking the area. Otherwise, you'll need to patch the lawn by sodding or reseeding the dead spots.

To patch with sod, remove all the damaged lawn and enough of the soil so the new turf will be level with the surrounding lawn. Loosen the newly exposed surface and level it. Then cut the sod to fit, lay it in place, tamp it down and water it.

To patch with seed, remove the damaged turf. Loosen and level the soil, then scatter the seeds. Lightly rake the seeds into the soil, and apply a high-phosphorus starter fertilizer, such as 5-10-5 or 16-20-0. Cover the seeded area with a layer of compost and water thoroughly. Keep the soil moist until the seeds sprout.

RENOVATING AN EXISTING LAWN

If your lawn is plagued by weeds, drought, thatch, compacted soil or dead or sparse grass, take heart. You may not need to reseed or resod—a lawn renovation program may be all you need to restore your lawn to its natural beauty. Here's a lawn renovation guide that addresses the most common lawn maladies.

Assessing the Damage

Begin your renovation by taking a look at your lawn and locating any problem areas.

Next, check for excessive thatch. Insert a spade about 6 in. into the ground and pull back the soil. If the layer of thatch between the bottom of the grass blades and the soil is more than ½ in. thick, you have a thatch problem.

ABOVE: *Even if your grass has serious problems, you can convert it into a vibrantly healthy lawn like this one, which provides a lush backdrop for flowering dogwood and azaleas.*

Check the moisture level by measuring the depth of dark, moist soil in your sample—it should extend at least 6 in. deep. If it doesn't, you'll need to replenish moisture to that level before you begin renovating your lawn.

Finally, conduct a comprehensive soil test. (Call your local extension service for information.) The soil test report will describe your soil's condition and any amendments required to support a lawn.

How to Renovate a Lawn

Step 1

Determine the kind and extent of weeds in your lawn. If weeds constitute more than 40 percent of the grass, your lawn needs more than a renovation program; you should remove it and start over from scratch. Otherwise, refer to pages 220-221, **The War on Weeds**, for information on getting rid of weeds.

Step 2

A. If you have excessive thatch buildup, you can remove it with a rented vertical mower (also called a verticutter, dethatcher or power rake). Set the tines on the vertical mower to rake about ¼ in. below the surface.

B. Push the vertical mower over the lawn in straight rows. Repeat the process, mowing in a grid pattern—first in one direction, then the other.

C. Rake up the loosened thatch with a leaf rake.

Use a rented vertical mower to remove excessive thatch.

Step 3

You can relieve compacted soil and improve drainage by removing small cores of soil from your lawn with an aerator.

A. Run the machine across the lawn in a grid pattern.

B. Allow the soil cores to dry and break up on the lawn.

C. Using the vertical mower, or a leaf rake, scratch the entire surface of the lawn to loosen the soil slightly.

Step 4

A. To prevent spills, set a broad-

Use an aerator to improve the soil drainage beneath the lawn.

cast spreader on a paved surface, then fill it with the fertilizer blend recommended in your soil test (or see **Figuring Fertilizer,** page 217).

B. Calibrate the spreader and apply the fertilizer according to the directions on the package.

C. Fill the broadcast spreader with a grass seed that's appropriate for your climate and site (see **Choosing the Right Grass for Your Yard,** page 234).

D. Topseed the entire lawn, working in a grid pattern.

REPAIRING BARE SPOTS

If your lawn is marred by bare spots, you'll need to determine their cause and take preventive measures before you topseed them. Here are some guidelines that can help you diagnose and treat bare areas in your lawn:

CAUSE	SOLUTION
Drought	Water the area to a depth of 6 to 8 in., then make sure it gets 1 to 1½ in. of moisture a week.
Compacted soil	Aerate the area, or till in an amendment, such as compost or peat moss.
Chemical burn	Remove several inches of topsoil from the bare area and patch with seed or sod.
Disease	Consult your local extension service for diagnosis and treatment.
Foot traffic	Install a path or stepping-stones to accommodate traffic.
Insects	Consult your local extension service for recommended treatment.

PUTTING IN A NEW LAWN

PREPARING THE SOIL

Soil preparation is a critical step in creating a new lawn or renovating an old one. The soil is the foundation on which grass grows, and proper preparation is necessary for strong, healthy root systems. Taking the time to prepare your soil now will save you time and money later.

The first step is to determine the condition of your soil. Start with a soil test on the site where you're putting in the new lawn. The test report will assess the nutrient levels of your soil and its capacity to support a lawn, and recommend any fertilizers or organic materials needed to fortify it.

Amending the Soil

If your soil fails the lawn compatibility test, you'll need to incorporate a layer of high-quality topsoil, compost or peat into the existing soil. Also,

even basically healthy soil may benefit from being amended with topsoil or organic material. Although this isn't as big a job as replacing the topsoil, it follows the same basic procedure.

Topsoil, or "black dirt," is sold in cubic yards and can be delivered to your home by a soil contractor. Measure your yard before ordering to make sure you order enough. Depending on how extensively you want to amend the soil, you'll want to add between 2 and 4 in. of new topsoil (see **Soil Coverage Chart,** opposite).

Leaving two distinct layers of soil on the gound can cause a lot of problems, so it's important to thoroughly rototill the new layer into the existing soil, 4 to 6 in. deep. If the existing soil is severely compacted, ask your soil contractor to "slice" the ground before adding the new

topsoil. This slicing is done by heavy machinery outfitted with a blade that makes deep cuts into the soil to loosen it.

Begin by spreading an even layer of the soil amendments over the area. Set the tiller so that it digs to a depth of 4 to 6 in. Till the surface, a small area at a time, working your way across the yard in the same pattern you use for mowing the grass. Once the entire area is tilled, level and regrade the soil as needed.

Grading Your Yard

Before you proceed, check to be sure your lawn is properly graded. The grade, or slope, of your yard determines how well water drains away from the house. A positive grade will carry water away, while a negative grade will drain water toward—and often inside—your home. When graded correctly, the 6 ft. next to your foundation should have a smooth, gradual slope away from the house of about ¾ in. per ft.

Here's how to grade your yard to prepare for new grass:

Step 1

Drive a pair of stakes into the soil: one at the base of your foundation, and another 8 ft. out into the yard, in a straight line.

Step 2

A. Attach a string fitted with a line level to the stakes; adjust the string until it's level.

B. Measure and flag the string with tape at 12-in. intervals.

Use stakes and a string level to correct the grade to ensure that water drains away from the house.

Use a rototiller to blend the recommended amendments into the soil.

measuring point, to get a smooth, gradual slope away from the house of ¾ in. per ft.

Step 5

Starting at the foundation, evenly distribute the soil over a small area with a garden rake. Measure down from the tape markings as you work to make sure that you're creating the desired even grade.

Step 6

A. Add and remove soil as needed, working away from the house, until the grade is evenly sloped.

B. Once you've completed one area, repeat this process for all other sections of the yard.

Smoothing the Surface

After the soil has been graded and amended, you'll need to lightly tamp it down. This final step will leave a smooth, even surface for seeding or sodding. Since you don't want to compress the soil too much,

Step 3

A. Measure down from the string at the tape flags, recording the measurements as you work.

B. Use these measurements as a guide for correcting the grade.

Step 4

Starting at the foundation of the house, add or subtract soil at each

it's important to apply the right amount of pressure. Fill a landscape drum one-third full with water, then roll it over the surface, walking in a row-by-row pattern.

To compact the soil, fill a landscape drum ⅓ full of water and roll it over the surface.

Soil Coverage Chart

If you're adding new topsoil or soil amendments, you'll need to calculate how much to buy. First, figure the square footage of the area you want to cover by multiplying its length by its width. Then check the table below for the amount of soil or amendments you'll need. Packaged amendments are usually sold by the cubic foot; bulk quantities and topsoil by the cubic yard (1 cubic yard is equal to 27 cubic feet).

Depth of Coverage:	Amt. required to cover 100 sq. ft.	Amt. required to cover 500 sq. ft.	Amt. required to cover 1000 sq. ft.
1 in.	9 cu. ft.	1⅔ cu. yds.	3⅓ cu. yds.
2 in.	16 cu. ft.	3 cu. yds.	6 cu. yds.
3 in.	1 cu. yd.	5 cu. yds.	10 cu. yds.
4 in.	1⅓ cu. yds.	6⅔ cu. yds.	13⅓ cu. yds.
5 in.	1⅔ cu. yds.	8⅓ cu. yds.	16⅔ cu. yds.
6 in.	2 cu. yds.	10 cu. yds.	20 cu. yds.

PUTTING IN A NEW LAWN *CONTINUED*

SODDING A LAWN

Installing sod is the quickest way to create a new lawn. Only a few hours of work can transform bare soil into a lush carpet of grass. However, the long-term success of a sodded lawn requires careful attention to several factors, including the quality of the sod, the preparation of the soil, installation technique and keeping the new sod well watered.

Although sod can be installed at any time from early spring through early fall, avoid laying it down during hot weather. Intense sun and dry heat can scorch and dry out new grass.

Sod can be purchased from sod farms, landscape supply stores and landscape contractors. Make sure that the price you're quoted includes delivery; most suppliers charge a fee for delivering small orders. For best results, buy sod that will be cut within 24 hours of delivery.

After the sod is delivered, keep it moist, but not soaked. Over-watered sod is difficult to install, and dried-out sod won't establish roots. Because it's susceptible to drying out, don't wait more than a day to install your sod. In the meantime, keep it rolled up in a cool, shaded area.

Before installing the sod, prepare your soil (see **Preparing the Soil**, page 228). The soil beneath the sod must be smooth and free of rocks and construction debris—the roots of the sod need to be in direct contact with the soil so they can dig in and grow. If your soil is dry, water it the night before you lay the sod to encourage quick root development.

SEED OR SOD: WHAT'S BEST FOR YOUR YARD?

Before you start a new lawn, you have to determine which installation method is best for you: seed or sod. Each has its benefits and drawbacks. You'll need to consider time, money, climate, upkeep and the amount of traffic over the lawn. Use this chart to choose the best way to put in your lawn:

SEED	PROS:
	• Inexpensive
	• Greater variety of grasses
	• Strong root systems develop quickly
	CONS:
	• Takes longer to develop complete coverage
	• Ideal times to plant are limited
	• Must be kept moist after planting
SOD	PROS:
	• Immediate results
	• Fewer weeds
	• Establishes better on slopes
	CONS:
	• Expensive
	• Limited variety of grasses
	• Labor-intensive

How to Install Sod

Step 1

Step 2

Step 3

Lay the first roll against a straight edge, such as a sidewalk. Lay the next roll as close as possible to the first.

Lift up the edges of adjoining sod pieces, then press them down together, blending the seam between the pieces.

Trim excess sod around curves with a sod cutter and use stakes to secure sod on sloped areas.

Step 1

A. Prepare the soil (see **Preparing the Soil**, page 228).

B. Begin laying the sod against a straight border, such as a walkway. If you don't have a straight surface to use as a guide, draw a reference line on the ground with agricultural lime. Unroll the first piece of sod and lay it down, using your fist to push it into the topsoil.

C. Lay the next roll as close as you can to the first piece, staggering the beginning of the roll slightly to avoid a running seam.

Step 2

A. To eliminate seams, lift up the edges of pieces that butt against each other and press the two edges down simultaneously so that they join, blending the two pieces together.

B. As you lay each new piece, cover the seams with ½ in. of topsoil to prevent the edges from drying out.

Step 3

A. Continue laying the sod in a staggered pattern. If you're sodding a slope, use wooden stakes to hold the sod in place. Use a sod knife to

trim excess sod from around trees, curves and corners.

Step 4

A. Once all the sod is installed, press it firmly into the soil by rolling it with a landscape drum half-filled with water.

B. Water the new sod until it's thoroughly saturated and keep it moist for the next three days. After that, water it as often as needed, increasing the frequency during extended hot, dry weather. (For more information on watering, see **10 Steps to a Beautiful Lawn**, pages 215-218.)

PUTTING IN A NEW LAWN *CONTINUED*

SEEDING A LAWN

Growing a beautiful new lawn from seed is not only rewarding, but also easier and less expensive than putting in a sod lawn.

A successful result requires only that you pay attention to a few simple guidelines that cover the time of year, type and quality of grass seed, condition of the soil and care of the area after seeding.

When seeding a lawn, timing is essential. The best time to seed is during the height of the grass growing season. In warmer climates, that's in spring. In colder climates, that's in early spring and early fall.

Fall is the best time to seed cold-climate lawns, because there are fewer weeds, cooler temperatures and more frequent rains to keep the seed from drying out.

Choosing Seed

Grass seed is available in three forms: straight (single variety), blends and mixtures. Blends contain different varieties of the same species, while mixtures combine different species. In blends and mixtures the strength of one grass compensates for the weakness of the other, so you get a more resilient lawn (see **Choosing the Right Grass for Your Yard,** page 234).

Warm-season grasses like Bermuda grass and zoysia are typically sold straight, because they don't tend to mix well. However, cool-season grasses are best planted in blends or mixtures.

Always match the seed you buy with your climate and site conditions—shade, moisture and so on. Read the label carefully before making your decision (see **Reading Lesson,** below). For example, if the label lists no variety names, only generic species, don't buy it. High-quality seed will have a high germination rate and a low percentage of weeds and inert matter.

Moisture

Rainfall also affects the success of a seeded lawn, and it can be tricky to work around Mother Nature. Check the weather forecast—you want the soil to remain moist so the seeds won't blow away, but you don't want to plant just before a heavy rainfall, either.

Once you've seeded the lawn, keep the soil moist for at least two weeks, or until the seeds germinate. Water the grass as needed, to ensure that it receives about 1 to 1½ in. a week, including rainfall. Don't overwater the area, though; too much water will only encourage fungal problems and root disease.

READING LESSON

```
        XYZ BRAND GENERAL MIXTURE

 LOT# TPG-1962593-0395        TESTED: MARCH 1995
 %PURITY      SEED                   %GERMINATION
 58.80     NASSAU KENTUCKY BLUEGRASS    85
 19.60     JAMESTOWN II CHEWINGS FESCUE 90
 19.60     PALMER II PERENNIAL RYEGRASS 90
    OTHER INGREDIENTS:  0.00% OTHER CROP SEEDS
   0.00% WEED SEED    2.00% INERT MATTER

          XYZ SUPER SEED CO.
            123 MAIN STREET
          ANYTOWN, USA 01234
```

When investing in a new lawn, it's important to buy high-quality seed. Seed packages provide a lot of information, including many clues about the quality of what's inside. Here are some tips for deciphering them:

Grass descriptions should include both a variety and a generic name. For example, the first listing on the sample label is Nassau Kentucky Bluegrass. Here, Nassau is the variety name, and Kentucky bluegrass is the generic name.

Annual grasses should not exceed 5 percent by weight of the varieties listed. Don't purchase any seed labeled "VNS," which means "varieties not stated."

The germination percentage should be at least 75 percent for Kentucky bluegrass and 85 percent for perennials, such as ryegrass, fine fescue and tall fescue.

Weed seed shouldn't exceed 0.3 percent to 0.5 percent by weight. Don't buy any grass seed that lists noxious weeds on the package label.

Other crop seed refers to other kinds of grass; it shouldn't exceed 1 percent by weight.

Inert matter (any substance that won't grow) shouldn't exceed 5 percent by weight. The lower this number, the better the seed mix.

Quality seed mixtures don't contain bent grass or rough bluegrass (*Poa trivialis*). These are weedy grasses that are difficult to control.

How to Seed a New Lawn

Step 1

Step 3

Set the broadcast spreader on a paved surface and fill it with the recommended amount of seed.

Roll a landscape drum over seed that has been lightly raked into the soil.

Step 1

A. Prepare the soil (see **Preparing the Soil**, page 228). If the soil is dry, water it the night before seeding.

B. Fill a broadcast spreader over a paved surface, such as a driveway, with the amount of grass recommended on the seed package.

Step 2

A. When you're ready to begin seeding, calibrate the spreader according to the recommendations on the seed package.

B. Apply the seed in two stages, following a grid pattern to ensure even coverage.

Step 3

A. Once the seed has been spread, use a metal rake to lightly rake the seed into the soil. When you're done, only 10 to 15 percent of the seeds should be visible.

B. Lightly compact the raked soil with a landscape drum half-filled with water. Water the yard until the soil is moist to a depth of 6 in.

PUTTING IN A NEW LAWN *CONTINUED*

CHOOSING THE RIGHT GRASS FOR YOUR YARD

Growing a carpet of lush green turf has never been easier, thanks to the hundreds of new hybrid "supergrasses" that look great and shrug off drought, insects and disease.

However, plant scientists have yet to develop a single grass that's best for all lawns and climates. To get a tough, handsome, low-maintenance lawn, you still need to sort through all the choices and select the best grass for your yard.

All lawn grasses are categorized as cool- or warm-season. Cool-season grasses grow fastest in fall and spring and slow down in summer and winter. They're at home in the cool, moist North. Warm-season grasses grow fastest during the heat of summer and turn brown as the weather cools. Warm-season grasses thrive in warm, hot climates.

If you live in Minneapolis or Miami, your choice is clear—but in many parts of the country both kinds of grass will flourish. Here's a zone-by-zone guide to the most promising new grasses.

Find your lawn climate zone on the map and read the recommendations below. (Some of the varieties listed may not be available in your area. Check with a local nursery or extension service for other recommendations.)

ZONE **1** Humid Northeast and Northwest

This zone is ideal for cool-season grasses, especially Kentucky bluegrass, perennial ryegrass and fine fescues.

In this zone, Kentucky bluegrass is the preeminent choice, with its fine texture, deep color, quick growth and outstanding cold hardiness.

There are many new hybrids that feature improved disease resistance. You can look for a blend of disease-resistant varieties, such as *Midnight* or *Unique,* or choose a variety that will remain a handsome dark green with less fertilizing, such as *Challenger, Cobalt, Livingston, Midnight, Opal,* or *Washington.*

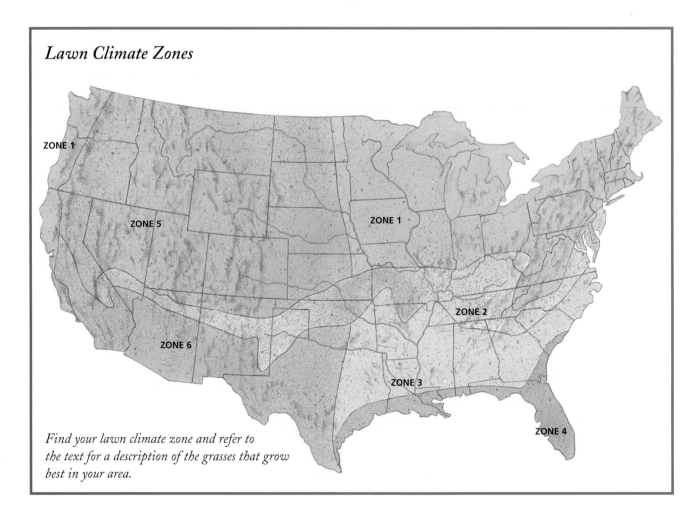

Lawn Climate Zones

Find your lawn climate zone and refer to the text for a description of the grasses that grow best in your area.

Perennial ryegrass is often mixed with Kentucky bluegrass to provide quick cover until the bluegrass establishes itself. Compared to older grasses, the new varieties are darker green, more disease-resistant and won't fray and brown after mowing. Some, such as *Divine, Stallion Select* and *Stallion Supreme,* are enhanced with endophytes—leaf-inhabiting fungi that repel or kill leaf-feeding insects.

Fine fescues are the best cool-season choice for shaded areas; they also require less mowing and fertilizing. The improved varieties *Aurora, Brigade, Discovery, Banner II* and *Flyer* are often combined with Kentucky bluegrass. *Supranova* requires less mowing and (when well irrigated) will tolerate deep shade and heavy traffic.

ZONE 2 Transition Zone

The transition zone is where the Southern and Northern lawn climate zones intersect. The best choice here will depend on your property. A south-facing slope exposed to intense sun and heat will favor a warm-season grass, while a cooler north-facing slope will prefer a cool-season grass.

Tall fescue, a cool-season grass, is ideal where the summers are too hot for other cool-season grasses and the winters too severe for warm-season grasses. It's planted widely in the East and the milder parts of the Southwest. Tall fescue tolerates foot traffic, heat, shade and drought. Avoid coarse, weedy older varieties, like *Kentucky 31* and *Alta.*

The new "turf-type" tall fescues have better texture, darker color and more compact growth. Look for blends with *Duster, Monarch, Tomahawk* and *Virtue;* or the varieties enhanced with endophytes: *Rebel III, Earth Save, Titan II* and *Tarheel.*

ZONES 3 & 4 Humid Southeast

Bermuda grass, zoysia and other warm-season grasses grow well in these areas, and St. Augustine grass will thrive in the warmest parts of Zone 4.

Bermuda grass is heat- and drought-tolerant, vigorous and fast-spreading—to the point where it may become invasive. There are two kinds: common Bermuda grass, which is planted by seed, and hybrid Bermuda grass, which is planted by sprigs or sod.

The hybrids, notably *Tifway* and *Tifgreen,* were developed for Southern golf courses. Although they look great, they require above-average care, including regular thatch removal.

The seeded varieties require less maintenance. Look for *Cheyenne, Del Sol, Primavera, Sahara, Sonesta, Sultan* and *Yuma,* which offer better color, density and texture than common Bermuda grass.

Zoysia is a good choice for most Southern lawns. It starts slowly, but once established it's relatively low-maintenance and tolerates traffic, heat and drought. Older varieties, like *Meyer,* turn brown early and are slow to green up in spring. Improved varieties, like *De Anza, El Toro, Emerald* and *Victoria,* offer faster growth, longer color and a finer texture.

St. Augustine grass is a good choice only in the mildest regions of the South—it can't tolerate prolonged temperatures below 25°F. Planted by sod or sprigs, it's coarse with broad leaves and spreads rapidly by surface runners. The variety *Floratam* is most common. New varieties like *Palmetto* and *Seville* have finer texture and better shade tolerance—but they're more prone to thatch, especially if overfertilized.

ZONE 5 Cool, Dry, West

The cool-season grasses described in Zone 1 will grow here, but they require supplemental irrigation.

If water is in short supply, buffalo grass is a promising alternative. It's a native prairie grass with unparalleled heat and drought resistance. Although it lacks the traditional, refined look of Kentucky bluegrass, it requires little maintenance once established. It browns with the first frost and is slow to green in spring, but is very cold-tolerant. Current research is producing interesting new varieties, such as *Bison* and *Cody.*

ZONE 6 Arid and Semiarid Southwest

The main difference between Zone 3 and Zone 6 is rainfall—there's lots of it there and not much here, making irrigation a crucial factor in this zone. If there's a good supply of water where you live, you can grow Zone 3 grasses. Bermuda grass is the best choice by far; the alternatives are zoysia and St. Augustine.

If your area lacks water, opt for buffalo grass (see Zone 5). At higher elevations—such as Prescott, Arizona, and Santa Fe, New Mexico—try cool-season Zone 1 grasses, like Kentucky bluegrass.

Vines & Ground Covers

Vines and ground covers decorate your landscape with living texture and color, while fulfilling some very practical needs.

Helpful Terms

Arbor: A garden shelter, often of lattice-work, on which climbing plants are grown.

Ground cover: A low-growing plant that forms a dense cover over the ground.

Prune: Cutting back sections or branches of a plant to improve its shape or health.

Soil erosion: When topsoil is depleted by processes such as wind or rainfall.

Vine: A plant with a flexible stem that climbs, clings or creeps.

Vines

Few plants deliver as many practical benefits as vines. Grown on a fence or a freestanding trellis, they can quickly provide natural privacy and cool summer shade for a deck or walkway. Vines can also dress up an arch or pillar with flowers, soften harsh structural lines and even hide an ugly view. The key to using vines is picking the right one for the right place and giving it the structural support it needs.

Choosing a Vine

Vines can be evergreen or deciduous; flowering or nonflowering; rampant or restrained. Choose a vine that's well suited to your climate and the available light and space.

Consider the purpose of planting the vine. Evergreen vines, such as bloodred trumpet, offer privacy and all-season color. Deciduous vines, like grape and wisteria, provide summer shade yet allow the winter sun to warm your home after their leaves have fallen.

Also, find out how fast the vine grows. A quick climber like silver lace vine can twine to 25 ft. or more in one season. However, a fast-growing vine will also quickly engulf other plants or structures, especially if it doesn't have enough room to spread out.

Buying and Planting Vines

Perennial vines are sold in 1-gal. or larger containers during the summer. In winter, you'll find deciduous vines, like grapes and roses, in bare root form at nurseries and garden centers.

Position most vines at least 1 ft. away from their support to allow enough room for their stems to develop. Vines planted in early summer also need thorough watering. Follow up with regular watering, especially during hot, dry spells.

If you plant vines against the house, the roof overhang could prevent rainwater from reaching the roots. If your roof doesn't have gutters, don't plant vines directly under the drip line; the constant dripping will injure them.

Once planted, most nonclinging vines need some guidance to help them start growing up the support. Often, using a few loose ties or simply wrapping the branch of a twining vine around the support will be sufficient.

Gold flame honeysuckle (Lonicera) is a vigorous vine with fragrant flowers that bloom from spring to frost. It reaches 12 to 15 ft. high and is hardy to -30°.

VINES CONTINUED

SEEKING THE SUN: HOW VINES CLIMB

Vines grow toward the sunlight they need in ingenious ways. Before choosing a vine, found out how it climbs and what kind of support structure it needs.

- Vines with twining stems will encircle vertical supports. They can maneuver themselves through and around an open fence or wire trellis, or coil up a single cable.
- Vines with twining tendrils will use them to reach out and wrap around anything nearby. They require a wire grid, wood lattice or other narrow crisscrossing support.
- Vines that cling use small suction disks and aerial roots to attach to any rough surface. These plants can damage soft brick or mortar and tear apart wood siding.

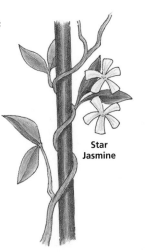

Star Jasmine

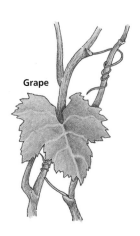

Grape

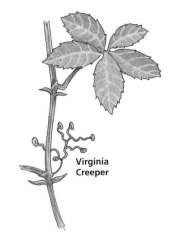

Virginia Creeper

TWINING
The entire stem twists and spirals around a support as it grows. Other examples include bittersweet, honeysuckle, silver lace vine and wisteria.

TWINING TENDRILS
Growths along stems or at leaf ends reach out and twine to support the rest of the plant. Other examples include coral vine, passionflower and trumpet vine.

CLINGING
Suction-cup discs, aerial roots or hooklike claws along the stems attach to flat surfaces. Other examples include Boston ivy, English ivy and coral vine.

PRUNING VINES

Vines that grow in confined spaces usually need pruning to keep them within bounds. Annual pruning will also help maximize flowering in many vines. The best time to prune depends on when the vine blooms:

- Vines that bloom in spring on the previous season's growth (like early flowering clematis and many climbing roses) should be pruned immediately after flowering. If you prune them too late, you'll remove next year's flower buds.

- Vines that flower on the current season's growth and bloom in midsummer and autumn (like silver lace vine, trumpet vine and climbing hydrangea) should be pruned in early spring.

- Vines that blossom or fruit on old growth (like wisteria and grape) should be pruned during their dormant season, shortly before their growth resumes in spring.

- Nonflowering woody vines (like English ivy and Boston ivy) should be pruned in late winter or early spring so that the cuts heal quickly and are soon covered by new growth.

SUPPORTING YOUR VINES

Trellises, pergolas and arches do more than just support vines; they can also keep tenacious plants from tearing apart your siding and other vulnerable surfaces.

No matter which support you choose, be sure it's large and sturdy enough to hold the mature vine, and put it in place before planting to avoid damaging the vine. You can build your own support or choose from a wide selection of prefabricated trellises and arches made of metal, PVC or wood.

If you're building your own structure, choose only weather-resistant materials. The wires used for cables or gridwork should be rustproof (plastic-coated or copper wire works well). When building a trellis or arbor, use only pressure-treated lumber or a decay-resistant wood, such as redwood or cedar heartwood. Here are some other support tips for vines:

- Secure trellises or latticework so they're positioned several inches away from the surface of wood siding. This protects the siding by promoting air circulation and also makes pruning easier. Use angle irons or small blocks of wood between the support and the siding to create the necessary space.

- Consider a hinged trellis, which lets you quickly move flexible-stemmed vines out of the way for painting and other maintenance. Hinge the trellis at the bottom and attach it at the top with metal hooks and eyes (see below).

- Tie vines to their supports with strong, stretchy materials that won't cut into growing branches. Strips of old nylon hosiery are an excellent choice. Always loop the ties in a figure-eight pattern that crosses between the stem and the support; this helps keep the vine stems from chafing or snapping in windy conditions.

- Don't use trees to support vigorous vines, such as bittersweet. Vines that grow into the top of a tree and shade its leaves can weaken or even kill it.

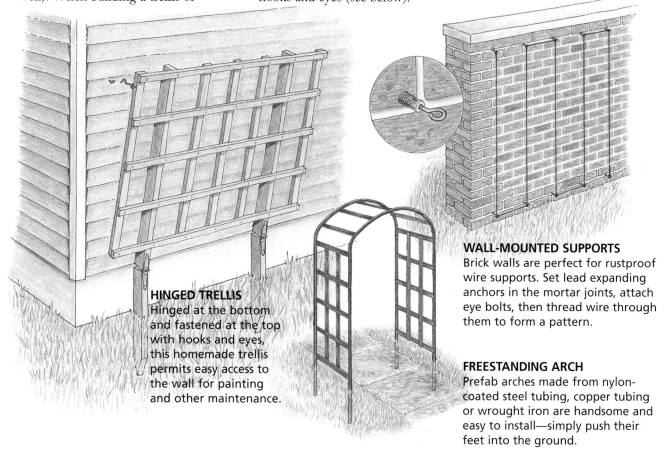

HINGED TRELLIS
Hinged at the bottom and fastened at the top with hooks and eyes, this homemade trellis permits easy access to the wall for painting and other maintenance.

WALL-MOUNTED SUPPORTS
Brick walls are perfect for rustproof wire supports. Set lead expanding anchors in the mortar joints, attach eye bolts, then thread wire through them to form a pattern.

FREESTANDING ARCH
Prefab arches made from nylon-coated steel tubing, copper tubing or wrought iron are handsome and easy to install—simply push their feet into the ground.

GROUND COVERS: FIVE SOLUTIONS FOR PROBLEM SITES

If your property includes deep shade, poor soil or steep slopes, it will be difficult to grow and maintain a healthy lawn. That's where ground covers come in.

Ground covers are a diverse group of dense, low-growing plants that include ground-hugging woody shrubs, vines and spreading perennials. Some are nearly as compact and

Junipers provide dense coverage on slopes. They also tolerate soils from acid to alkaline in climates ranging from cool to hot and from moist to dry.

uniform as a lawn, while others grow into a jumbled mass several feet high.

Here are some typical problems that make grass-growing difficult, and suggested ground covers that thrive in those same conditions. Before buying, check with a local nursery for planting requirements and winter hardiness.

Plantain lilies are made for the shade. Their varied and dramatic foliage creates a sea of green.

PROBLEM: **Steep Slopes**

1 Growing and caring for plants on slopes is a real challenge. The soil tends to be shallow or poor, and as water runs off the slope, it erodes any topsoil that remains so it isn't available to support plants. The following plants require relatively little watering or feeding and provide excellent erosion control:

- Aaron's beard *(Hypericum calycinum)*
- Bougainvillea *(Bougainvillea)*
- Broom *(Genista lydia)*
- Junipers *(Juniperus)*
- Mahonias *(Mahonia)*
- Manzanitas *(Arctostaphylos)*
- Wild lilacs *(Ceanothus)*
- Winter creeper *(Euonymus fortunei)*

PROBLEM: **Too Much Shade**

2 Few grass varieties grow well in light shade and none grows well in heavy shade—but dozens of ground covers thrive in both. The plants listed below are good choices under a dense tree, around shrubs or on the north side of a house:

- Carpet bugle *(Ajuga reptans)*
- Creeping lilyturf *(Liriope spicata)*
- Dead nettle *(Lamium maculatum)*
- English ivy *(Hedera helix)*
- Japanese spurge *(Pachysandra terminalis)*
- Periwinkle *(Vinca minor)*
- Plantain lilies *(Hosta)*
- Sweet woodruff *(Galium odoratum)*

PROBLEM: **Limited Water**

3 Lack of moisture can make it difficult to grow a lawn, especially where watering is regulated. These ground covers look lush and grow well in arid gardens, although some may need occasional watering in very hot or dry climates.

- Cotoneasters *(Cotoneaster)*
- Coyote brush *(Baccharis pilularis)*
- Germander *(Teucrium chamaedrys)*
- Gazanias *(Gazania)*
- Lavender cotton *(Santolina chamaecyparissus)*
- Mexican daisy *(Erigeron karvinskianus)*
- Snow-in-summer *(Cerastium tomentosum)*
- Woolly yarrow *(Achillea tomentosa)*

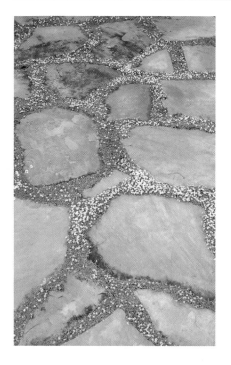

This blue star creeper (left) flows around paving stones and sports light blue blossoms in late spring and summer. Goldmoss sedum (above) finds a suitable home between stepping stones. Its yellow flowers bloom in late spring.

PROBLEM: Stark Surfaces

Concrete pathways, flagstone patios, rough-hewn timber steps and other hard surfaces can appear cold and imposing. Tucking ground-hugging plants between paving stones or at the edges of a paved area softens these surfaces and unites them with the surrounding landscape. The plants listed below can provide a carpet of greenery. Although they'll survive occasional footsteps, they won't tolerate heavy foot traffic.

- Blue star creeper *(Pratia pedunculata)*
- Heronsbill *(Erodium reichardii, E. chamaedryoides)*
- Indian mock strawberry *(Duchesnea indica)*
- Irish moss *(Sagina subulata)*
- Moneywort *(Lysimachia nummularia)*
- Stonecrops *(Sedum)*
- Thymes *(Thymus)*
- Wall rock cress *(Arabis caucasica)*

PROBLEM: Under a Pine Tree

Covering the ground under a needle evergreen is always a challenge. Some of the problems include dense shade, dry soil, competition from tree roots and the constant rain of pine needles. However, there are some attractive ground covers that can tolerate these tough conditions, including:

- Bishop's hat *(Epimedium)*
- Archangel *(Lamiastrum)*
- Sweet woodruff *(Galium odoratum)*

QUICK TIPS

Planting Ground Covers

- Before planting, amend the soil with organic material and remove weeds. You can either pull the weeds by hand or apply an herbicide (follow package directions).
- Space plants appropriately, according to each plant's requirements.
- After planting, spread a 2- to 3-in.-deep layer of organic mulch between the new plants as a weed deterrent and to help control erosion.
- If planting on a slope, use a biodegradable jute netting to secure the soil until the plants spread.
- To help control erosion, plant ground covers in a triangular, staggered or terraced pattern and keep the area well mulched.
- Water newly planted ground covers deeply and regularly. Even drought-tolerant plants will need extra water for at least the first two seasons.

Shrubs & Trees

Trees and shrubs are permanent design elements that can add the practical benefits of shade, privacy and seasonal color to your landscape.

QUICK REFERENCE

Helpful Terms

Bare root: Dormant plants that are sold without any soil around their roots.

Deciduous: Plants (especially trees and shrubs) that lose their leaves in the fall.

Evergreen: Plants (especially trees and shrubs) that keep their leaves year-round.

Pruning: Cutting back the branches of a tree or shrub to improve its look or health.

Winter hardiness: The lowest winter temperature that a given plant can survive.

BUYING SHRUBS AND TREES

Choose trees and shrubs to fit the scale, climate, soil and environmental conditions of your site. When you're ready to buy, you'll find that they're available in these three forms:

CONTAINER PLANTS are sold in the pot in which they are grown. Container-grown plants are available throughout the growing season and can be planted anytime the soil can be worked. Before planting, water regularly to prevent the roots from drying out. If the plant is difficult to remove, snip the sides of the container.

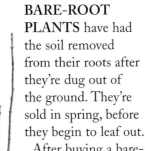

BARE-ROOT PLANTS have had the soil removed from their roots after they're dug out of the ground. They're sold in spring, before they begin to leaf out.

After buying a bare-root plant, soak the roots in water for at least one hour but not more than 24 hours, and plant immediately. Spread the roots out in the hole and fill it with soil to ensure that no air pockets remain around the roots.

BALLED & BURLAPPED PLANTS (also called B & B) have had their roots pruned into a compact root ball that's wrapped in burlap. Balled-and-burlapped plants are sold throughout the growing season and can be planted anytime the ground can be worked. Keep the root ball moist until planting.

To plant, place the tree or shrub in its planting hole, then cut the twine and loosen the burlap. Pry or cut away as much of the burlap as you can without damaging either your back or the root ball.

BARE-ROOT BENEFITS

Nurseries commonly sell dormant bare-root plants in winter and early spring. There are several reasons to consider them:

Bare-root plants cost 15 to 25 percent less than container plants. Although that may not mean much on a single tree, it adds up when you're buying many trees or shrubs.

Since bare-root plants take up less space than container plants, nurseries can offer more varieties and they'll often special-order a plant you can't find.

Bare-root trees and shrubs are easier to carry and transport than container plants.

Bare-root plants adapt more easily to your garden, since they aren't used to container soil. Their roots also develop faster; while the roots of container plants are often cramped and overgrown, bare roots are free to spread out immediately.

Shop early in the season, and buy before plants start to leaf out. Select plants with plump, well-developed roots. And—especially in the case of trees—buy big. Larger plants will fruit or flower sooner. Also, look for plants that are displayed with their roots sunk into moist sand or sawdust, which keeps them from drying out. Avoid plants that have their roots wrapped in plastic bags—the roots must be severely pruned to fit inside the bag.

SHRUBS

The best way to ensure that the shrubs in your yard thrive is to select them carefully, plant them correctly, prune them as needed and protect them from winter damage.

Choose the Right Shrub

Before you go shopping for a new shrub, consider the following points:

Soil Type

Does your soil stay wet or dry out quickly? What's its pH? Does it feel light and sandy, or firm and sticky? Some shrubs, such as red choke-berry and cotoneaster, will tolerate a wide range of soils. Others need acidic soil or excellent drainage.

Light Requirements

How much sunlight does the site receive during the day and over the year? Some shrubs grow well in either sun or shade, but sunny spots will usually produce more intense fall color and more abundant fruit.

Slope and Exposure

Is the ground level or steep? Is the area wind-whipped or sheltered? Fragrant sumac is among the shrubs with great fall color that tolerate a broad range of conditions, including wind. It will also help stabilize slopes with its suckering habit and stems that root readily where they touch the ground.

Space

How large is the planting area? Don't plant a shrub that grows 12 ft. wide in a 4 × 4-ft. space. Most shrubs look better and bear more fruit when they're allowed to reach their natural size and shape. Also, why spend your weekends pruning if you don't have to?

You can curve a small hedge around a shrub to form both a border and a barrier.

Winter-Hardiness

Choose only plants that can handle your winters. To be sure, you can check with a local nursery or extension agent.

Purpose

Design your plantings to meet specific needs: Mass tall, dense shrubs together to create a privacy screen. Position mid-size shrubs to link trees and buildings with the rest of the yard. Use fall foliage to sustain a yard's appeal after flowers have faded. Choose plants with lush green summertime foliage as a soothing backdrop for flower beds.

Plant the Right Way

In mild regions where the soil seldom freezes, fall is prime shrub-planting time. In colder areas, you can plant container-grown deciduous shrubs until about a month before the soil freezes. However, it's safest to plant them in the early spring to get them off to a good start. Use the instructions on page 245 as a guide for planting shrubs.

It's important not to plant too deep. Otherwise, if the soil settles after planting and watering, water will collect on the plants's roots or at its base, which can lead to decay or root suffocation. To prevent the plant from settling, place on a plateau of unloosened soil on the bottom of the planting hole.

After planting and watering, spread a 2- to 4-in. layer of organic mulch around the shrub, being sure to keep it away from the base the plant. Mulch that rests against a plant's trunk or stems may cause the bark to rot and attract insects and disease organisms.

Prune Every Year

Annual pruning helps shrubs stay robust yet compact. Recommended pruning techniques vary depending on the plant involved, but here are some general guidelines. (Consult a nursery or

In spring, use pruning shears to remove dead branches from shrubs.

arboretum for more detailed advice.)

To maximize flowering, prune flowering shrubs right after they've bloomed each year. The flowers on early blooming shrubs come from the growth of the previous summer or fall. If you prune too long after the new growth has occurred, you'll lose many of the flower buds and have fewer flowers the following spring.

How to Prune

Begin by removing any weak, diseased or dead branches from the shrub. This includes any split branches or branches that cross or rub together.

Next, remove one-fourth to one-third of the oldest branches of vigorously growing shrubs by

How to Plant a Shrub

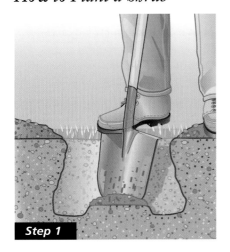

Step 1

Step 2

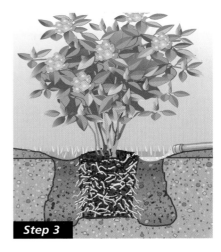

Step 3

Step 1

Dig a hole, tapering the sides outward. Make the hole 1 or 2 in. shallower than the root ball and dig out around the bottom of the hole to create a planting plateau. The bottom of the hole should be twice as wide as the root ball.

Step 2

Remove the plant from its container. Gently loosen the roots and uncoil any that are circling or twisted. Set the plant in the hole on the soil plateau. The top of the root ball should be about 1 in. above ground level.

Step 3

Fill in around the root ball with unamended backfill soil. Mound the soil slightly around the planting hole to create a watering moat. Irrigate gently, so that water stays in the moat, away from the base of the shrub.

SHRUBS *CONTINUED*

cutting them at ground level. This selective pruning method will completely renew the shrub every three to four years.

Prevent Winter Damage

Some evergreens are susceptible to winter stress that can lead to browning, bleaching or other discoloration. Hemlock, yew and arborvitae are especially prone to this problem.

A number of factors can cause an evergreen to succumb to winter damage:

- Sun and wind can cause the foliage to lose excessive water, which can't be replaced by roots in frozen soil.
- Warm, sunny winter days can stir an evergreen to initiate new growth. But when the sunlight

fades, the temperature falls rapidly, damaging or killing foliage.

- Bright, cold winter days can kill chlorophyll, causing bleaching. Plants can't replace chlorophyll at temperatures below 28°F.
- Severe cold in early fall or spring can kill or injure young trees that aren't acclimated to the cold.

To minimize winter injury, prop pine boughs against or over an evergreen to protect it from the wind and sun.

You can also protect a susceptible shrub or tree with a simple burlap barrier (see photo). You can surround the entire plant, or shield only its south, west or windward sides, which are most likely to suffer from winter damage. Leave the top

A simple burlap covering like this one can protect your evergreens from the disfiguring effects of a harsh winter.

open to ensure that light and air can reach the tree from above.

Preventative measures include planting evergreens in spots that are protected from the bright winter sun and excessive wind, such as the north and east sides of the house.

HOW TO DESIGN WITH SHRUBS

This symphony of evergreen texture and color includes global arborvitae, creeping juniper and Austrian pine.

Pay attention to foliage texture and size, as well as color. These strongly influence the overall appearance of a shrub and how well it complements the neighboring plants. You can make individual plants stand out by juxtaposing shrubs with contrasting textures.

For a yard you can admire at all times of the year, combine shrubs with different peak seasons or plant shrubs with multi-seasonal appeal. For example, witch hazel offers showy, spiderlike yellow-red flowers in winter and spring, and displays a kaleidoscope of warm colors in fall.

Avoid the jarring look that can be created by planting one each of several different shrubs. Instead, group several shrubs of the same type within a planting or repeat them throughout your landscape.

SHRUBS FOR FALL COLOR

When we think of fall color, shade trees usually come to mind first. While it's hard to deny the majestic beauty of a sugar maple in its glory, yards today just don't have enough room for one of these giants. However, shrubs fit the scale of almost every yard—and the leaves, fruits and berries of many shrubs can also provide spectacular fall color.

Shrubs offer many advantages over trees. Most cost less than trees, plus they mature more quickly and provide good color the first fall after planting. Shrubs can also do double-duty by providing screens, barriers, ground covers or spring flowers for your yard.

The sixteen shrubs listed below are all easy-maintenance plants that offer great fall color; the list includes choices for all areas of the country. Use this list as a starting point, and check with your neighbors and local nurseries for other regional favorites. (All plants are deciduous, unless otherwise noted.)

Cranberry bush *(Viburnum trilobum)* gets its name from its showy red autumn fruit. In spring it displays flat, lacy clusters of white flowers. In fall its maple-like leaves range from yellow to red-purple. This shrub reaches up to 15 ft. high and wide. The variety 'Compactum' grows 6 ft. tall. Hardy to -50°F.

A related shrub, similar in appearance, is the European cranberry bush, *V. opulus.*

Dwarf fothergilla graces the landscape in fall with a striking leaf mosaic in a rainbow of warm colors.

Cranberry cotoneaster *(Cotoneaster apiculatus)* is a low, wide-spreading shrub that reaches up to 3 ft. high and 3 to 6 ft. wide. Its dark, glossy green summer foliage turns shades of red or purple in fall. Its white or pinkish springtime flowers are followed by bright red berries that ripen in late summer and usually persist for several months. Hardy to -30°F.

Dwarf fothergilla *(Fothergilla gardenii)* is grown mainly for its intense yellow and orange-red fall foliage. In spring it bears brushlike clusters of honey-scented white flowers. These shrubs typically reach 2 to 3 ft. high with a 3-ft. spread.

F. major is a related species similar to *F. gardenii* but larger, up to 9 ft. tall. They both prefer acid soil. Hardy to -30°F.

SHRUBS FOR FALL COLOR *CONTINUED*

Firethorns *(Pyracantha)* are a group of shrubs practically unrivaled for their breathtaking fall fruit display. The large, dense clusters of pea-size fruits range from red to orange to yellow, depending on the species and variety. The size and shape of firethorns varies from sprawling ground covers to 18-ft. giants. Nearly all have needle-like thorns. Leaves are evergreen to semideciduous. Hardiness varies.

Fragrant sumac *(Rhus aromatica)* grows 3 to 5 ft. tall and sprawls much wider. Its attractive, 3-in. glossy green leaves release a fragrance when touched or crushed. The fall leaf color in orange, red and purple tones lasts for several weeks. The 'Gro-low' variety reaches only 2 ft. high and spreads 6 to 8 ft. Hardy to -40°F.

Heavenly bamboo *(Nandina domestica)* is a feathery, upright, 6- to 8-ft. shrub, but it can easily be kept smaller. It bears showy

Bronze-red foliage and red berries compete for attention on this 'Rose Glow' Japanese barberry.

white flowers in midsummer, followed by orange-red pea-sized fruit in fall. Its fine-textured foliage is a dark, glossy green in summer, reddish purple in fall and sometimes brilliant red in winter. The shrub is evergreen in all but the coldest part of its range. Low-growing varieties are available. Hardy to 0°F.

Japanese barberry *(Berberis thunbergii)* is a dense, rounded shrub with spiny branches up to 6 ft. high. Its small rounded leaves turn yellow, orange and red in fall. It has beadlike bright red berries from fall through winter. You can get varieties that have purplish foliage throughout the growing season, as well as dwarf forms. Hardy to -30°F.

Japanese maples *(Acer palmatum)* grow slowly to 20 ft. and may take the form of trees or multistemmed shrubs. Their delicate, deeply cut leaves grow 2 to 4 in. long. Typically, the young spring growth is red, the summer leaves are soft green and the fall foliage is scarlet, orange or yellow. Many varieties are available with a range of forms and leaf colors. Hardy to -20°F.

Summersweet's golden leaves electrify a fall landscape. The color develops in October and can remain for weeks.

Oakleaf hydrangea *(Hydrangea quercifolia)* is handsome in all seasons. Its two most outstanding features are large, showy, cone-shaped clusters of white flowers in early summer and bronze or crimson, 8-in. oaklike leaves in fall. It grows 4 to 6 ft. high with an equal or greater spread. Hardy to -20°F.

Purple Beautyberry *(Callicarpa dichotoma)* is known for its show-stopping fall display—clusters of ⅛-in. fruits in an unusual lilac-violet color. These graceful plants with arching branches reach 4 ft. tall and wider. *C. d. albifructus* is a white-fruited form. In cold-winter areas, they may freeze to the ground, but they come back from the roots. Hardy to -20°F.

Red chokeberry *(Aronia)* grows 6 to 8 ft. high and spreads 3 to 5 ft. wide. Bright red fruits develop in profusion along the branches in late summer and persist well into winter. Its fall leaf color is a bright red-purple that lasts for several weeks. Black chokeberry *(A. melanocarpa)* is similar, but the ripe fruit is black-ish purple. Hardy to -30°F.

Rugosa roses *(Rosa rugosa)* are vigorous, hardy shrub roses with prickly stems that grow 3 to 8 ft. high. Fragrant, 3- to 4-in. blossoms range from white to pink to deep purplish red. The fall payoff is a bright red tomato-shaped fruit, each an inch or more across. Hardy to -50°F.

Summersweet *(Clethra alnifolia)* grows 10 ft. tall with thin but strong vertical branches. Four- to 6-in.-long spires of tiny, fragrant white flowers bloom on the branch tips in summer. The 2- to 4-in. leaves turn yellow to golden in fall. Hardy to -40°F.

Winged euony-mus, also called burning bush *(Euonymus alata)*, is prized for its fiery red fall foliage. The plant grows 15 to 20 ft. high and wide. The variety 'Compacta' reaches 6 to 10 ft. high. Hardy to -30°F.

Winterberry *(Ilex verticillata)* bears generous crops of bright red fruit that ripen in fall and can last all winter. Plants grow 6 to 10 ft. tall with 3-in.-long oval leaves. 'Red Sprite' is a dwarf variety that reaches 4 ft. high. Hardy to -30°F.

The colorful orange highlights of witch hazel rise above the pinkish leaves of a 'Rose Glow' Japanese barberry.

Witch hazel *(Hamamelis intermedia)* grows to 15 ft. high with an equal or greater spread. Its spider-like winter flowers on bare stems range from yellow to orange to red. Depending on the variety, the fall foliage may be a single color or may combine yellow, orange and red on the same plant. Hardy to -20°F.

HOW TO SHOP FOR COLORFUL SHRUBS

Since leaf and fruit color can vary even within one type of plant, it's smart to shop for colorful plants when they're at their peak, so you can see them all and choose the ones that appeal to you the most.

When buying shrubs that have decorative fruit, remember that some plants make berries by themselves, but others need a pollinating plant. Each holly plant, for example, is either male or female. The females make the berries, but they usually need a male plant nearby. The nursery can tell you which plants will need a pollinator.

Also, when buying container plants, don't buy the biggest plants in the nursery. The biggest plants may be overgrown or root-bound—not the best. In most cases, a smaller, healthy plant will adapt to your garden more quickly and soon catch up in size to a larger plant.

HEDGES

Hedges can take many forms, depending on the purpose and style you have in mind. An informal hedge of flowering shrubs will add seasonal color, while a formal hedge of closely planted evergreens will form a dense privacy screen. Whatever kind of hedge you want, you can ensure lush, uniform growth by following proper planting and maintenance procedures.

Hedge plant choices generally fall into two groups: fast-growing and steady-growing. Fast-growing shrubs quickly form a solid hedge, but their rapid growth requires frequent pruning. Steady-growing shrubs require less frequent prunings, but take several years to grow into a solid wall.

Match your plants to your climate. Temperature, wind exposure, snow cover and soil type can influence hardiness. Also find out the plant's light and moisture needs and its mature size. A nursery professional or extension agent can help you sort this out.

Pick plants that are well suited to perform the function you have in mind when they reach maturity:

- Evergreens are the best choice for privacy since they stay dense all winter.
- To lure birds, plant an informal, fruit-yielding shrub, like firethorn.
- For a touch of color, choose plants with flowers, fruit or bright fall foliage.
- Hedges that grow less than 2 ft. high, such as lavender or germander, work best as edging for paths and casual plantings.
- Waist-high shrubs, such as informal nandina or clipped boxwood, can help separate and define gardens.
- Spiny-leafed holly or thorn-bearing plants, such as barberry and flowering quince, can discourage intruders when planted under windows.
- Arborvitae and hemlock grow to more than 6 ft., the perfect height to create a living wall or a windbreak.

Once you've made your choices, check a few local nurseries to compare prices and quality before you buy.

BELOW: *Flowering hedges like these roses provide a wall of seasonal color. They need less maintenance than evergreen hedges, and their thorny shrubs discourage intruders.*

PLANTING HEDGE SHRUBS

Proper planting is key to the success of a hedge. When you plant is also an important factor. In cold regions, plant container-grown shrubs in spring. In warm regions, plant them in early fall.

It's easy to plant hedges too close to walkways or boundaries so that they end up blocking paths or encroaching on a neighbor's yard. To avoid this, set the distance between the hedge and any boundary at half the shrub's mature width.

For a hedgerow, the space between plants should be about a quarter to a third of their mature height. For example, space 4-ft.-high plants 15 to 18 in. apart and 2-ft.-high plants 7 to 10 in. apart.

If you're planting large shrubs, dig individual holes, and follow the instructions for planting shrubs on page 245. However, if you're planting smaller shrubs that need to be placed close together, you may find it easier to dig a continuous trench. Begin as follows.

Step 1

Use stakes and string to outline a ditch that's as wide as the containers that hold the shrubs.

Step 2

Dig a planting trench that's an inch or two shorter than the root balls.

Step 3

Arrange the shrubs in the trench and gently spread their roots. From this point, follow the instructions on page 245.

Pruning and Maintenance

Pruning helps keep hedges healthy and dense all the way to the ground. Begin training the shrubs into a hedge by pruning them the first

A hedge's height at maturity helps to determine its function. Hemlock shrubs can reach 6 ft. or more; planted as a dense wall, they can block both strong winds and prying eyes.

year. Don't overprune the shrubs—cut no more than 2 in. from the last pruning.

You can start pruning as soon as the plants are in the ground. Here are some pruning tips:

- Cut back informal deciduous plants by a third, but don't top the plant. Instead, cut individual branches, following the plant's natural shape. Wait a full season before repruning.
- If formal deciduous hedges aren't bushy down to the base, prune to within 6 in. of the ground. This forces new stems to sprout very low on the plant. Wait a few months, then prune again lightly.
- Cut only the branch tips on needled evergreens. Usually the leader is left unpruned.
- The most important rule of shaping is to taper the hedge shrubs so that their bottoms are wider than their tops. This lets sunlight reach the lower

branches, which encourages uniform growth.

Since most hedge plants are closely spaced, their roots compete for water and nutrients. To keep them well fed, water and fertilize them regularly. (Apply a complete, slow-release fertilizer every spring.) Once the plants are well established, taper off the watering, especially with drought-tolerant shrubs.

QUICK TIPS

Heeling In Hedge Shrubs

If you can't plant your bare-root shrubs immediately, "heel" them in by digging a hole or trench for storage. Lean the plants at a 45-degree angle and cover the roots completely with soil. Keep them moist and don't leave them heeled in for more than three to four weeks.

*T*REES

Adding trees to your property can be a big investment, not only financially, but also in terms of the space you allocate, the time and effort involved in planting and maintaining it and the permanence of your decision once the tree is established. For all these reasons, it's important to choose the tree and its location carefully, so you'll both be satisfied for many years to come.

Choose the Right Tree

To find out which trees are best suited for your yard, educate yourself. Consult the best local gardening authorities you can find; these may include nursery staff, landscape architects or horticulturists at public gardens. With their help, answer these ten questions about any tree you're considering:

1. Does the tree thrive in your climate?
2. Will it get enough sun or shade in your yard?
3. Is your soil suitable?

4. When the tree is mature, will it fit the space without interfering with other features or neighboring yards?
5. Is the tree a favorite of animal pests that are common in your area, like deer or rabbits?
6. How long does the tree live? Some decorative flowering fruit trees live only ten to fifteen years, which means you may have to replace them eventually. Other trees live for generations.
7. Is the tree messy? Does it drop unacceptable amounts of leaves, twigs or fruits? You wouldn't want to plant an olive tree that will drop loads of juicy fruit onto a patio or entryway.
8. Do the roots mind their manners? Some tree roots aggressively seek out drainage and sewer lines, and others will buckle paving. Find out before you plant.
9. Are the branches strong, or do they tend to split or break apart? Trees with brittle wood, like locusts, are susceptible to storm damage.

LEFT: *This elegant front yard features several ash trees and a clump of river birch next to the front door.*

10. Does the tree require frequent pruning? Most trees require some pruning at first, but some need regular attention even once mature; others do not.

By getting the answers to these ten questions before you plant, you'll increase the chances that your trees will thrive and you'll be satisfied with the results.

Fertilizing a Tree

To determine if you need to fertilize your trees, have your soil tested. Bear in mind that trees growing on a fertilized lawn rarely need additional fertilizer—overfeeding is far more likely than underfeeding.

Soluble fertilizer can cause a spurt of rapid growth, and too much can harm a tree. Fast-growing, overfertilized trees can end up with small, inefficient root systems. Overfeeding also makes trees more susceptible to stress and pests. The lush growth of overfertilized trees actually invites certain pests, such as aphids and scale insects.

Planting a Tree

A properly dug planting hole is the best gift you can give a new tree, but soil preparation and technique are important as well. Here are some steps you can follow for planting a tree:

Step 1

Till or spade the soil over the entire planting site, which should be about five times as wide as the root ball. Remove all weeds and turf.

NAME THAT TREE

Perhaps you've noticed a neighbor's tree and imagined how nice it would look in your yard. How can you find out its name, so you can plant one, too? Start by asking your neighbor. The next step is to show a small branch to experts at a local nursery, botanical garden or extension service.

Another approach is to order the National Arbor Day Foundation's 70-page guide *What Tree Is That?* This inexpensive booklet details 135 trees common in the eastern and central U.S. Its step-by-step format makes identifying trees easy. Contact The National Arbor Day Foundation, 100 Arbor Ave., Member Services, Nebraska City, NE 68410; (402) 474-5655.

Step 2

Dig a hole in the center of the site. Make the bottom of the hole three times the width of the root ball. Slant the sides outward and leave a pedestal of undisturbed soil at the center of the hole, as shown.

Step 3

Don't add fertilizer or amendments to the hole or to the soil you use to fill it. If you do, the roots might not grow beyond the amended area.

Step 4

Place the tree on the pedestal, with the roots spread horizontally, rather than extending downward. Cut or pull apart any of the roots that

are closely surrounding or girdling the base of the stem. The tree should end up at the same level as it was growing in the nursery container. The one exception is heavy clay soil—here you should place the tree 1 in. higher than it was growing in the container.

Step 5

Fill soil snugly around the roots without tamping or compacting it. Once the tree is planted, gently water the entire planting site until it's fully soaked. Then spread pine straw or other organic mulch over the surface of the soil. To promote air circulation and discourage disease, keep the mulch away from the trunk of the tree.

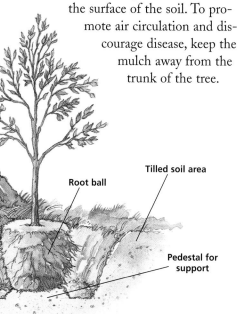

Normal soil level

Root ball

Tilled soil area

Pedestal for support

PRUNING TREES

Trees can add as much as 14 percent to the value of your property. They also reduce noise, trim air conditioning bills and fight soil erosion and air pollution—which is why mature trees can fetch from $1,000 to $10,000.

However, to protect that investment, sooner or later most trees will need pruning to maintain their appearance and health. Pruning makes trees healthier, safer and more attractive by strengthening their branch structure and eliminating any diseased or damaged limbs.

What's the right way to prune a tree? Although different trees require different techniques, there are some rules for pruning the ashes, birches, maples and other deciduous ornamental trees that grace many yards.

When to Prune a Tree

The best time to prune most deciduous trees is during late winter and early spring, when they're dormant. Dormant-season pruning encourages vigorous growth in the spring, and cuts seal rapidly once the tree starts growing. Pruning a leafless tree also makes it easy to see what you're cutting and simplifies cleanup.

Some trees, such as maple, birch, dogwood, elm and walnut, will ooze sap when pruned in late winter and early spring. Although this isn't as harmful as it sounds, you can minimize it by pruning these trees in late fall or early winter.

How much and how often you need to prune depends on the tree and how it grows. Some, such as

ginkgo and katsura, which have symmetrical growth patterns and grow at a moderate rate, need little or no pruning. Trees that grow more quickly need frequent attention because they may develop weak wood or have limbs with narrow V-shape crotches.

Making the Cut

The right cuts in the right places encourage desirable new growth along the trunk and branches. Properly made cuts also close quickly, discouraging rot and insect invasion. Likewise, the wrong cuts at the wrong points can weaken a

Risky Business

Some pruning jobs may put your safety or the health of the tree at risk. Call an arborist if you're faced with any of the following situations:

- A branch you need to remove is unreachable with a pole pruner.
- Storm damage has left heavy, broken limbs dangling in the tree top.
- Weak or split branches need to be stabilized with cabling or bracing.
- A branch near a power line needs to be removed.
- Specialized equipment, knowledge or experience are needed to restore a large tree.

To find a certified arborist in your community, contact the International Society of Arboriculture, P.O. Box 3129, Champaign, IL 61826; 217/355-9411; *www.ag.uiuc.edu/~isa.*

tree's structure, damage its bark and create large wounds that are slow to heal.

The illustration on the opposite page shows what to cut and why. Here's how to do it:

- When pruning dead wood, always cut back to healthy wood. Trim a healthy branch back to another healthy branch or a dormant bud. Also, when cutting to a bud, choose one that points outward. That way, the branch the bud produces will grow out from the trunk, rather than inward, where it will cross other branches.
- When cutting to another branch, position the thin cutting blade of the hand pruners or loppers closest to the branch that will remain on the tree. This method makes the resulting stubs as short as possible.
- Remove large limbs, water sprouts or suckers by cutting back to the trunk, another branch or the ground. This approach discourages new shoots and helps the remaining limbs grow stronger.
- When cutting a branch back to the main trunk, don't cut it flush. Instead, cut only up to the branch collar—the wrinkled or swollen area at the branch base. Otherwise, the wound will take longer to close, inviting insects and disease. Avoid tearing bark from the main trunk when removing large, heavy limbs by using the three-cut method shown on page 256, **How to Cut a Limb.**

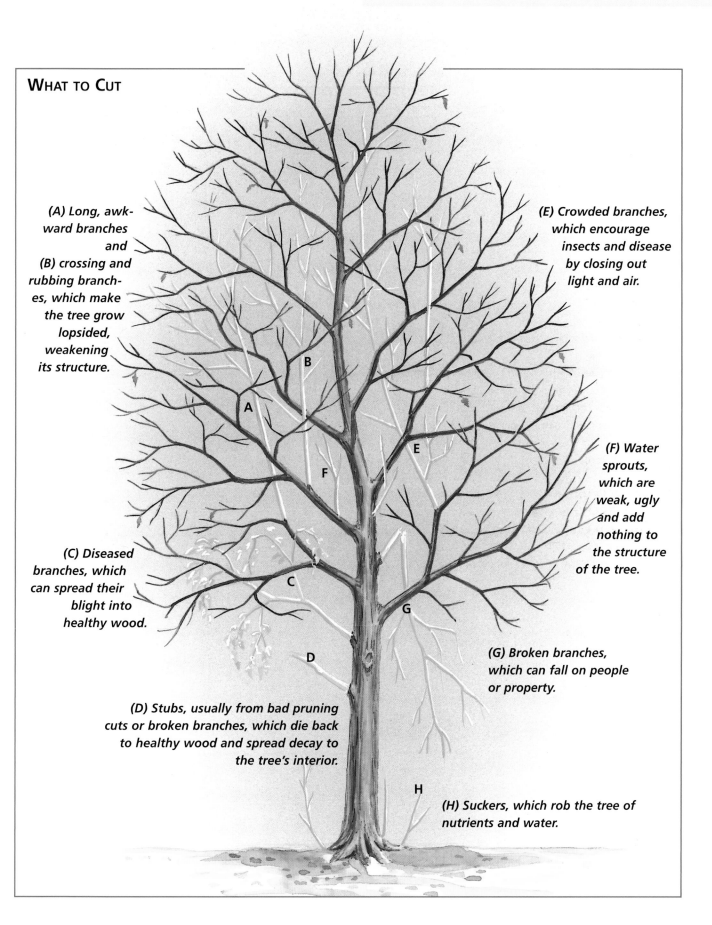

WHAT TO CUT

(A) Long, awkward branches and (B) crossing and rubbing branches, which make the tree grow lopsided, weakening its structure.

(E) Crowded branches, which encourage insects and disease by closing out light and air.

(F) Water sprouts, which are weak, ugly and add nothing to the structure of the tree.

(C) Diseased branches, which can spread their blight into healthy wood.

(G) Broken branches, which can fall on people or property.

(D) Stubs, usually from bad pruning cuts or broken branches, which die back to healthy wood and spread decay to the tree's interior.

(H) Suckers, which rob the tree of nutrients and water.

PRUNING TO A BUD

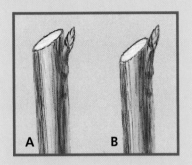

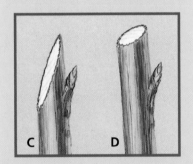

When pruning back to a bud, cut just above the bud. The cut should slope upward in the same direction as the bud (A). Incorrect cuts include those too close to the bud (B), too sloped (C) and too far away from the bud (D).

HOW TO CUT A LIMB

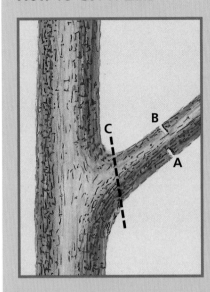 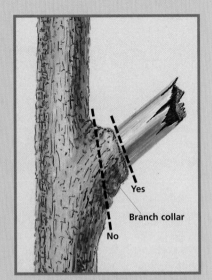

ABOVE LEFT: *This three-cut method will remove a heavy branch without damaging the tree. Using a pruning saw, make the first cut (A) 1 to 2 ft. out from the trunk. Cut from the bottom a third of the way through. Make the second cut (B) on top of the branch, about 1 in. farther out. The branch will break between the two cuts. Then make the third cut (C) just outside the branch collar.*

ABOVE RIGHT: *Remove a branch by cutting as close to the branch collar as possible without injuring it. Cutting into the collar enlarges the wound and promotes decay.*

4 MOST COMMON PRUNING MISTAKES

1 **Removing large parts of the treetop.** Known as topping, this makes trees ugly and unsafe, since the regrowth is weakly attached to the trunk. Topping can also kill a tree.

2 **Pruning too much.** Don't remove more than a quarter of a tree's live branches at one time, or more than a third in one year. Overcutting weakens a tree and tends to stimulate vigorous regrowth, which creates yet another big pruning job next year.

3 **Leaving stubs.** These are often the result of cutting too far from a dormant bud or another branch. Stubs die back, inviting decay and disease.

4 **Covering pruning wounds with paint, shellac or asphalt.** This once-common practice serves no purpose, and can damage a tree by holding in moisture and causing decay.

TRAINING YOUNG TREES

The best pruning method is one that prevents problems by shaping a tree while it's still young. Early pruning will promote a balanced, open branch structure and a healthy tree.

Prune lightly, if at all, at planting time and during the first year. At this time, remove only damaged branches and exposed roots. Prune more extensively during the next four to six years to gradually accentuate the tree's natural branching structure (see illustration). Most trees require a strong main stem, or leader, that extends up through the crown of the tree. Remove any vertical shoots that compete with the leader.

First Winter:

Remove only damaged growth or badly crossing branches in the upper part of the trunk. Shorten long side branches to about 1 ft. on the lower part, cutting back to their own side branches or to buds.

Second and Third Winters:

Remove any badly positioned or crossing branches in the upper part of the trunk. Shorten

but do not remove side branches on the lower trunk.

Fourth Winter:

Thin out any badly placed branches in the crown. Remove side branches from the trunk below the scaffold, or primary branches.

Central leader

Scaffold branch

REMOVING AN OLD TREE

Sometimes a tree or shrub has to go, no matter how much time or money you have put into it. There are five good reasons you might need to remove a tree or shrub:

1. It's a safety hazard. A diseased or dying tree might threaten your house or a neighbor's house, especially if it's losing branches. Although a declining tree could take years to die, it's best to remove it before it falls. If you're concerned about the health and safety of a tree, hire an arborist to evaluate whether it should be removed.

2. It's out of scale. If a tree or shrub is encroaching on your walkway or blocking the view from your living room, don't try to constantly trim it to correct the problem; remove it. This kind of pruning is a waste of time and can make the tree look unnatural and misshapen.

3. It's stunted. An improperly sited tree or shrub may survive, but it will rarely thrive. For example, a sun-loving shrub that's been planted in a shady spot will languish without blooming. If possible, relocate it to a sunnier location and plant a shade-tolerant shrub in its place.

4. It attracts pests. It's often more practical to eliminate a tree or shrub than to repeatedly use heavy applications of pesticides to keep it healthy. Replace the plant with one that's better suited to your climate and site.

5. It looks dated. Your yard, like the interior of your home, needs periodic updating and remodeling. An outdoor renovation might involve swapping old trees and shrubs for new ones. Here, it pays to hire a pro—in this case, a landscape designer or architect.

Specialty Gardens

Container gardens, shade gardens and water gardens are popular options for those who want to go beyond the boundaries of traditional landscaping.

Helpful Terms

Aquatic plants: Plants that grow in water or in containers that are set in the water.

Garden pond: A small decorative pond designed to support a water garden.

Potting mix: Growing medium for container plants; most mixes are lightweight and retain water well.

Shade tolerance: The degree of shade that a plant can tolerate and still flourish.

CONTAINER GARDENS

Container gardening is the quickest, simplest way to fill your yard with flowers, decorative foliage and even vegetables, shrubs and small trees. Even a single pot of red geraniums on a patio, deck or doorstep can brighten an otherwise drab space. Several containers grouped together in a staggered pattern can create an impression of depth and picturesque variety.

Container gardens are small, portable and versatile enough to be located virtually anywhere, even in unexpected spots, such as on stairs or pedestals and next to benches. Because the containers can be moved around, you can rearrange them to suit any mood or occasion.

Another benefit of gardening in containers is convenience. Buying young plants and growing them in pots is the perfect solution if you lack the time, space or soil quality required for conventional gardening. However, growing plants in containers isn't the same as growing them in the ground. For example, since container-grown plants can't spread out in search of water and nutrients, you need to provide these essentials on a regular basis.

Here are some tips for planting, watering and fertilizing container plants and selecting plants and containers.

Planting: The Right Soil

One of the most important aspects of planting in containers is selecting the medium that your plants will grow in. You don't want to use garden soil—it's too dense and holds too much water, which can drown or suffocate roots, and it's also likely to contain pests and diseases. Most container plants grow best in a lightweight, porous potting mix. It should hold water well yet allow any excess to drain off quickly.

There are lots of potting mediums on the market. When shopping, look for the word "professional" on labels of the mixes you're considering. This term is used to indicate the top-quality mix in the product line.

Potting mediums include both soil-based and soilless mixes. Since soilless mixes weigh less, they're the best choice for raised and hanging planters that might otherwise be too heavy to install, or for large containers that you may want to move around.

A good soil-based mix has to drain efficiently, yet hold moisture well.

Combining equal parts of packaged garden soil, compost or peat moss, and vermiculite (which improves soil aeration) creates a well-balanced medium for general planting. If the plants you've chosen like to keep their roots dry, substitute sand or perlite for the vermiculite.

You can ask the staff at your nursery for their favorite potting mix. If you want to concoct your own, start with a packaged mix that contains peat moss and vermiculite or perlite, then blend in an equal amount of packaged topsoil. Another option is to combine equal parts packaged topsoil, milled peat moss and perlite.

CONTAINER GARDENS *CONTINUED*

Watering

Since container gardens lose moisture faster than in-ground plantings, they must be watered more frequently. In hot, windy weather you may need to water once a day or more.

Check the soil with your finger; the soil should remain moist just below the surface. Each time you water, saturate the container—keep adding water until it begins to flow out the drainage holes. Here are some tips and techniques that can make your container watering chores easier and less frequent:

• Use a self-watering plastic container with a reservoir—a well at the bottom that roots can draw moisture from without drowning. These devices reduce the frequency of watering and prevent overwatering at the same time.

• Use nonporous containers, such as glazed pottery; they retain moisture longer than porous containers. If you do use a porous container, such as a wicker basket, line it with perforated plastic.

• If you water your pots with a hose, use a watering wand to reach hanging containers more easily. Use a nozzle with a fine spray to avoid dislodging the potting medium.

• Use a drip irrigation system to water several containers efficiently. Add an automatic timer to make watering even easier.

• Group containers close together so they shield each other from drying sun and wind; this will slow moisture loss.

• Mulch large containers to slow moisture loss. Use chipped or shredded bark or other organic materials that allow the soil to breathe (see **Mulching**, pages 194-195).

• When planting, blend water-retaining polymers into the potting medium; this will give you extra time between watering sessions.

This cheerful grouping of bougainvillea (in hanging basket) and geraniums, marigolds and decorative greens (in pots) brightens the entryway of a house.

Fertilizing

The frequent watering that container plants require also washes nutrients out of the potting medium, making it essential to add fertilizer. There are two ways to fertilize container plants. Either method will work, but don't do both—overfeeding your plants can kill them.

The first approach is to blend a timed-release fertilizer into the potting mix before planting. A single application of timed-release fertilizer can feed plants for up to nine months. The second approach is to fertilize weekly with a water-soluble fertilizer diluted to half its recommended strength.

A picnic basket filled with favorite annuals makes a unique planting container. Plant the flowers in pots, and place a dish on the bottom of the basket to catch any water seepage. The blooms in this picnic basket are yellow marigolds and deep pink moss roses.

Choosing and Combining Plants

For a simple effect, try a few pots of easy-to-grow annuals, and use one plant per pot. However, a mixture of plants will give you far more room for creative experimentation. Here are some tips that can help you combine plants successfully:

• **Combine plants with similar requirements**. For example, alyssum, coleus, lobelia and impatiens all thrive in light shade, while celosia, petunia and verbena all love the sun.

• **Stagger plant heights**. Place taller plants in the middle or back of the pot and shorter or cascading plants at the edge of the container. The result will be a full, rounded bouquet.

• **Space plants closer than in open ground**. For example, place annuals 4 in. apart or even closer in an 18-in. container. This will force plants to grow upward and outward.

• **Include foliage plants**. Caladium, sweet potato vine and coleus offer color, while ferns, ivy, variegated vinca and ornamental grasses offer interesting forms and textures.

• **Repeat colors**. Use a simple color scheme. For example, an attractive combination for a shady porch might be white-flowering wax begonias, white-flowering New Guinea impatiens and white variegated caladium.

ABOVE: *Container gardening isn't just for flowers and decorative foliage. Some small trees, such as this dwarf crab apple, also thrive in pots.*

LEFT: *This cheerful planting features yellow coreopsis, orange marigolds, purple lobelia and white sweet alyssum.*

CONTAINER GARDENS *CONTINUED*

CHOOSING PLANTING CONTAINERS

When choosing a planting container, aim to complement your plants and the style and materials of your landscape design. Make sure that every pot provides room for roots and good drainage—check for drainage holes. If the pot lacks them, drill them yourself, or plant in a pot that has drainage holes and fit it inside a larger pot without drainage. You can also raise pots on bricks, blocks or decorative "pot feet" to further improve drainage and air circulation. If you're placing the containers on a wood deck, put trays under the pots to protect the deck from water drainage.

Here are some of the many container choices you're likely to find in garden centers and mail-order catalogs.

1. Wine barrels. Oak wine barrels are attractive and make excellent plant containers. Their main drawback is that a 35-gal. half-barrel can be tough to move once it's filled with plants and wet soil.

2. Plastic window boxes. Self-watering plastic window boxes come in various sizes and are durable and lightweight. They're made of nonporous plastic that retains soil moisture well.

3. Polyurethane planters. Polyurethane planters are available in many styles. (The one shown resembles sandstone but weighs 90 percent less.) They resist chipping and tolerate freezing temperatures well.

4. Clay pots. These traditional containers offer a natural, understated look that fits nearly all garden settings. But unglazed clay pots are porous and breakable. Sizes and prices vary considerably.

5. Bronze-imbedded fiberglass planters. These bronze-imbedded fiberglass planters develop a rich verdigris patina as they age. Like plastic, they're lightweight, durable and nonporous.

2. Plastic window box

1. Wine barrel

5. Bronze-imbedded fiberglass planter

3. Polyurethane planter

4. Clay pots

How to Plant a Container Garden

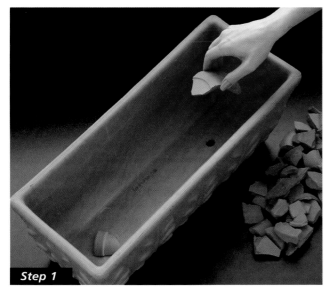

Step 1

Step 1
Place pieces of broken pottery in the bottom of the container so that they arch over each drainage hole. This will help prevent soil from washing out of the hole.

Step 2
Place a layer of potting medium on the bottom of the container. With the plants still in their containers, test-fit them to finalize the arrangement and spacing.

Step 3
Set the plants in position and surround them with potting mix; their root balls should be ½ to 1 in. below the rim of the container. Fill in all the remaining space with the potting mix. Press it gently in place with your hands to eliminate air pockets.

Step 3

Materials
- **Planting container**
- **Potting medium (see page 259)**
- **Pottery shards**
- **Plants**
- **Sheet moss or mulch (optional)**
- **Saucer or tray (if pot will be on a wood surface)**

Step 4
Cover the soil with a layer of moss or mulch to help retain moisture. Water thoroughly. Place the container outdoors in the shade for a few days, to help the plants recover from transplanting. If the container will be placed on a wood surface, put a saucer or tray beneath it.

CONTAINER GARDENS *CONTINUED*

MOSS HANGING BASKET

Hanging planters are an excellent way to add color without taking up ground space, and some of the most attractive hanging containers are wire basket frames lined with sphagnum moss. The wire frame allows you to plant flowers not only on top of the basket, but also along its sides. As the plants grow, they cover the wires, creating an unusually lush, full appearance. Although this kind of basket can be challenging to create and maintain, your efforts will pay off in a strikingly beautiful addition to your yard.

In selecting plants for a hanging basket, choose a combination of bushy and trailing plants that complement each other. The basket project shown here uses pansies, ivy geraniums and vinca in pink and purple tones.

Key	Materials	Color/Size	Qty
A)	Ivy Geranium	Pink	5
B)	Pansy	Purple	7
C)	Vinca major	Green	3
	Hanging wire basket	12" dia.	1
	Sheet sphagnum moss		1 sq. yd.
	Plastic 2 mil thick		2½ sq. ft.
	Sterile potting mix		4 lb.

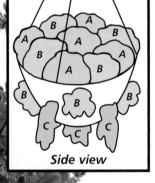

Side view

PANSIES provide colorful blooms throughout the summer.

VINCA is a trailing vine with smooth green leaves. Some kinds are variegated, with pale green and yellow leaves. They trail nicely out of the basket, giving it a fuller appearance.

IVY GERANIUMS have colorful flowers that bloom all summer and attractive leaves that add an interesting texture to the arrangement.

How to Create a Moss Hanging Basket

Step 1

Step 2

Step 3

Step 1

A. Cover the wire basket with dry sphagnum moss. Lay a large piece over the bottom first, then tear off smaller pieces to fit along the sides, overlapping the bottom piece and extending to the top of the basket.

B. Line the moss with plastic. Working from inside, make small drainage slits through the bottom of the lining. Next, cut X-shaped planting slits in the sides of the lining. Fill the basket with soil up to the bottom of the slits. Secure a hanging wire or chains to the basket.

Step 2

A. Loosely wrap a piece of plastic around the vinca and pansies that you'll be inserting in the sides of the basket. This will make it easier to pull them through the planting slits.

B. Working from the inside, thread the wrapped plants through the slits. Pull away the plastic wrap and carefully spread the roots apart, inside the basket. Fill the basket halfway with potting mix.

Step 3

A. Arrange the geraniums and pansies in the top of the basket, working from the outer rim toward the center. Distribute them evenly so the finished basket will hang level. Fill the basket with potting mix, leaving ½ in. at the top.

B. Cover the soil surface between the plants with sphagnum moss, to improve moisture retention between waterings. Hang the basket from a wall bracket or ceiling hook in the desired location. Water it thoroughly.

MAINTAINING A MOSS HANGING BASKET

Like other container plantings, hanging baskets need frequent watering and feeding. Although the plastic liner between the moss and the potting mix helps retain moisture, it's still important to check the basket daily and water it whenever the soil feels dry to the touch. However, also avoid overwatering; the plants will suffer if the soil becomes waterlogged. Feed the basket by adding a slow-release fertilizer to the potting mix when preparing the basket or by applying a diluted solution of water-soluble fertilizer each time you water the plants.

To promote flower production and dense foliage, pinch back the plants regularly. Trim off any dead flowers and leaves as they appear as well as any excessive growth.

In the fall, bring the basket indoors and leave it in a sunny window for the winter. If you prefer, you can compost the plants and potting mix and save the moss and basket to reuse next year.

SHADE GARDENS

If you're like most homeowners, you have a shady area somewhere in your yard that will support only a sparse lawn. However, shade gardening means far more than dealing with intractable lawn grass. Plants that flourish in low light conditions can transform a shady spot into a landscaping showcase—a cool, lush retreat in which to kick back and relax on even the hottest days.

Landscaping in the shade isn't the same as landscaping in sunny areas. Here are some tips that can help you create a shade garden that you'll be proud to display.

Adding Light

Start by making sure you're taking full advantage of all the light you can get. Overgrown trees are the most obvious barriers to sunlight. You can often prune a tree to let more light through without risking either its health or its appearance. For example, removing just a few lower limbs can let in a lot more light. Another option is to thin the tree canopy by selectively removing branches. This job is best done by a licensed arborist, who will know how to improve the form of the tree in the process of thinning it. Never cut off the top of a tree—this looks bad, harms the tree and stimulates weak growth that can create more shade than you had before.

Living with Tree Roots

Shade trees often have large surface roots. In addition to getting in the way of planting, these roots starve smaller plants by depleting the surrounding soil of water and nutrients. Don't dig out the offending roots or bury them deep and plant over them—both of these options may kill the tree. Two safer solutions are:

Plant in Containers

Plant annuals, perennials or shrubs in containers and provide the water and nutrients they need (see **Container Gardens**, pages 259-265).

Plant Between Roots

You can avoid digging into surface tree roots by planting pockets of ground-hugging, shallow-rooted plants between the roots of a large tree (see photo above). Since these plants will be competing with the tree's roots for water in shallow soil, you may need to water them more frequently than you would otherwise.

Surface tree roots can create a maze of planting pockets for primroses and other shallow-rooted plants.

Help Shade Plants Grow

Here are some more tips that can help your shade garden flourish:

Improve Air Circulation

The moist soil and reduced air movement found in shady spots invite molds and fungus. Space plants farther apart than you would in the sun to ensure air circulation and reduce competition for light and nutrients.

Water as Needed

Since shaded soil stays moist longer than soil exposed to direct sunlight, some shade gardens will need to be watered less frequently—in fact, too much moisture will lead to disease. However, shady spots may also be dry, especially if a building or tree canopy is blocking rainwater or trees are drawing water from the soil. In dry shade conditions, give plants plenty of water.

Add Organic Matter

Many shade-loving plants are native forest dwellers that like light, airy soil—and you can help them thrive by mimicking a forest floor: Before planting, work compost or rotted manure into the top 4 to 6 in. of the soil. After planting, lay down a 2- to 3-in. layer of pine needle or shredded leaf mulch. As the mulch decays it will also enrich the soil (see **Mulching**, pages 194-195).

PICKING PLANTS FOR SHADE GARDENS

Not all shade is the same, and different plants will tolerate different types and levels of shade. For example, lawn grass will tolerate filtered shade but will die in the heavy shade cast by a dense tree canopy. Some perennials, on the other hand, will flourish in these conditions. But in general, the deeper the shade, the fewer the plants that will thrive in the area.

A plant's shade tolerance also varies with the climate and site conditions. For example, a plant that needs full sun in cool northern regions might tolerate, or even require, afternoon shade in a more southerly area.

Refer to the chart below for some suggested shade plants. The plants are listed alphabetically by their common names, followed by their botanical names. For perennials, shrubs and trees, the chart also notes the minimum winter temperature that the plant can tolerate, and whether it is deciduous (D) or evergreen (E). Also, check with your local extension service or nursery to confirm which plants are best for your region and growing conditions.

PLANTS FOR SHADE			
Annuals	**Perennials**	**Shrubs**	**Trees**
These plants can quickly brighten a shady garden with colorful flowers or foliage. They complete their life cycle in one year and then die.	These shade-loving perennials offer interesting flowers or foliage and return every year.	These plants form the backbone of a shade garden, giving it structure and stature.	These small trees (under 40 ft.) can grow beneath a thin canopy of tall trees. They add interest to a shade garden by providing varying heights.
Amethyst flower (*Browallia*)	Bleeding heart (*Dicentra spectabilis*): -35°	Camellia (*Camellia japonica*): 10° (most); E	Cornelian cherry (*Cornus mas*): -30°; D
Black-eyed Susan vine (*Thunbergia alata*)	Caladium (*Caladium bicolor*): frost tender	Daphne (*Daphne*): hardness varies; D and E	Eastern redbud (*Cercis canadensis*): -20°; D
Coleus (*Coleus*)	Coral bells (*Heuchera sanguinea*): -40°	Holly (*Ilex*): hardiness varies; D and E	Flowering dogwood (*Cornus florida*): -20°, D
Forget-me-not (*Myosotis sylvatica*)	Columbine (*Aquilegia*): hardiness varies	Hydrangea (*Hydrangea*): hardiness varies; D	Japanese maple (*Acer palmatum*): -20°; D
Impatiens (*Impatiens wallerana*)	False spirea (*Astilbe*): -25°	Kerria (*Kerria japonica*): -20°, D	Katsura tree (*Cercidiphyllum japonicum*): -30°; D
Lobelia (*Lobelia erinus*)	Globeflower (*Trollius*): -30°	Mountain laural (*Kalmia latifolia*): -20°; E	Serviceberry (*Amelanchier*): hardiness varies; D
Love-in-a-mist (*Nigella damascena*)	Hosta (*Hosta*): -35°	Pieris (*Pieris*): hardiness varies; E	Silverbell (*Halesia*): -20°; D
Nicotiana (*Nicotiana alata*)	Japanese painted fern (*Athyrium*): -35°	Rhododendron, azalea (*Rhododendron*): hardiness varies; D and E	
Pansy (*Viola wittrockiana*)	Lady's mantle (*Alchemilla mollis*): -40°	Viburnum (*Viburnum*): hardiness varies; D and E	
Scarlet sage (*Salvia splendens*)	Lenten rose (*Helleborus*): hardiness varies	Witch hazel (*Hamamelis*): hardiness varies; D	
Wishbone flower (*Torenia fournieri*)	Lungwort (*Pulmonaria*): -35°		
	Meadow rue (*Thalictrum*): -20°		
	Primrose (*Primula*): hardiness varies		
	Virginia bluebells (*Mertensia virginica*): -40°		

Water Gardens

A water garden can be a refreshing retreat from the stresses of the world, whether it's a simple tub on a patio or a lavish in-ground pond with plants, bubbling fountains and darting goldfish. Water gardening is popular because it delivers something many people are looking for: a beautiful place to relax without the maintenance required by a lawn or flower garden. There's no need for hoeing, mowing or raking. All you need to do is start right, sit back and let nature do its thing.

You can put in a garden pond any time, as long as the ground isn't frozen or overly wet. Generally speaking, you can dig and install an average pond in a weekend, but it will take additional time to landscape it properly.

Selecting a Site

For a successful garden pond, you need to select the right site. Although the pond will naturally become a focal point in your yard, it should also blend in with its surroundings. Unless you're planning a secluded garden oasis, locate the pond near an existing deck or patio where you can relax and enjoy it. You can also consider putting a water garden in a spot where nothing else seems to grow.

Select a level site. Sloping ground requires a lot of digging and isn't a natural setting for a pond. Also, don't build a water garden directly under overhanging trees, since falling leaves and other debris will foul the water and tree roots may make excavation difficult.

Look for a sunny location with good drainage, since aquatic plants bloom best if they have six to eight hours of direct sunlight each day. Avoid low-lying areas where runoff may flow into the pond. If possible, locate the pond next to a hedge or building that will provide some shelter from the wind.

LEFT: *The sound of splashing water masks unwanted neigborhood noises from beyond this serene garden retreat.*

For an informal, natural-looking pond, use a variety of colors and textures, including stone, water lilies, upright plants and goldfish.

The pond should be within garden-hose length of a spigot so you can fill it easily, and electrical service must be available nearby to power the pond's pump, filtration systems and lighting fixtures. (Outdoor outlets that operate electrical devices near water must be equipped with a ground-fault circuit-interrupter.)

Don't forget to check your local building code for any regulations about the size and depth of the pond and whether you need a fence around it. You may be able to avoid building a fence if the pond is less than a certain depth.

Planning the Pond

The next step is to choose a style, design and size. For example, do you want a formal water garden or an informal one? Formal ponds are usually large, formed in simple geometric shapes, bordered in stone, brick or cement and located near a garden wall or terrace.

Informal ponds can be any size. Their shape is usually free-form and designed to look like part of the natural landscape. They may feature native plants and an edging of rocks or fieldstone.

Next, consider whether you want fish in your pond. For goldfish, you'll need at least 18 in. of water (some fish require deeper water). In cold climates, ponds usually need a deep end (perhaps 24 in. in an 18-in. pond) to create a place for the fish to hibernate in winter. You'll also need to use a liner that's rated "fish grade."

Plants don't require as much water as fish. Water lilies need about 6 to

WATER ACCENTS IN YOUR GARDEN

If a full-scale garden pond isn't practical in your yard, you can use small accent pools to echo the tranquil, relaxing atmosphere of a bigger pond.

Small accent pools can be as simple as a birdbath, a barrel planter or a vinyl tub that you convert into a water garden. Position these mini-ponds in featured spots in the garden, along a path or near a bench.

Barrel planters are available at lawn and garden stores. Depending on the kind of barrel, you may need to make it watertight. Cypress, cedar and redwood barrels with tongue-and-groove construction are self-sealing. All you have to do is fill them with water until the wood swells, which creates a watertight seal. This usually takes about 24 hours.

Vintage whiskey barrels, usually made of white oak, can also be used for water gardens and they're self-sealing as well. However, you'll need to scrub and rinse the interior well to remove any acids or alcohol before you add water or plants.

Other barrels can be made watertight either by lining them with heavy-duty plastic sheeting secured with staples or by sealing the seams with a marine-grade sealant and letting it cure for a few days.

For a larger garden, use a vinyl tub and construct a simple surround for it with dimensional cedar lumber. Large all-purpose tubs are available at home supply stores. Cedar lumber is rough on one side and finished on the other; you can use either side on the outside.

Finally, fill your mini-pond with a pleasing arangement of water-loving plants, such as water iris or water lilies.

WATER GARDENS *CONTINUED*

8 in. of water above their roots. Floating plants like duckweed and water hyacinth don't need even that much.

If your pond will be on the small side (less than 1,000 gals.), figure that plants will cover about 70 percent of the water surface. Larger ponds will be closer to 50 percent.

When deciding on the size of your pond, remember that you'll need to have a border around the perimeter. Because of this, the completed pond will probably look smaller than you expected. In fact, the biggest complaint that pond experts hear is "I made my pond too small." Make your pond as large as possible, considering your yard and budget. You can do much more with a larger pond, and a larger pond can

actually be easier to maintain than a smaller pond.

Choosing a Liner

Modern materials have greatly simplified pond building and made it more affordable. Do-it-yourself kits are readily available at home centers and gardening specialty shops.

There are two kinds of pond kits: those with flexible liners and those with rigid liners. When you use a flexible pond liner, your range of designs is unlimited; when you use a preformed liner, you must use one of the available sizes and shapes.

A flexible liner is basically a sheet of strong plastic that is used to line the pond excavation. Flexible liners made from polyvinyl chloride

(PVC) are economical, but they can become brittle in just a few years. Rubber liners often are a better choice. Although they're more costly, the added durability is worth it.

A rigid liner is a preformed fiberglass tub you place in the ground. Rigid liners are very easy to install but generally more expensive than the flexible type. Furthermore, they may crack in very cold weather.

A typical pond kit, including a flexible liner, pump, filter and a small fountain, may cost as little as $300. Adding fish, plantings or special effects like waterfalls can push the cost to between $500 and $700. The costs vary depending on the size and the type of the liner and accessories you choose.

. . . .

How to Install a Garden Pond with a Flexible Liner

You can design a garden pond that's as simple or as lavish as you like. Here's one that can be installed in a weekend. (For instructions on adding plants and fish, see **Adding Plants, Fish and Snails**, page 272.)

Step 1

A. Outline the pond with a hose or a heavy rope. For a natural look, avoid sharp angles, corners and symmetrical shapes. The pond should have at least 15 sq. ft. of surface area and be at least 18 in. deep.

B. Excavate the pond to a depth of about 1 ft. Dig the sides of the pond so they slope slightly toward the center. Excavate the center of the pond to its maximum depth plus 2 in. Leave a 1-ft.-wide shelf inside the perimeter to hold aquatic planters. The pond bed should be flat, and the walls should slope downward from the shelf.

Step 2

A. Lay a straight board across the pond and place a carpenter's level on it. Check all the sides to make sure the edges are level. If not, adjust the surrounding ground by digging, filling and packing soil until it's level.

Step 1

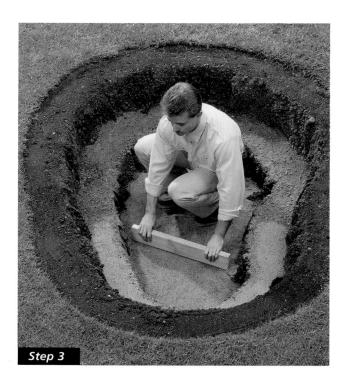

Step 3

Step 4

B. Once the excavation is completed and the site is level, dig a shallow bed around the perimeter of the pond to hold the border flagstones (coping stones).

Step 3

Remove all stones, roots and sharp objects from the bed of the pond and smooth out the soil base. Next, spread a 2-in. layer of wet sand on the level area of the pond bed. Pack the sand with a tamper, then smooth it with a length of 2×4.

Step 4

Place the flexible liner in the pond bed, folding and tucking it so it conforms to the shape of the hole. Smooth the liner as much as possible, avoiding any sharp creases. Set a few stones on the overhang to hold the liner in place. Too many stones will cause the liner to stretch rather than settle into the hole when it's filled with water.

Step 5

Fill the pond up to the top with water. Smooth out any large creases or wrinkles that develop as the water level rises. Remove the holding stones after the pond is full, and allow the liner to settle for a day. Using scissors, trim the liner so it overhangs the edges of the pond by about 1 ft. all around the perimeter.

Step 6

Spread a mixture of 20 parts sand and one part dry mortar in a shallow layer on top of the liner overhang and spray it with a light mist. Set the coping stones into the sand so they overhang the edge of the pond by about 2 in. Position one of the stones so that it's ½ in. lower than the rest, to serve as an overflow point for excess water.

Step 6

Water Gardens *continued*

The right mixture of aquatic plants, fish and snails will keep your garden pond ecosystem healthy and attractive.

fish waste and decaying plants, and turn it into the oxygen that's essential for fish. Add one pot of submerged plants for every 1 to 2 sq. ft. of pond surface. Our 5 × 10-ft. sample pond would hold 25 to 50 pots of submerged plants (six stems to a pot).

Upright Bog Plants

This group includes ornamental grasses and rushes as well as plants with showy flowers, such as water iris and pickerel rush. They all grow in damp soil or shallow water and most grow in soil-filled containers, which you raise to the right height on bricks, large stones or cinder blocks. Use about one pot of upright plants for every 10 sq. ft. of pond surface. Our 5 × 10-ft. sample pond would hold about five containers of upright plants (three plants to a container).

ADDING PLANTS, FISH AND SNAILS

The right combination of plants, fish and snails will do more than add life and beauty to your pond—these life forms are essential for maintaining the pond's water clarity and ecological balance.

Buy plants and fish at specialty stores where the staff is knowledgeable about garden ponds. When buying plants, check their hardiness. For example, water lilies can be frost-tender or winter-hardy, depending on the species. And like land plants, certain aquatic plants are invasive and even banned in some areas.

Start with plants from each of the three basic plant groups—submerged plants, floating plants and upright plants.

Floating Plants

This group includes water lilies (*Nymphaea*) and water clover (*Marsilea mutica*). These plants shade the pond's surface and keep the water cool. Some have roots submerged in soil; others have roots that dangle in the water. Their leaves should cover no more than a third of the water surface. For example, a 5 × 10-ft. pond might hold three to five water lilies.

Submerged Plants

The workhorses of this group are *Egeria* (also known as *Elodea* and *Anacharis*) and *Cabomba*. They help control algae and consume carbon dioxide and nitrogen from

Night-blooming tropical water lilies, like this 'Texas Shell Pink', open at dusk and remain open until late morning.

Fish

Add goldfish at least one week after you add the plants. Fish are an important addition to the pond; besides charming the eye, they help maintain the ecological balance of the pond and consume pests such as mosquito larvae. However, don't overdo it. Too many fish is the most common cause of murky water. You want to stock up to about 1 in. of fish per 5 gals. of water. This would be about thirty-five 4-in.-long fish for a 24-in.-deep 5 × 10-ft. pond (roughly 700 gals.).

If you simply let fish feed naturally, they won't grow or reproduce very well. It's a good idea to feed them daily; give them as much food as they can eat in 5 to 10 minutes. That way, they'll get enough nutrition, but they'll still eat enough to keep the pond clean. Stop feeding when the water temperature drops below 40° to 45°F.

Snails

Garden ponds also need snails, which scavenge algae and decaying matter from plants and containers. Add one black Japanese water snail for every 1 to 2 sq. ft. of surface area, or 25 snails for a 50-sq.-ft. pond.

Once you've stocked the pond, don't be alarmed if the water turns a murky green. New ponds typically go through a murky stage that may take four to six weeks to clear.

A hardy bog plant, pickerel rush grows to 30 in. tall.

Garden Pond Maintenance Tips

Make containers for aquatic plants by drilling 1-in. holes in plastic planters and lining them with landscape fabric. The holes allow water to circulate past the roots of the plants.

Replenish pond water regularly, especially during hot, dry weather. Rainwater is preferable to tap water, especially if the pond is stocked with fish. Collect rainwater in a barrel or let tap water sit for at least three days before adding it to the pond.

Use chemicals sparingly. Little maintenance other than a yearly cleaning is needed for well-balanced ponds.

Water-quality problems, like algae buildup, can be treated with diluted chemical products sold in pet stores.

Fish, hardy lilies and other plants become dormant in winter. Ice is a problem because it forms a seal over the water, cutting off their oxygen supply. A pond de-icer is a worthwhile purchase that can protect your pond investment.

Bring plants indoors if your pond freezes for more than a week or two during the winter. Cut back plant stems and store dormant plants in a dry, dark location.

Bring pond plants indoors in winter.

Gardening Resources

Want to learn more? Supplement the gardening information in this book with these additional resources, which include mail-order catalogs, books, web sites and extension agents.

CATALOGS

Almost everyone finds a seed catalog in the mail occasionally, but many people have no idea how many mail-order catalogs there really are.

Landscaping catalogs fall into four categories: seeds, plants & bulbs, water gardens and tools & supplies. Most of the catalogs are free, and companies that do charge often refund the money with your first order. Here's a selection of what we think are some of the best mail-order landscaping catalogs—all free, unless otherwise noted.

Plants and Bulbs

A growing number of catalogs now offer garden-ready starter plants as well as seed. Most mail-order nurseries focus on permanent landscape plants, especially perennials.

Antique Rose Emporium
9300 Lueckemeyer Rd.
Brenham, TX 77833
800/441-0002; fax: 409/836-0928
www.garden.com
Short catalog: free; more detailed: $5.

Busse Gardens
5873 Oliver Ave. SW
Cokato, MN 55321-4229
800/544-3192; 320/286-2654
fax: 320/286-6601
bussegardens@cmgate.com
Catalog: $2.

Carroll Gardens
444 East Main St.
Westminster, MD 21157
800/638-6334; fax: 410/876-7336
Catalog: $3.

Forestfarm
990 Tetherow Rd.
Williams, OR 97544-9599
541/846-7269; fax: 541/846-6963
www.forestfarm.com
Catalog: $4.

Heronswood Nursery, Ltd.
7530 N.E. 288th St.
Kingston, WA 98346
360/297-4172; fax: 360/297-8321
www.heronswood.com
Catalog: $5.

John Scheepers
23 Tulip Dr.
Bantam, CT 06750
860/567-0838; fax: 860/567-5323
www.johnscheepers.com
Catalog: free

Klehm Nursery
4210 N. Duncan Rd.
Champaign, IL 61821
800/553-3715; fax: 217/373-8403
www.klehm.com
Catalog: free or $4 (refundable)

Mellinger's, Inc.
2310 W. South Range Rd.
North Lima, OH 44452
800/321-7444; fax: 330/549-3716
www.mellingers.com
Catalog: free

Santa Barbara Heirloom Seedling Nursery
Box 4235
Santa Barbara, CA 93140
805/968-5444; fax: 805/562-1248
www.heirloom.com/heirloom/
Catalog: $1, refundable

Spring Hill Nurseries
6523 N. Galena Rd.
Peoria, IL 61656
800/582-8527; fax: 800/991-2852
Catalog: free

Stark Brothers Nurseries
Box 10, Hwy. 54 W
Louisiana, MO 63353
800/325-4180; fax: 573/754-5290
www.starkbros.com
Catalog: free

Wayside Gardens
1 Garden Lane
Hodges, SC 29695-0001
800/845-1124; fax: 800/457-9712
www.waysidegardens.com
Catalog: free

White Flower Farm
Box 50
Litchfield, CT 06759-0050
800/503-9624; 860/496-9600
fax: 860/496-1418
www.whiteflowerfarm.com
Catalog: free

Seeds

Planting from seed allows you to choose from many varieties available in seed catalogs. Some specialize by type of plant; others by region.

W. Atlee Burpee & Co.
300 Park Ave.
Warminster, PA 18974
800/333-5808; fax: 800/487-5530
http://garden.burpee.com (catalog)
Catalog: free

The Cook's Garden
Box 535
Londonderry, VT 05148
800/457-9703
fax: 800/457-9705
www.cooksgarden.com
Catalog: free

Johnny's Selected Seeds
Foss Hill Rd.
Albion, ME 04910
207/437-4301; fax: 207/437-2165
www.johnnyseeds.com
Catalog: free

Park Seed Company
Cokesbury Rd.
Greenwood, SC 29647-0001
800/845-3369; fax: 800/275-9941
www.parkseed.com
Catalog: free

Shepherd's Garden Seeds
30 Irene St.
Torrington, CT 06790
860/482-3638; fax: 860/482-0532
www.shepherdseeds.com
Catalog: free

Southern Exposure Seed Exchange
Box 170
Earlysville, VA 22936
804/973-4703; fax: 804/973-8717
www.southernexposure.com
Catalog: $2.

Territorial Seed Company
20 Palmer Ave.
Cottage Grove, OR 97424
541/942-9547; fax: 888/657-3131
www.territorial/seed.com
Catalog: free

Tools and Supplies

The catalogs in this group range from upscale garden boutiques to basic suppliers who sell to farmers, landscapers and homeowners.

Earthmade Products
Box 609
Jasper, IN 47547-0609
800/843-1819; fax: 800/817-8251
www.earthmade.com
Catalog: free

Gardener's Supply Company Watering Guide
128 Intervale Rd.
Burlington, VT 05401
800/955-3370; fax: 800/551-6712
www.gardeners.com
Catalog: free

Harmony Farm Supply
Box 460
Graton, CA 95444
707/823-9125; fax: 707/823-1734
www.harmonyfarm.com
Catalog: $2 (refundable)

Kinsman Company
PO Box 357 River Rd.
Point Pleasant, PA 18950
800/733-4146; fax: 215/297-0450
www.kinsmangarden.com
Catalog: free

Langenbach
PO Box 2200
Galesburg, IL 61402-2200
800/362-1991; fax: 800/362-4490
www.langenbach.com (catalog)
Catalog: free

Lee Valley Tools Ltd.
Box 1780
Ogdensburg, NY 13669-6780
800/871-8158; fax: 800/513-7885
www.leevalley.com
Catalog (gardening): free

The Natural Gardening Company
217 San Anselmo Ave.
San Anselmo, CA 94960
707/766-9303; fax: 707/766-9747
www.naturalgardening.com
Catalog: free

Peaceful Valley Farm Supply
110 Spring Hill Drive
Grass Valley, CA 95945
530/272-4769; fax: 530/272-4794
www.groworganic.com
Catalog: free

The Urban Farmer Store
2833 Vicente St.
San Francisco, CA 94116
800/753-3747; fax: 415/661-7826
Catalog: free

Water Gardening

Although many nurseries are offering an increasing variety of aquatic plants and supplies, catalogs still provide the best selection.

Lilypons Water Gardens
6800 Lilypons Rd.
PO Box 10
Buckeystown, MD 21717-0010
800/723-7667; fax: 800/879-5459
www.lilypons.com
Catalog: free

Slocum Water Gardens
1101 Cypress Gardens Blvd.
Winter Haven, FL 33884-1932
941/293-7151; fax: 800/322-1896
Catalog: $3.

Van Ness Water Gardens
2460 N. Euclid Ave.
Upland, CA 91784-1199
800/205-2425; fax: 909/949/7217
www.vnwg.com (catalog)
Catalog: free

BE A SMART SHOPPER

Catalog shopping is one place where surprise packages are rarely welcome. Some simple precautions can help ensure that you get the seeds, plants or tools you want at the price you expected.

- The more you know about a product, the better your chances of getting the best quality for the price. Compare products in different catalogs, and compare catalog supplies with those sold at nurseries and garden centers.

- Include shipping charges when calculating the cost of a mail-order product. Often the relative cost of shipping decreases as the value of your order goes up. And remember, if you aren't satisfied with a product, you'll probably have to pay to ship it back. Clear up any uncertainties by calling customer service before ordering.

- Buy only plants that are hardy in your climate. Nursery catalogs should indicate the hardiness zone for each plant they sell.

- When ordering for the first time from a nursery catalog, place a small order so you can see if you like the products and packing methods.

- When plants arrive, open the package immediately and remove any plastic or other covering; make sure the soil is moist. Follow any instructions on handling plants.

- Buy only from nurseries that guarantee their plants are true to the catalog description and will arrive in a healthy condition.

BOOKS

For more detailed information on gardening, landscaping and outdoor projects, start with our library of recommended books.

Gardening

All About Lawns
by Cathy Haas, Michael MacCaskey
Ortho Books
112 pages. $9.95

Burpee Complete Gardener
by Maureen Heffernan, et al.
Macmillan
432 pages. $29.95

Color in Your Garden
by Penelope Hobhouse
Little, Brown & Company
240 pages. $50.00

Encyclopedia of Gardening
American Horticultural Society
DK Publishing
648 pages. $59.95

The Essential Garden Book: Getting Back to Basics
by Terrance Conran & Dan Pearson
Three Rivers Press
272 pages. $40.00

Garden Design
by Robin Williams
Reader's Digest
208 pages. $32.95

Garden Primer
by Barbara Damrosch
Workman Publishing
673 pages. $16.95

Gardening for Dummies
by Michael MacCaskey & editors of the National Gardening Association
IDG Books Worldwide
335 pages. $16.99

The Natural Garden
by Ken Druse
Clarkson N. Potter, Inc.
296 pages. $40.00

Principles of Gardening
by Hugh Johnson
Fireside Books
272 pages. $17.95

Shade Gardening
Ortho Books
96 pages. $9.95

Sunset National Garden Book
Sunset Books
656 pages. $34.95

Sunset Western Garden Book
Sunset Books
624 pages. $34.95

Taylor's Master Guide to Gardening
by Rita Buchanan
Houghton Mifflin Co.
612 pages. $60.00

Wyman's Gardening Encyclopedia, 2nd ed.
by Donald Wyman
Macmillan Publishing
1221 pages. $55.00

Landscaping

Designing Your Outdoor Home
Creative Publishing international
112 pages. $14.95

Home Masonry Repairs & Projects
Creative Publishing international
128 pages. $14.95

Landscape Design & Construction
Creative Publishing international
128 pages. $14.95

A Portfolio of Landscape Ideas
Creative Publishing international
96 pages. $9.95

A Portfolio of Water Garden & Specialty Landscape Ideas
Creative Publishing international
96 pages. $9.95

Step-by-Step Landscaping
Better Homes & Gardens Books
336 pages. $14.95

Outdoor Projects

Building Your Outdoor Home
Creative Publishing international
112 pages. $14.95

Complete Guide to Decks
Creative Publishing international
256 pages. $19.95

Decks & Patios for Dummies
by Robert Beckstrom & editors of the National Gardening Association
IDG Books Worldwide
356 pages. $16.99

Fences & Gates Quick Guide
Creative Homeowner Press
80 pages. $7.95

Fences, Gates & Trellises
Creative Homeowner Press
159 pages. $14.95

Patio Plans
Ortho Books
96 pages. $11.95

Patios & Walks Quick Guide
Creative Homeowner Press
80 pages. $7.95

Porch and Patio Essentials: Black & Decker Quick Steps
Creative Publishing international
80 pages. $9.95

A Portfolio of Fence & Gate Ideas
Creative Publishing international
96 pages. $9.95

Step-by-Step Deck Projects
Better Homes & Gardens Books
112 pages. $12.95

Step-by-Step Outdoor Projects
Better Homes & Gardens Books
112 pages. $12.95

Storage Sheds Quick Guide
Creative Homeowner Press
80 pages. $7.95

WEB SITES

It's easy to get lost on the information highway, but this list of sites can give you a head start.

Gardening Sites

Adventures in Gardening
www.gardenguy.com
Links, information, book reviews, Q & A from "the garden guy."

Ambrose Gardens
www.ambrosegardens.com
Tips & info for northern gardens: plants, planning, design, Q & A.

Garden Escape
www.garden.com
Advice, weekly magazine, shopping, chat room, design info.

Garden Mart
www.gardenmart.com
Search thousands of garden retailers, chat, get professional advice.

GardenNet
www.GardenNet.com
Directory of articles, books, catalogs and other garden resources.

GardenTown
www.GardenTown.com
Chat room, glossary.

Garden Web
www.gardenweb.com
Calendar of gardening events; online merchant directory; glossary, links.

Gardening
www.bhglive.com/gardening/index.html
Shopping, discussion groups, tips.

Gardening in Shade
www.suite101.com/topics/page.cfm/222
Gardening in shady spots. Weekly feature articles; archives; links.

Gardening Links
www.geocities.com/RainForest/1329/index.html
Web index: gardening information, resources, home pages, guides, tips.

Hometime
Hometime.com/projects/deckprch.htm#deck
Hometime TV show site: projects, summaries & highlights of the show.

Joe & Mindy's WebGarden
www.nhn.ou.edu/howard/garden.html
Gardening tips, articles; links.

New York Botanical Garden
www.pathfinder.com/vg/Gardens/NYBG/index.html
Garden tours and information. Link to Time Life Plant Encyclopedia.

Ortho Online
www.ortho.com
Information on grasses, growing tips, Rose Encyclopedia, glossary, links.

The Scotts Company
www.scottscompany.com
Lawn & garden tips from a supplier of lawn & garden products.

Virtual Garden: Garden Guru
pathfinder.com/vg/features/guruwebcolumns.html
Columns on timely subjects from recognized garden writers.

Sites For Kids

Kids' Valley Garden
www.arnprior.com/kidsgarden/index.htm
Click on smiling tree to get gardening tips for kids. Links to other kid sites.

KinderGarden
aggie-horticulture.tamu.edu/Kindergarden/Kinder.htm
Texas A&M site helps parents and teachers garden with children.

Databases

Extension Bulletin Database
www.hcs.ohio-state.edu/factsheet.html
Horticultural information from 46 colleges & universities; over 20,000 pages; frequently updated.

Time Life Electronic Encyclopedia of Plants
www.pathfinder.com/@@S3vZBQ'A1811rCGh/vg/TimeLife/CG/vg-search.html
Searchable illustrated database of almost 3,000 species.

Landscape Design and Project Sites

Decks and Patios
www.marsweb.com/dtr/patios.htm
Forty-three suggestions for building outdoor projects.

Home Design How-To Guides
www.Sierra.com/Sierrahome/homedesign/howto
Illustrated step-by-step instructions for a myriad of outdoor projects.

Planning the Home Landscape
www.aggie-horticulture.tamu.edu/extension/homelandscape/home.html
Landscape design and project diagrams and discussions.

Rebecca's Garden
www.rebeccasgarden.com
TV show: projects, planning, gardening tips, chat room, garden supplies.

Extension Service Links

Links to Online Resources
www.hortnet.com/toextensions.html
Link to your state extension service site (38 states), Journal of Extension.

Associations

American Hemerocallis Society
www.daylilies.org/daylilies.html

American Horticultural Society
www.ahs.org

American Rose Society
www.ars.org

National Gardening Association
www.garden.org/nga

Perennial Plant Association
www.perennialplant.org

EXTENSION AGENTS

Every lawn and garden article seems to tell you to call your "local extension agent" for landscaping and garden advice. But who are these garden gurus, and how do you find them?

Extension agents are scientists who usually hold advanced degrees in fields ranging from agriculture to horticulture and forestry. They work out of county extension offices affiliated with each state's land grant university. Each office offers a range of resources on lawn care, landscape maintenance and gardening. Most offices will even test your soil for a minimal fee.

Here is a listing of state extension agents. These offices can help you locate your own county extension agent.

Alabama
Cooperative Extension System
Alabama A&M University (AAMU)
P.O. Box 967
Normal, AL 35762
256-851-5710; fax: 256-851-5840

Auburn University (AU)
Duncan Hall
Auburn, AL 36849
334-844-4444; fax: 334-844-5544

Alaska
Alaska Cooperative Extension
University of Alaska Fairbanks
P.O. Box 756180
Fairbanks, AK 99775-6180
907-474-7246; fax: 907-474-6971

Arizona
Cooperative Extension
University of Arizona
College of Agriculture
301 Forbes Bldg
Tucson, AZ 85721-0036
520-621-7205; fax: 520-621-1314

Arkansas
Cooperative Extension Service
University of Arkansas
P.O. Box 391
Little Rock, AR 72203
501-671-2000; fax: 501-671-2301

California
Cooperative Extension Service
University of California
Alameda County
1131 Harbor Bay Parkway, Suite 131
Alameda, CA 94502
510-567-6812; fax: 510-567-6813

Colorado
Cooperative Extension
Colorado State University
1 Administration Building
Fort Collins, CO 80523-4040
970-491-6281; fax: 970-491-6208

Connecticut
Cooperative Extension System
The University of Connecticut
1380 Storrs Rd.
Storrs, CT 06269
860-486-6271; fax: 860-486-6338

Delaware
Cooperative Extension System
University of Delaware
531 South College Ave.
Newark, DE 19717-1303
302-831-2504; fax: 302-831-6758

District of Columbia
State Office
Cooperative Extension Service
University of the District of Columbia
4250 Connecticut Ave. NW
Washington, DC 20008
202-274-7115; fax: 202-274-7130

Florida
Cooperative Extension Service
University of Florida
Horticulture Sciences
1038 McCarty Hall
Gainesville, FL 32611-0210
352-392-1928; fax: 352-392-3583

Georgia
Cooperative Extension Service
The University of Georgia
101 Conner Hall
Athens, GA 30602
706-542-3924;
fax (Dir. office): 706-542-0803

Hawaii
Cooperative Extension Service
University of Hawaii at Manoa
Ohau County
962 Second St.
Pearl City, HI 96782
808-453-6055; fax: 808-453-6052

Idaho
Cooperative Extension System
University of Idaho
P.S.E.S. AG SCI 242
Moscow, ID 83844-2339
208-885-6639; fax: 208-885-7760

Illinois
Cooperative Extension Service
University of Illinois
1301 W. Gregory Dr.
214 Mumford Hall
Urbana, IL 61801
217-333-2660; fax: 217-244-5403

Indiana
Cooperative Extension Service
Purdue University
1140 Agricultural Administration
West Lafayette, IN 47907-1140
765-494-8489; fax: 765-494-0391

Iowa
Cooperative Extension Service
Iowa State University
218 Beardshear Hall
Ames, IA 50011
515-294-4576; fax: 515-294-4715

Kansas
Cooperative Extension Service
Kansas State University
123 Umberger Hall
Manhattan, KS 66506
785-532-5820; fax: 785-532-6290

Kentucky
Cooperative Extension Service
University of Kentucky
College of Agriculture
Lexington, KY 40546
606-257-1846; fax: 606-323-1991

Louisiana
Cooperative Extension Service
Louisiana State University
P.O. Box 25100
Baton Rouge, LA 70894-5100
504-388-6083; fax: 504-388-4225

Maine
Cooperative Extension
University of Maine
5741 Libby Hall
Orono, ME 04469-5741
207-581-3188; fax: 207-581-1301

Minnesota
Extension Service
University of Minnesota
240 Coffey Hall
St. Paul, MN 55108
612-624-1222; fax: 612-625-6227

Mississippi
Cooperative Extension Service
Mississippi State University
Box 9601
Mississippi State, MS 39762
601-325-3036; fax: 601-325-8407

Missouri
Cooperative Extension Service
University of Missouri
309 University Hall
Columbia, MO 65211
573-882-7754; fax: 573-884-4204

Lincoln University of Missouri (LU)
Cooperative Extension, P.O. Box 29
Jefferson City, MO 65102-0029
573-681-5543; fax: 573-681-5546

Montana
Extension Service
Montana State University
Culbertson Hall
Bozeman, MT 59717
406-994-6641; fax: 406-994-1756

Nebraska
Cooperative Extension Division
University of Nebraska
211 Agricultural Hall
Lincoln, NE 68583-0703
402-472-2966; fax: 402-472-5557

Nevada
Cooperative Extension
2345 Red Rock St., Suite 330
Las Vegas, NV 89146-3157
702-251-7531; fax: 702-251-7536

New Hampshire
UNH Cooperative Extension
59 College Rd., Taylor Hall
Durham, NH 03824-3587
603-862-1520; fax: 603-862-1585

New Jersey
Rutgers Cooperative Extension
Middlesex County
390 George St., 8th floor
New Brunswick, NJ 08901
732-745-3443; fax: 732-745-3478

New Mexico
Cooperative Extension Service
New Mexico State University
Box 30003, Dept. 3AE
Las Cruces, NM 88003
505-646-3015; fax: 505-646-5975

New York
Cornell Cooperative Extension
Roberts Hall
Ithaca, NY 14853-4203
607-255-1791; fax: 607-255-9998

North Carolina
Extension Service
North Carolina State University
Box 7602
Raleigh, NC 27695-7602
919-515-2811; fax: 919-515-3135

A & T State University (A&T)
C.H. Moore Research Facility
P.O. Box 21928
Greensboro, NC 27420-1928
336-334-7956; fax: 336-334-7027

North Dakota
NDSU Extension Service
North Dakota State University
315 Morrill Hall, Box 5437
Fargo, ND 58105-5437
701-231-8944; fax: 701-231-8520

Ohio
Ohio State University Extension
Ohio State University 2120 Fyffe Rd.
Columbus, OH 43210-1084
614-292-4067; fax: 614-688-3807

Oklahoma
Cooperative Extension Service
Oklahoma State University
139 Agricultural Hall
Stillwater, OK 74078
405-744-5398; fax: 405-744-5339

Oregon
Oregon State University
Extension Service
102 Ballard Extension Hall
Corvallis, OR 97331-3606
541-737-2711; fax: 541-737-4423

Pennsylvania
Cooperative Extension Service
Pennsylvania State University
201 Ag Administration Bldg.
University Park, PA 16802-2600
814-865-2541; fax: 814-863-6139

Puerto Rico
University of Puerto Rico
Mayaguez Campus, P.O. Box 9031
College of Agricultural Sciences
Agricultural Extension Service
Mayaguez, PR 00681
787-833-2665; fax: 787-265-4130

Rhode Island
Cooperative Extension
University of Rhode Island
Woodward Hall
Kingston, RI 02881
401-874-2900; fax: 401-874-2259

South Carolina
Cooperative Extension Service
Clemson University & SC State
   College
103 Barre Hall
Clemson, SC 29634
864-656-3382; fax: 864-656-5819

South Dakota
Cooperative Extension Service
Box 2207D
Brookings, SD 57007
605-688-4792; fax: 605-688-6733

Tennessee
Agricultural Extension Service
University of Tennessee
P.O. Box 1071
Knoxville, TN 37901-1071
423-974-7114; fax: 423-974-1068

Texas
Cooperative Extension Service
Texas A&M University
104 Jack K. Williams Admin. Bldg.
College Station, TX 77843-7101
409-845-7808; fax: 409-845-9542

Utah
Cooperative Extension Service
Utah State University
4305 University Blvd.
Logan, UT 84322-4305
435-797-7777; fax: 435-797-2644

Vermont
Extension System
University of Vermont
College of Agriculture
601 Main St.
Burlington, VT 05401-3439
802-656-2990: fax: 802-656-8642

Virginia
Cooperative Extension Service
Virginia Tech
101 Hutcheson Hall
Blacksburg, VA 24061
540-231-5299; fax: 540-231-5545

Virginia State University (VSU)
Box 9081
Petersburg, VA 23806
804-524-5871; fax: 804-524-5259

Washington
WSU Cooperative Extension
College of Agriculture and Home
   Economics
P.O. Box 646230
Washington State University
Pullman, Washington 99164-6230
509-335-2811; fax: 509-335-2926

West Virginia
Extension Service
West Virginia University
P.O. Box 6031
Morgantown, WV 26506
304-293-5691; fax: 304-293-7163

Wisconsin
Cooperative Extension
University of Wisconsin
432 N. Lake St., Room 601
Madison, WI 53706-1498
608-263-2775; fax: 608-265-4545

Wyoming
Cooperative Extension Service
University of Wyoming
P.O. Box 3354
Laramie, WY 82071-3354
307-766-5124; fax: 307-766-3998

HOT LINES

Here are some hotline numbers you can call for free lawn and garden advice:

National Pesticide Network: 800-858-7378/fax: 541-737-0761. 9:30 a.m. to 7:30 p.m. EST. Health and environmental effects of pesticides, safe use, cleanup and disposal of pesticides.

Ferry-Morse Seeds: 800-283-3400. 8 a.m. to 4:45 p.m. CST. Planting, maintaining and harvesting vegetables.

Scotts Consumer Service Help Line: 800-543-8873. Hours vary seasonally. Experts answer lawn care questions.

INDEX

CONTRIBUTORS

(Note: T=Top, C=Center, B=Bottom, L=Left, R=Right)

Anchor Wall Systems: p. 142
tel: 800-473-4452
http://www.anchorwall.com

Tad Anderson Landscape Design: pp.
182-183, 184, 242, 258
tel: 612-473-8387
http://www.land-design.com

Armstrong World Industries: p. 39T
tel: 888-ARM-STRONG
http://www.armstrongfloors.com

Bachman's Landscape Services: pp.
146, 244
tel: 612-861-7653
http://www.bachmans.com

Better Barns / Geoffrey Gross,
photographer: p. 179 all
tel: 888-266-1960

Bruce Laminate Floors: p. 41B
tel: 214-887-2100
http://www.brucelaminatefloors.com

California Redwood Association:
pp. 140-141, 154, 170
tel: 415-382-0662
http://www.calredwood.org

Cole Sewell Corporation: p. 94
tel: 651-605-4600

Crossville Ceramics: pp. 48-49, 50
tel: 931-484-2110
http://www.crossville-ceramics.com

Dutch Gardens: p. 212C
tel: 800-818-3861

Four Seasons Solar Products Corp.: pp.
60-61
tel: 800-FOUR SEASONS
http://www.four-seasons-
sunrooms.com

Handy Home Products: p. 178
tel: 800-221-1849
http://www.handyhome.com

Idaho Wood Lighting: cover: BC; p. 164
tel: 800-635-1100
http://www.idahowood.com

Intermatic Incorporated p. 165T
tel: 815-675-2321
http://www.intermatic.com

Lilypons Water Gardens: pp. 269, 272B
tel: 301-874-5503
http://www.lilypons.com

Mannington Resilient Floors: pp. 30,
31, 34T, 36, 38
tel: 856-935-3000
http://www.mannington.com

Progress Lighting: p. 165B
tel: 864-599-6000
http://www.progresslighting.com

Robern, Inc.: p. 24
tel: 215-826-9800
http://www.robern.com

Shanker Industries, Inc.: p. 45T
tel: 516-766-4477

Simpson Door Company: p. 85
tel: 800-952-4057
http://www.simpsondoor.com

The Stanley Works: p. 84
tel: 800-STANLEY
http://www.stanleyworks.com

USG Corporation: p. 44 both
tel: 312-606-4122
http://www.usg.com

U.S. Structures/Archadeck: pp. 130-131
tel: 888-OUR-DECK
http://www.archadeck.com

Ventana USA: back cover: T
tel: 724-325-3400
http://www.ventanainternational.com

Wall Magic by Wagner Spray Tech
Corp.: p. 10T
tel: 800-328-8251
http://www.wagnerspraytech.com

Walpole Woodworkers: p. 177
tel: 800-343-6948
http://www.walpolewoodworkers.com

Weatherend Estate Furniture: p. 134
tel: 800-456-6483
http://www.weatherend.com

Weber Horticultural Design: p. 133L
P.O. Box 5264
Minnetonka, MN 55343-2264

Wood-Mode Inc.: pp. 100-101, 116
tel: 570-374-2711
http://www.wood-mode.com

PHOTOGRAPHY CREDITS

(Note: T=Top, C=Center, B=Bottom, L=Left, R=Right)

Alderman Studios
High Point, NC
© Alderman Studios: pp. 118 both,
120-121 all

Carolyn Bates
© Carolyn Bates: p. 7

Woody Cady
Bethesda, MD
© Woody Cady: pp. 25, 172

David Cavagnaro
Decorah, IA
© David Cavagnaro: p. 220

Walter Chandoha
Annandale, NJ
© Walter Chandoha: pp. 200, 217T, 268

Crandall & Crandall
Dana Point, CA
© Crandall & Crandall: pp. 161T, 168,
173, 207B, 210BR, 225L

Stephen Cridland
Portland, OR
© Stephen Cridland: p. 26

John Decker
Belmont, MA
© John Decker: back cover: B;
pp. 174-176 all

Chris Eden
Seattle, WA
© Chris Eden / Eden Arts: pp. 42, 43B

Derek Fell
Gardenville, PA
© Derek Fell: pp. 201, 226, 240B, 241R,
266

Bob Firth
Shakopee, MN
© Bob Firth: p. 99 both

David Hamsley
New York, NY
© David Hamsley: pp. 233BR, 262

PHOTOGRAPHY CREDITS (CONTINUED)

Grant Heilman Photography, Inc.
Lititz, PA
© Grant Heilman Photography, Inc.:
Larry Lefever: cover TL, p. 236;
Stanley Schoenberger: p. 273T

Merle Henkenius
Lincoln, NE
© Merle Henkenius: pp. 54-55 all

Saxon Holt
Novato, CA
© Saxon Holt: pp. 136T, 148T, 190-193
all, 196B, 199, 202 all, 206, 208BR, 209,
210BL, 214, 240T, 250, 251, 261 both

Roy Inman Photography
Lenexa, KS
© Roy Inman Photography: pp. 32-33 all,
46-47 all, 72-73 all, 76-79 all

Thomas H. Jones
King of Prussia, PA
© Thomas H. Jones: pp. 20-21 all

Jeff Krueger Photography
St. Paul, MN
© Jeff Krueger Photography: p. 98

Mark A. Madsen
Bloomington, MN
© Mark A. Madsen: pp. 166, 167L, 230

Charles Mann
Santa Fe, NM
© Charles Mann: pp. 198, 208T

Lisa Masson
Arlington, VA
© Lisa Masson: p. 6

Bill Mathews
Overland Park, KS
© Bill Mathews: pp. 160, 161B

Joshua McHugh
New York, NY
© Joshua McHugh: 188, 189T, 212BL,
246T

Karen Melvin / Keith Waters & Associ-
ates, Inc., Architect
Minneapolis, MN
© Karen Melvin: pp. 28-29

Melabee M. Miller
Hillside, NJ
© Melabee M. Miller: pp. 22, 62, 82-83

John Nasta
New York, NY
© John Nasta: pp. 4-5, 103BL, 114, 155-
157 all

Eric Nelson, Ph.D.
Ithaca, NY
© Eric Nelson, Ph. D.: pp. 224, 225R

Jerry Pavia
Bonner's Ferry, ID
© Jerry Pavia: pp. 136B, 139, 147, 148B,
212T, 237, 241L, 272T

Joan Pavia
Bonner's Ferry, ID
© Joan Pavia: p. 238B

Robert Perron / Steve Lasar, Architect
Branford, CT
© Robert Perron: p. 63B

Tom Philbin III
Kings Park, NY
© Tom Philbin III: p. 162 all

Tim Proctor & Associates, Inc. / Man-
nington Resilient Floors
Burlington, NJ
© Tim Proctor: pp. 30, 31, 34T, 36, 38

Smith-Baer Photography
Port Chester, NY
© Smith-Baer Photography: pp. 18, 19
51, 52-53 all, 56-57 all, 63T, 68-69 all,
75 all, 90-93 all, 96-97 all, 112-113 all,
128-129 all

Keith Talley
Temple, TX
© Keith Talley: pp. 58-59 all

Michael S. Thompson
Eugene, OR
© Michael S. Thompson: pp. 133T,
137TR, 138, 208 BL, 208BC, 210 TR,
247, 248 both, 249

Andrew Van Dis
Berkeley, CA
© Andrew Van Dis: p. 27

Jessie Walker
Glencoe, IL
© Jessie Walker: pp. 23, 102

Wil Zehr / Residential Construction
Consultants
Champaign, IL
© Wil Zehr Photography: p. 81 all

ILLUSTRATION CREDITS

(Note: T=Top, C=Center, B=Bottom, L=Left, R=Right)

© Susan Johnson Carlson: pp. 221-223
all, 234

© Andrew Christie: p. 27

© Creative Publishing international,
Inc. (John T. Drigot): p. 105

© Arlo Faber: pp. 115, 172, 173

© Mario Ferro: p. 20, 21, 117

© Narda Lebo: p. 253

© Greg Mason: p. 39

© Tom Moore: pp. 80, 215 both, 218

© Paul Perrault and Trevor Johnston:
p. 43

© George Retseck: pp. 255-257 all

© Rodney J. Stokes: pp. 238 all, 239

© Ian Worpole: pp. 24B, 25B, 245 all

Creative Publishing international, Inc.
offers a variety of how-to books.
For information write or visit our website:
  Creative Publishing international, Inc.
  Subscriber Books
  5900 Green Oak Drive
  Minnetonka, MN 55343

www.howtobookstore.com